geography 360°

Ann Bowen and John Pallister

Foundation Book 2

www.heinemann.co.uk
✓ Free online support
✓ Useful weblinks
✓ 24 hour online ordering

01865 888058

Heinemann
Inspiring generations

Heinemann Educational Publishers
Halley Court, Jordan Hill, Oxford OX2 8EJ
Part of Harcourt Education

Heinemann is the registered trademark of
Harcourt Education Limited

Harcourt Education Limited, 2005

First published 2005

10 09 08 07 06 05
10 9 8 7 6 5 4 3 2 1

British Library Cataloguing in Publication Data is available
from the British Library on request.

ISBN 0 435 35655 0

Copyright notice

All rights reserved. No part of this publication may be reproduced in any form or by any means (including photocopying or storing it in any medium by electronic means and whether or not transiently or incidentally to some other use of this publication) without the written permission of the copyright owner, except in accordance with the provisions of the Copyright, Designs and Patents Act 1988 or under the terms of a licence issued by the Copyright Licensing Agency, 90 Tottenham Court Road, London W1T 4LP. Applications for the copyright owner's written permission should be addressed to the publisher.

Edited by Caroline Hannan
Designed by hicksdesign and typeset and illustrated by HL Studios
Original illustrations © Harcourt Education Limited, 2005
Printed and bound in Italy by Printer Trento S.r.l.
Cover photo: © Getty Images
Picture research by Beatrice Ray

Acknowledgements

Maps and extracts

This product includes mapping data licensed from Ordnance Survey® with the permission of the Controller of Her Majesty's Stationery Office, © Crown copyright. All rights reserved. Licence no. 100000230.
Page 20 Source B: US Census Bureau. Pages 24, 25 Sources A, D: Home Office. Pages 26, 27 Sources A and B, page 41 Source C: BBC News. Page 49 Sources B and C: World Tourism Organization. Page 54 Sources A and B, page 55 Sources D, E and F: United Kingdom Tourism Survey. Page 58 Source B: wordtravels.com. Page 67 Source E: Daily Telegraph. Page 140 Source A: Mail on Sunday. Page 142 Source A: Independent. Page 143 Source C: Guardian.

Photos

Pages 7, 9, 22, 26, 30, 34, 36, 44, 47, 48, 51, 52, 56, 60, 137: Alamy. Page 117: Cafedirect. Pages 12, 13, 15, 17, 34, 52, 58, 82, 136: Corbis. Pages 7, 22, 41: Empics. Pages 6, 7, 9, 15, 25, 27, 28, 31, 44, 52, 72, 75, 111, 130, 131, 132, 134, 137: Getty. Pages 5, 32, 128, 129, 135: Harcourt Education. Pages 7, 28, 50, 51: Lonely Planet Images. Page 40: NERC Satellite Receiving Station. Page 9: Oxford Scientific Films. Pages 5, 9, 15, 32, 128, 129, 135: Photodisc. Page 138: Reuters. Pages 6, 7: Robert Harding. Page: 119: Roundabout. Page 22: Syed Jan Sabawoon. Pages 59, 60: Travel Ink. Photographs on all other pages kindly supplied by author John Pallister.

Every effort has been made to contact copyright holders of material reproduced in this book. Any omissions will be rectified in subsequent printings if notice is given to the publishers.

Websites

On pages where you are asked to go to
www.heinemann.co.uk/hotlinks
to complete a task or download information, please insert the code **6550P** at the website.

Contents

1 Introducing Europe — 5
Where is Europe? — 6
What does Europe look like? — 8
What is the EU? — 10
Living in the EU — 12
Assessing 360° Investigation – what are the advantages and disadvantages of Country X's membership of the EU? — 14

2 Who are the Europeans? — 15
Where do people live in Europe? — 16
Population change – it's a numbers game — 18
What is a population pyramid? — 20
People on the move — 22
Asylum-seekers in Europe — 24
Feelings running high! — 26
Poland – a new entrant to the EU — 28
Assessing 360° Who are the Europeans? — 30

3 Europe's weather and climate — 31
What is weather? — 32
How and why does the sky change? — 34
Feeling the pressure? — 36
Why does the weather change? — 38
Satellites help forecast the weather — 40
Europe's climates — 42
How does the climate affect us? — 44
Assessing 360° Choosing where to go on holiday — 46

4 Tourism – good or bad? — 47
What is tourism? — 48
Tourism – just how important is it? — 50
Europe's tourist attractions — 52
UK tourism — 54
Visiting an island in Europe: Menorca — 56
Visiting a poorer country: Jamaica — 58
Managing tourism — 60
Assessing 360° Tourism – good or bad? — 62

5 Rivers and floods — 63
Water cycle – processes — 64
Water cycle – stores and water supply — 66
Rivers in the uplands — 68
Rivers in the lowlands — 70
Why do rivers flood? — 72
The Boscastle flood in August 2004 — 74
Flood prevention measures — 76
Investigating rivers using fieldwork — 78
How can the results from river fieldwork be used? — 80
Assessing 360° Can river flooding in the UK be stopped? — 82

6 Italy — 83
Physical background — 84
Does Italy have a 'North and South'? — 86
Why is the North wealthy? — 88
Why is the South poor? — 90
Can the gap between South and North be closed? — 92
Italy – a great place to visit — 94
Venice and that sinking feeling — 96
An ageing population – Italy's economic time bomb — 98
Assessing 360° Pensions time bomb in the EU – what can governments do? — 100

7	**Rich world, poor world**	**101**	
	Are you rich or poor?	102	
	How are differences in wealth between countries measured?	104	
	What is development?	106	
	Other measures of development	108	
	Why are poor countries poor?	110	
	Other problems for people living in the tropics	112	
	Why are countries in sub-Saharan Africa poorest of all?	114	
	Is world trade fair?	116	
	What a difference clean water makes	118	
	Are poor countries caught in a trade and poverty trap?	120	
	Assessing 360° Rich country, poor country	122	
8	**South and East Asia**	**123**	
	Asia – the big continent	124	
	Asia – continent of many people	126	
	Japan – geography and people	128	
	Japan – industrial powerhouse of Asia	130	
	South Korea – country of chaebols	132	
	China – geography and history of development	134	
	China – the giant stirs	136	
	The sub-continent – India, Pakistan and Bangladesh	138	
	Old India awakes	140	
	Bangladesh – struggling with its geography	142	
	Assessing 360° Taking a different look at the world	144	

SKILLS in geography — **145**

How to use an atlas 1 — 145
How to use an atlas 2 — 145
How to give a four-figure grid reference — 145
How to give a six-figure grid reference — 145
How to draw a cross-section — 146
How to draw a divided bar graph — 146
How to draw a pictograph — 146
How to draw a pie graph — 147
How to draw a block graph — 147
How to draw a line graph — 147
How to draw a vertical bar graph — 148
How to draw a climate graph — 148
How to draw a scatter graph — 149
How to draw a population pyramid — 150
How to draw a block bar graph — 150
How to draw a living graph — 151
How to draw a shading (choropleth) map — 151
How to draw a flow map — 152
How to measure distances on a map — 152
How to draw a pictorial or mental map — 153
How to draw a sketch map — 154
How to draw a labelled sketch from a photograph — 154
How to draw a time column — 155
How to draw a spider diagram — 155

Knowing your levels — **156**
Glossary — **158**
Index — **160**

» 1 Introducing Europe

Can you pick out Europe on this satellite view of part of the world?
Where does Europe start and finish?

Learning objectives

What are you going to learn about in this chapter?
- How far does Europe stretch?
- What is the European Union?
- What does Europe look like?
- How was the European Union formed?

Where is Europe?

> Understanding where Europe is
> Analysing information in photographs

Could you draw the boundaries of Europe on to a map? Map **A** shows the continent of Europe. To the west lies the Atlantic Ocean, to the north the Arctic Ocean, and to the south the Mediterranean Sea.

It is often more difficult to work out where Europe ends in the east, where Europe meets Asia. This boundary is formed by the Ural Mountains that run from north to south through the Russian Federation – so only part of Russia is in Europe. Turkey is split between Europe and Asia. Turkey's largest city Istanbul is in Europe, but most of its land area is in Asia. The North Sea and the English Channel separate the British Isles from mainland Europe.

A A political map of Europe

Activities

1 In a pair or small group, choose *one* of photographs **B–H**. Make sure that every photograph is studied by a group in the class. Note down the key features of the photograph.

   a) Where do you think the photograph may have been taken in Europe? Give reasons for your answer.

   b) Working with another small group, compare your two photographs. List the similarities and differences. Check that the other group agrees with your description of the photograph.

   c) As a class, discuss what you think of when you hear the word *Europe*. Do these images match your ideas of what Europe looks like?

2 Read the following statements about Europe. Decide which statements are true and which are false.

   - Europe is a continent.
   - Europe is a group of countries.
   - The European countries are all next to each other with no sea between them.
   - Only part of the Russian Federation is in Europe.
   - Europe stretches from the Atlantic Ocean in the west to the Ural Mountains in the east.

3 If you had a free choice, where in Europe would you prefer to live? Why? Give *three* reasons.

1 Introducing Europe   7

What does Europe look like?

> Recognising the different landscapes of Europe
> Learning about the major rivers and seas of Europe

Europe is almost triangular in shape. It is often called a **peninsula** because it is surrounded on three sides by the sea (see map **A**). To the north-west the land is made up of old, hard rocks while the centre of Europe has much younger rocks and many lowland plains. To the south there are ranges of mountains such as the Alps. Some of these high mountains are covered in ice and snow, forming glaciers and ice caps.

A The physical geography of Europe

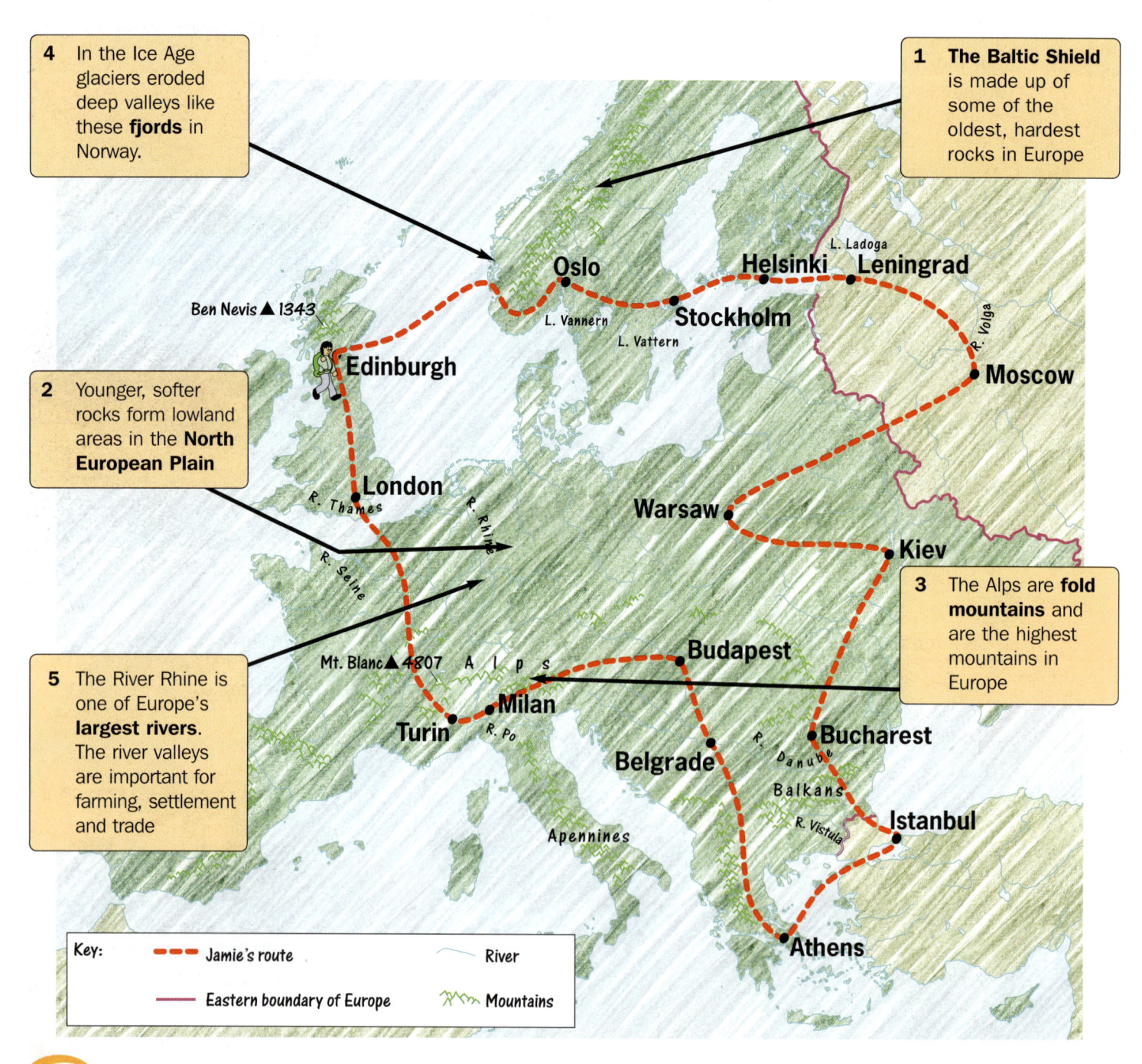

4. In the Ice Age glaciers eroded deep valleys like these **fjords** in Norway.

1. **The Baltic Shield** is made up of some of the oldest, hardest rocks in Europe

2. Younger, softer rocks form lowland areas in the **North European Plain**

3. The Alps are **fold mountains** and are the highest mountains in Europe

5. The River Rhine is one of Europe's **largest rivers**. The river valleys are important for farming, settlement and trade

Key:
- – – – Jamie's route
- ——— Eastern boundary of Europe
- ～～～ River
- ⋀⋀⋀ Mountains

8 geography 360° Foundation Book 2

Activities

1. Make a copy of the table below. Using an atlas to help you, put each of the names below into the correct column. The first one has been done for you.

   Alps   Italy   Rhine   Thames   Urals
   Iberia (Spain and Portugal)   Pennines   Rhône
   Pyrenees   Scandinavia   Danube

European mountains	European rivers	Peninsulas
Alps		

2. a) Look at the photos on this page. Match each item on this list of physical features to the correct photo.
   - Mountains
   - Glaciers
   - Rivers
   - Flat, fertile farmland
   - Fjords

   b) Choose *one* photograph from this spread. Draw a sketch of the photograph and label the physical features. Add the title: 'The physical characteristics of …'. (See pages 145–155 of *SKILLS in geography* for more help.)

3. **Jamie's European holiday**

   a) Jamie lives in Edinburgh and is going to take a long holiday after his exams. He hopes to travel in Europe – you can see his planned route on map **A**. Describe Jamie's route through Europe.

   b) Jamie wants to try some activities on his trip. Use an atlas and match each of the activities below to a landscape Jamie will visit:
   - Visiting ancient ruins
   - Skiing
   - Sailing
   - Rock climbing
   - Cycling in lowland areas.

Key words

Fold mountains – mountains formed by rocks being folded and uplifted
Landscape – the natural scenery of an area and what it looks like
Peninsula – an area of land surrounded on three sides by the sea
Physical geography – the natural features on the Earth's surface

1 Introducing Europe   9

What is the EU?

> Understanding how the European Union was formed
> **Practising your map skills**

A The countries of the EU

Key
Members of the EU

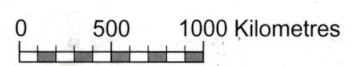

Key words

EU – the European Union, many countries in Europe have joined
Trade – the selling of goods between countries
Treaty – an agreement between different countries

Map **A** shows the countries that belong to the **EU**. Throughout history countries have signed agreements or **treaties** for many reasons, such as the environment and **trade**. The European Union grew from a trading agreement between the Benelux countries (**Be**lgium, The **Ne**therlands and **Lux**embourg) in 1948.

Source **B** shows a simple history of the development of the European Union. Today the EU has 25 member states. More countries wish to join the EU because it opens up new chances for jobs and new places to live. It also helps promote human rights and environmental standards.

1948	Benelux countries (**Be**lgium, **Ne**therlands and **Lux**embourg) formed an agreement to trade with each other.
1952	France, West Germany and Italy joined with the Benelux countries.
1957	These six countries formed the EEC – European Economic Community or 'Common Market' – to co-operate on trade. The organisation became known as the European Community or EC.
1973	The United Kingdom, Denmark and Eire joined the EC to make nine members.
1981	Greece joined the EC.
1986	Spain and Portugal joined to make twelve members.
1990	East Germany reunites with West Germany and becomes part of the EC.
1993	The single European market was created. People from EC countries could work, study, trade or travel anywhere within the EC.

geography 360° Foundation Book 2

1995	Austria, Finland and Sweden joined – fifteen members.
2002	The launch of the Euro – the single currency was adopted by twelve of the member states.
2004	Ten more countries joined – Cyprus, the Czech Republic, Estonia, Hungary, Latvia, Lithuania, Malta, Poland, Slovakia, Slovenia.
2007	Bulgaria, Croatia, Macedonia, Romania and Turkey hope to join.

B A simple history of the EU

The EU is vast and it needs a huge amount of money to make it work. Member countries pay money to the EU headquarters in Brussels according to how much they can afford. This money is raised from taxes paid on goods. In the UK it is called Value Added Tax or VAT. The EU divides the money up into different funds. Source **C** shows where the money went in 2004.

Agriculture	42%
Regional development and Social Fund	36%
Internal policies, e.g. security, research, transport, energy	8%
External action, e.g. aid to other countries such as Iraq	8%
Administration	5%
Other	1%

C How the EU spends its money (2004)

Activities

1. Use source **B** and an outline map of Europe. Shade in the countries to show the decade in which they joined the EU (see key below). Remember to include the islands that belong to each country. Begin with the six countries that formed the EEC in 1957.

   Key
   1950–1959   1980–1989
   1960–1969   1990–1999
   1970–1979   2000–2010

   (See pages 145–155 of *SKILLS in geography* for more help.)

2. Write out and complete these sentences using source **B**.

   a) The first six countries to form the EU were _____ _____ _____ _____ _____ _____ .
   These countries are located *in the centre/on the edges* of Europe and are *neighbours/far apart*.

   b) In 1973 three countries joined; they were _____ _____ _____ .

   c) By 1986 there were ____ members. Three more countries had joined since 1973; they were _____ _____ _____ .

   d) In 1995, _____ _____ _____ joined, making ____ members.

   e) In 2004 _____ more countries joined, mostly from *eastern/western* Europe.

3. The main EU buildings are in Strasbourg, Luxembourg and Brussels. Find these cities in an atlas. Why do you think these cities were chosen as the main meeting places?

4. a) Draw a pie chart (see pages 145–155 of *SKILLS in geography* for more help) to show the information in source **C**.

   b) What is most money spent on?

1 Introducing Europe

Living in the EU

> Using GDP to show if some parts of the European Union are more developed than others
> Creating spider diagrams

You might think that all European countries are rich but there can be big differences. Table **A** shows some key characteristics of six European Union countries. **GDP** means Gross Domestic Product and shows how rich a country is. To work it out, all the money a country earns from producing goods and services is divided by its total population (see **B**).

Country	Population (millions)	GDP per head (US $)	Unemployment (%)	When joined EU
Belguim	10.29	29 200	7.2	1957
France	60.18	26 000	9.1	1957
Finland	5.19	25 800	8.5	1995
Portugal	10.10	19 400	4.7	1986
Poland	38.62	9 700	18.1	2004
UK	60.09	25 500	5.2	1973

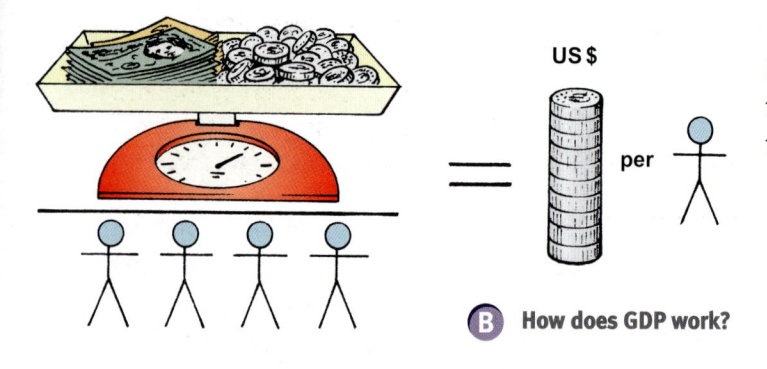

A Key characteristics of six EU countries, 2002–3

People from different countries in the EU can see things very differently. You can see how three people feel about the EU in source **C**.

B How does GDP work?

YOUR VOICE: EU ENLARGEMENT

Marcin Jasinski, 18, Warsaw, Poland

I feel disappointed that we will not have complete equality with earlier members

Although I am glad that Poland can join the EU, I feel disappointed that we will not have complete equality with earlier members.

We have many skilled workers with much to contribute who do not have jobs because unemployment is high. Of the EU countries, Poles will only be allowed to work in the UK and Ireland. This seems unfair.

João Rodrigues Lopes, 28, Lisbon, Portugal

The benefits of joining the EU seem obvious to me. Although not everyone agrees, I believe that European expansion is a good thing. It will be a step forward to unite Europe as a single democratic body.

I believe that European expansion is a good thing

Anna Naudi, 78, Mosta, Malta

I am pleased to see Europe being enlarged to include Malta and other countries. After living through Nazi occupation and the threat of communism, I think that belonging to the EU will be a blessing.

I think that belonging to the EU will be a blessing

C Three views on the expansion of the EU

Activities

1. a) Using the worksheet from your teacher, complete a table like the one below. Rank the countries according to the percentage (%) unemployment, starting with the lowest.

Rank	Country according to unemployment (lowest first)
1	Netherlands
2	Cyprus (GC)
3	Sweden
4	

    b) Colour the countries in your table that joined the EU in 2004.

2. a) On an outline map of Europe draw a choropleth or shading map to show the GDP of countries. Use the following key:

    Key
    0–9999
    10 000–19 999
    20 000–29 999
    30 000 and over

    (See pages 145–155 of *SKILLS in geography* for more help.)

    b) On the map underline the names of those countries that joined the EU in 2004.

    c) Discuss in pairs or small groups what you think the advantages of the EU are. Share at *least one* of your advantages with the rest of the class. As a whole class create a spider diagram to show your opinions.

Key word

GDP (Gross domestic product) – the amount of money a country makes from the production of goods and services divided by the total population; the higher the GDP, the richer the country

SKILLS

How to draw a spider diagram

1. Draw a circle (the 'body') in the middle of your page. Write the title in it, e.g. 'Advantages of the EU'.
2. Draw lines ('legs') away from the circle.
3. Write an advantage at the end of each line.
4. You could draw a small sketch beside each advantage.

For more help see page 155 of *SKILLS in geography*.

1 Introducing Europe

Assessing 360°

Investigation – what are the advantages and disadvantages of Country X's membership of the EU?

You are going to investigate one of the countries that joined the EU in 2004: Cyprus, the Czech Republic, Estonia, Hungary, Latvia, Lithuania, Malta, Poland, Slovakia or Slovenia.

First choose your country and check your choice with your teacher.

You should not produce more than four sides of A4. Remember to include maps, diagrams, photographs and graphs. Make sure that you include the stages in Box **A**.

To help you, take a look at the websites about Europe on the Hotlinks site (see page 2).

Use the mark scheme from your teacher to help you assess your work.

It is important to set out your work clearly. You should include a *beginning*, a *middle* and *an end*.

1 A beginning
- A front cover – the title, a picture or map, your name and class.
- A contents list – of all headings in the work.
- An introduction – what is your investigation about, which country are you studying and why did you choose it?

2 A middle
Here describe the characteristics of your country. Use the checklist below to make sure that you have included information about the following themes:
- The physical geography of the country – mountains, lowlands, deserts, natural vegetation, rivers, lakes and seas, the climate, etc. A map would be a good idea here.
- Any natural hazards, e.g. earthquakes, volcanoes, floods, drought.
- The human geography – population, cities, culture, religion and economy (agriculture, industry, tourism, etc.)
- What advantages will the country bring to the EU?
- What does the country hope to gain from membership of the EU?

3 An end
Write a conclusion to summarise the advantages of the country's membership of the EU for the country and the EU as a whole.
And finally...
Always include a bibliography – this is a list of books, websites and other information used to produce your investigation.

A Organising your investigation

» 2 Who are the Europeans?

On the world scale Europe has a high population, but some places have lots of people and others have very few. Study these photographs. Can you suggest why there are lots of people in some places and not very many in others?

Learning objectives
What are you going to learn about in this chapter?
> How the population is spread over Europe
> How Europe's population has changed over time
> The groups that make up Europe's population
> The migration of people in Europe
> The similarities and differences between the UK and Poland

High density population: Paris, France

Low density population: Uig, Scotland

Where do people live in Europe?

> Understanding why some places have lots of people and some have very few
> Learning how to measure populations

Key words

Core region – area most attractive for settlement and most densely populated in a region

Distribution – how the population of an area is spread

Periphery – areas in a region that do not have very many people and do not favour settlement

Population – the people who live in a place

Population density – the number of people per square kilometre

How to work out population density

Population density is the number of people living in an country per square kilometre. You can work out this out by using the formula:

$$\text{Population density} = \frac{\text{Number of people in the country}}{\text{Country's total area (km}^2\text{)}}$$

For example: if there are 58 million people living in France, and the area is 544 000 km^2, then the population density is 106 people per square kilometre.

HOW DO WE MEASURE POPULATION?

The **distribution** of **population** is the way people are spread across a landscape. The density shows how many people live in an area. Source **A** shows the difference between density and distribution.

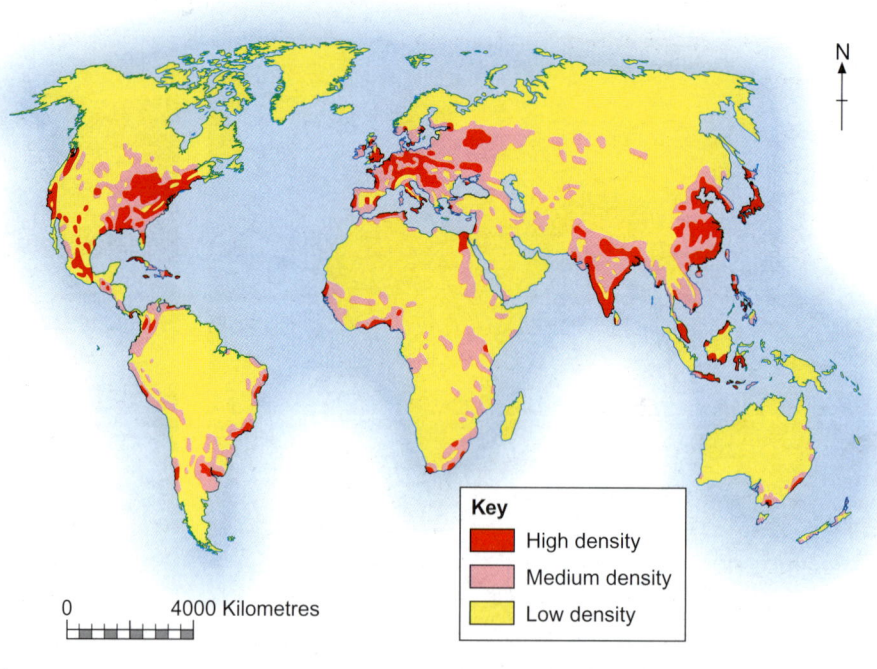

A Population distribution and density

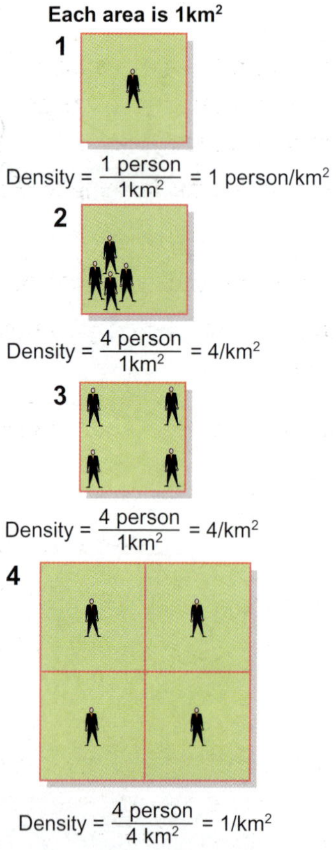

Each area is 1km^2

1. Density = $\frac{1 \text{ person}}{1 \text{km}^2}$ = 1 person/km^2

2. Density = $\frac{4 \text{ person}}{1 \text{km}^2}$ = 4/km^2

3. Density = $\frac{4 \text{ person}}{1 \text{km}^2}$ = 4/km^2

4. Density = $\frac{4 \text{ person}}{4 \text{km}^2}$ = 1/km^2

The population densities in 1 and 4 are the same, 1/km^2, although the area is larger in 4.

The population densities in 2 and 3 are the same, 4/km^2, but notice how the distribution is different. In 2, people are clustered together but in 3 they are more spread out.

B Where people live worldwide

Key:
- High density
- Medium density
- Low density

Map B shows where people live in the world. Areas with a lot of people (densely populated) are Europe, south-east Asia and the north-east of North America. But these regions are not densely populated everywhere. The distribution or spread of the population is very uneven. There are areas of low, medium and high population density.

C Where people live in Europe

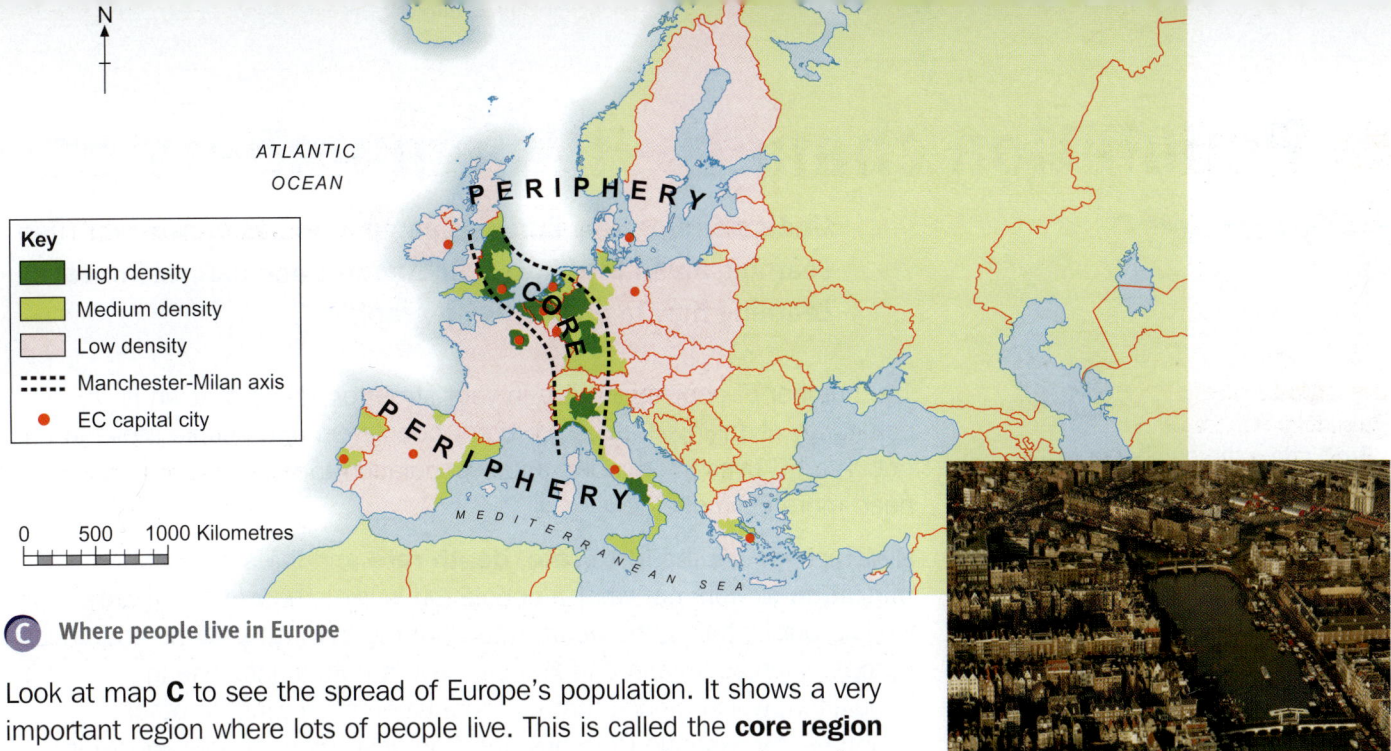

Look at map **C** to see the spread of Europe's population. It shows a very important region where lots of people live. This is called the **core region** (see photo **D**). The core region has many advantages for people, such as flat, fertile land, a water supply and a good climate. Other parts of Europe, such as Scandinavia and upland Britain, have very low population densities. These areas do not attract people because they have poor soils, steep slopes or a cold climate. These regions are called the **periphery**.

D Aerial photograph of Amsterdam, part of the densely populated Manchester–Milan axis

Activities

1. Find the area where you live on map **C**.
   a) What type of population density does your local area have?
   b) Is your area part of the core or periphery?

2. In this activity you are going to complete a choropleth or shading map of Europe (see pages 145–155 of *SKILLS in geography* for more help).
   a) Look at the Worksheet table that your teacher will give you. Complete the table column to show the densities of population for the European countries.
   b) Use an outline map of Europe. Choose *one* colour to complete your key for the map: colour lightly for densities below 100 people per km²; colour more heavily for densities between 101 and 200 people per km² and heavily for those with densities over 201. Then use the shades you chose to colour in the map to show the population densities in the table.
   c) Can you recognise the core and periphery? Write *core* and *periphery* in the correct places on your map.

3. Study this list of factors affecting population density. Copy them into a table like the one below. The table has been started for you.
   - A moderate climate good for farming and people
   - Thin, rocky soils
   - High steep land where tractors cannot be used
   - Gently sloping land where it is easy to build roads and railways

High density of population	Low density of population
A moderate climate with no extremes	

4. Think about your own local area. Which of the factors in the list above apply to it? Complete the paragraph below.

   My local area has a *high / medium / low* population density because it has *a moderate climate good for farming and people / thin, rocky soils / high steep land where tractors cannot be used / gently sloping land where it is easy to build roads and railways.*

2 Who are the Europeans?

Population change – it's a numbers game

> Understanding why Europe's population has grown over time
> Learning about birth rates, death rates and natural increase
> Learning how to draw a living graph

Key words

Birth rate – the number of births per 1000 people per year
Death rate – the number of deaths per 1000 people per year
Migration – the movement of people
Natural decrease – when death rate is greater than birth rate
Natural increase – when birth rate is greater than death rate; birth rate minus death rate is the growth rate of the population

The number of people who live in your street or village or town is constantly changing. Babies are born, people die and people move in and out. The EU uses information about population to decide which regions need more EU money.

Geographers use the **birth rate, death rate** and the amount of **migration** to work out what a population is like. The **natural increase** is worked out by taking the death rate from the birth rate. Some countries in Europe, such as Ireland and France, have a natural increase in population, which means that the population is growing. In other countries, for example Germany and Romania, more people are dying than are being born so there is a **natural decrease** in population.

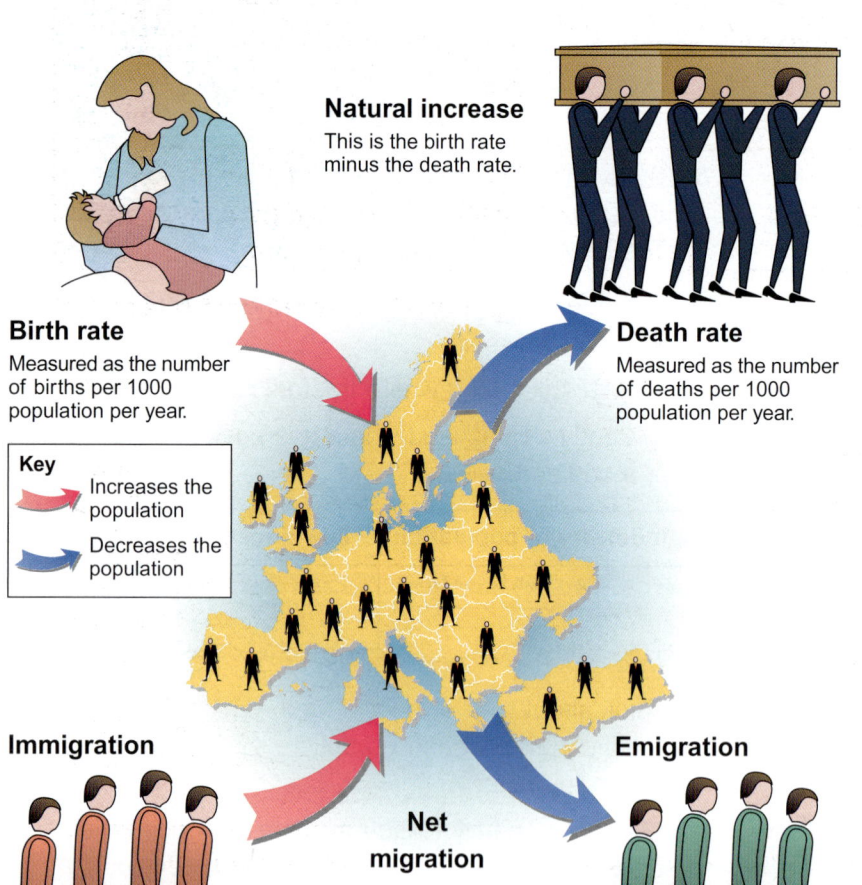

Population changes can also occur if people move into or out of a country or region. This is called migration.

Figure **B** and source **C** show how the population has changed in Europe.

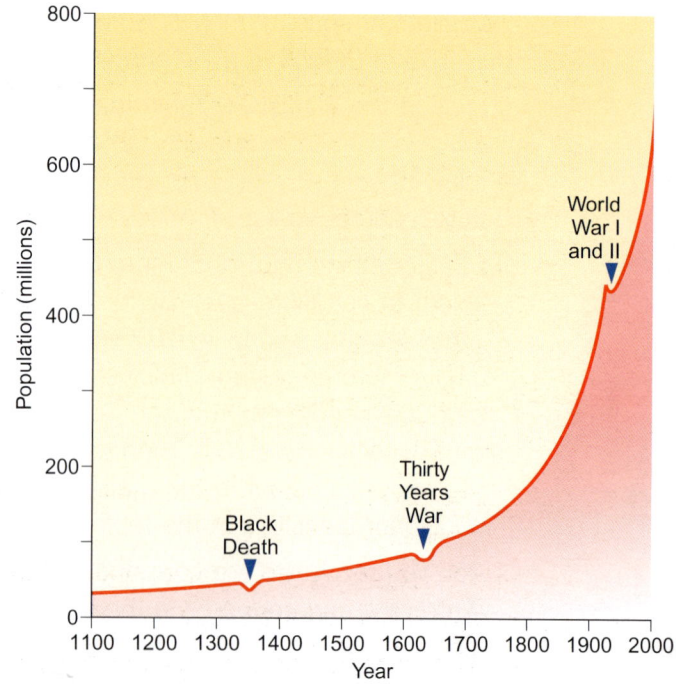

Birth rate
Measured as the number of births per 1000 population per year.

Natural increase
This is the birth rate minus the death rate.

Death rate
Measured as the number of deaths per 1000 population per year.

Key
→ Increases the population
→ Decreases the population

Immigration

Emigration

Net migration

A Factors causing population change in Europe

B Population change in Europe

18 geography 360° Foundation Book 2

The population grew very slowly up until about 1750. At this time both birth rates and death rates were high.

From 1750 to 1950 the population grew more quickly because medical care and water supplies improved.

In the late twentieth century the population stabilised. But in some European countries the populations have begun to decrease. Birth rates have fallen below death rates. We say that the population is below replacement level. Some countries are now encouraging higher birth rates so that the population begins to grow again. People are also living longer so the population is ageing – there are fewer young people and more older people.

C shows some of the reasons why birth and death rates have fallen.

Better health care	Better food	Pensions and sick pay
Better education	Family planning	Improved water supply

C Why did the population in Europe change?

Activities

1 How the population in Europe has grown

Use a copy of graph **B**. Make your graph into a living graph by adding these notes in the correct places:

- 1750   The Industrial Revolution begins
- 1800   Death rates start to fall
- 1600   Birth rates and death rates high
- 1950   Birth rates falling
- 2000   Birth rates and death rates are low

2 Use your graph.

a) Describe the graph's shape: is it a straight line? Is it an 'S' shape? Does it go up or down?

b) Can you imagine how your graph will look by 2500? What sorts of changes would there be?

c) When was Europe's population growing very slowly? When was it growing very quickly?

SKILLS

How to draw a living graph

1 Draw your graph outline and label the axes. Put the years along the bottom and the population up the side.
2 Plot the graph to show how the population has changed over time.
3 Add the labels in the correct places on the graph.
4 Add a title to your graph.

For more help see page 151 of *SKILLS in geography*

2 Who are the Europeans?

What is a population pyramid?

> Learning about the age–sex structure of populations
> Learning how to draw population pyramids and why they have different shapes

Key words

Gender – the sex of a person, male or female
Life expectancy – the average age to which people in a country are expected to live
Population pyramid – a graph showing the population structure of an area, country or region
Population structure – the numbers of males and females in different age groups in a population

Think about the place where you live. How many people in the local area are male? How many are female? How many are young people, adults or elderly? Dividing up the population by age and **gender** shows the **population structure**. A population pyramid (**A**) is often drawn to show the age structure of a population.

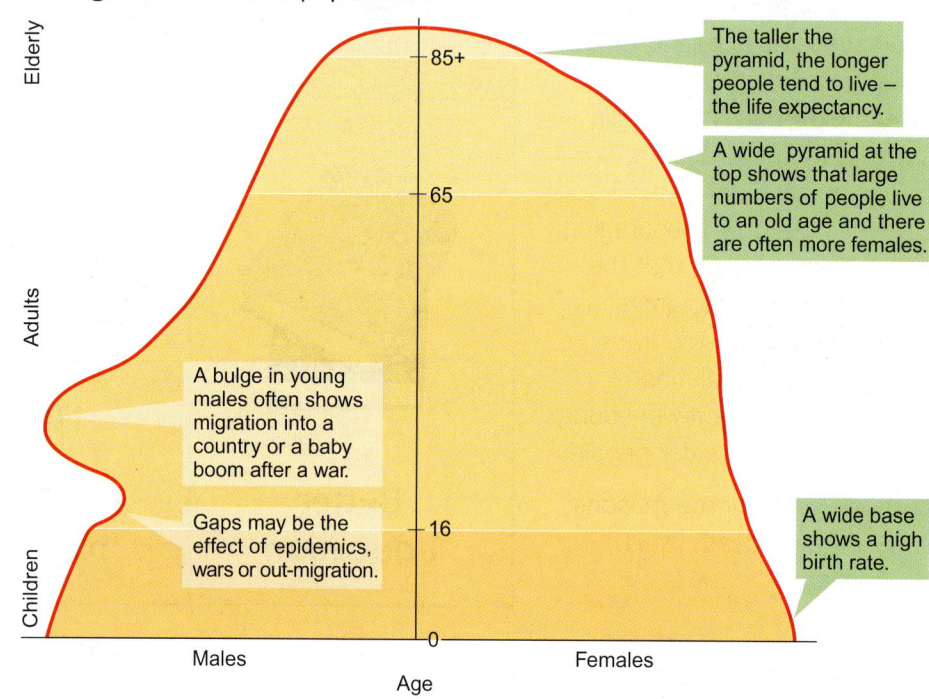

The taller the pyramid, the longer people tend to live – the life expectancy.

A wide pyramid at the top shows that large numbers of people live to an old age and there are often more females.

A bulge in young males often shows migration into a country or a baby boom after a war.

Gaps may be the effect of epidemics, wars or out-migration.

A wide base shows a high birth rate.

A What is a population pyramid?

Different places have different population pyramids. A population pyramid can tell us about the population history of a country. Look at the pyramid for Germany in **B**.

You can see that Germany has a lot of elderly women. Population pyramids often show larger numbers of elderly females because women usually live longer (they have a longer **life expectancy**). In many European countries there are gaps on the male side because men died in the World Wars. You can see pyramids with different shapes in **C**.

Fewer males of this age due to World Wars I and II
Fewer births in this age group due to World War II
More boys than girls are born
More females living longer than males
Baby boom after World War II and influx of migrant workers
A narrow base so birth rate is falling

Source: US Census Bureau, International Data Base

B Population pyramid for Germany, 2002

20 geography 360° Foundation Book 2

WHAT CHANGES PYRAMID SHAPES?

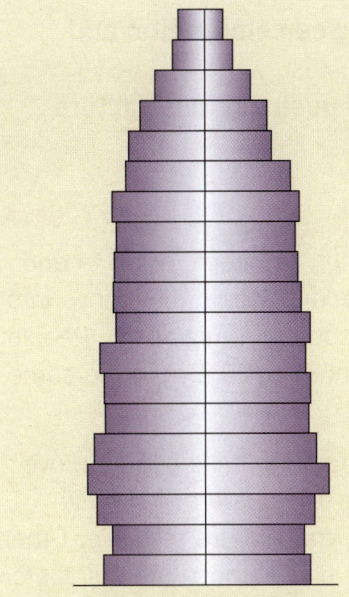

(i) A pyramid may have a narrow base if the birth rate is less than the death rate. Births may have fallen due to improved birth control or women staying in education and having a career. This is happening in some European countries.

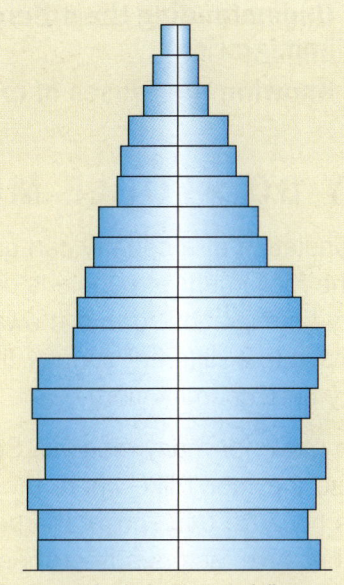

(ii) There may be bulges, especially among young adults in countries where there is high immigration. These may be because young males have moved into the country looking for work and a higher standard of living.

(iii) In some pyramids the shape may be triangular. This indicates that there are high birth and death rates. This is usually in less developed regions.

C The different shapes of population pyramids

Activities

1. a) Use the information in **D** to draw a population pyramid for the UK. Use the *SKILLS* box to help you.
   b) Add these labels in the best places:
   - More young males than females
   - More elderly females than males
   - Gap in males
   - Narrow base

2. Go to the Hotlinks site (see page 2) to find the Census data for 2001 on the Internet.
   a) How many men and women of different age groups are there in your area? You could choose your town, ward or county.
   b) Draw a population pyramid for the data.
   c) What are the similarities and differences between your pyramid and the one for the UK as a whole? Suggest why they are different.

3. Go to the Hotlinks site to find population pyramids for countries around the world. Choose *one* country and study the pyramids for 2000, 2025 and 2050. If you can, print them off. Label the pyramids to show the key information.

Age	Males	Females
0–14	9.6	9.2
15–29	9.4	9.4
30–44	11.1	11.5
45–59	9.4	9.5
60–74	6.3	7.0
75–89	2.6	4.3
90+	0.2	0.5

D Population (in millions) for the UK, 2000

SKILLS

How to draw a population pyramid

1. Show the male population on the left and the female on the right.
2. Draw a horizontal axis with 0 in the middle. The scale can be in either percentages or numbers.
3. Draw a vertical axis from the 0. Divide into age groups, e.g. 0–4, 5–9, 10–14, etc.
4. Draw bars horizontally for each age group and gender.
5. Label the axes and add a title.

For more help see page 150 of *SKILLS in geography*

People on the move

> Understanding the differences between emigration and immigration
>
> Knowing the causes of migration – push and pull factors

WHY DO PEOPLE MOVE?

The population of a country can quickly change as people move in and out. The movement of people is called migration. People may move into a country (immigration) or move away from a country (emigration). People may move to a different country (international migration) or in the same country (internal migration).

People move for many reasons. Sometimes factors make people move because they don't like where they are living. These are called *push factors* because they 'push' the person away from where they live. Others move because factors attract them to a new place. These are *pull factors* because they 'pull' the person towards the new place. Table **A** shows some push and pull factors.

In some cases people move because they are forced to (photo **B**). **Refugees** are people forced to move out of their country because of push factors such as famine or civil war.

Key word

Refugee – a person who is forced to move to another country, usually as a result of civil war, persecution or a natural disaster

Push factors	Pull factors
• Harsh climate	• Well paid jobs
• Lack of services	• Entertainment
• Natural disasters, e.g. famine, earthquake, flood	• Education
• Civil war	• Moving to be with relatives
	• Health care and welfare benefits

A Reasons for migration

B Afghan refugees outside United Nations camp in Kabul, Afghanistan

C Where is this family moving to – around the corner or abroad? Why are they moving?

Look at map **D**. It shows some migrations over time. Some people migrated from poor to rich countries; some migrated to escape war. Some moved because of their religious beliefs. Some were taken and sold against their will. But migrations happen all the time. In 2004, people from Sudan in Africa were forced to move out of their homes while British people chose to leave for the sunshine in Australia and Spain.

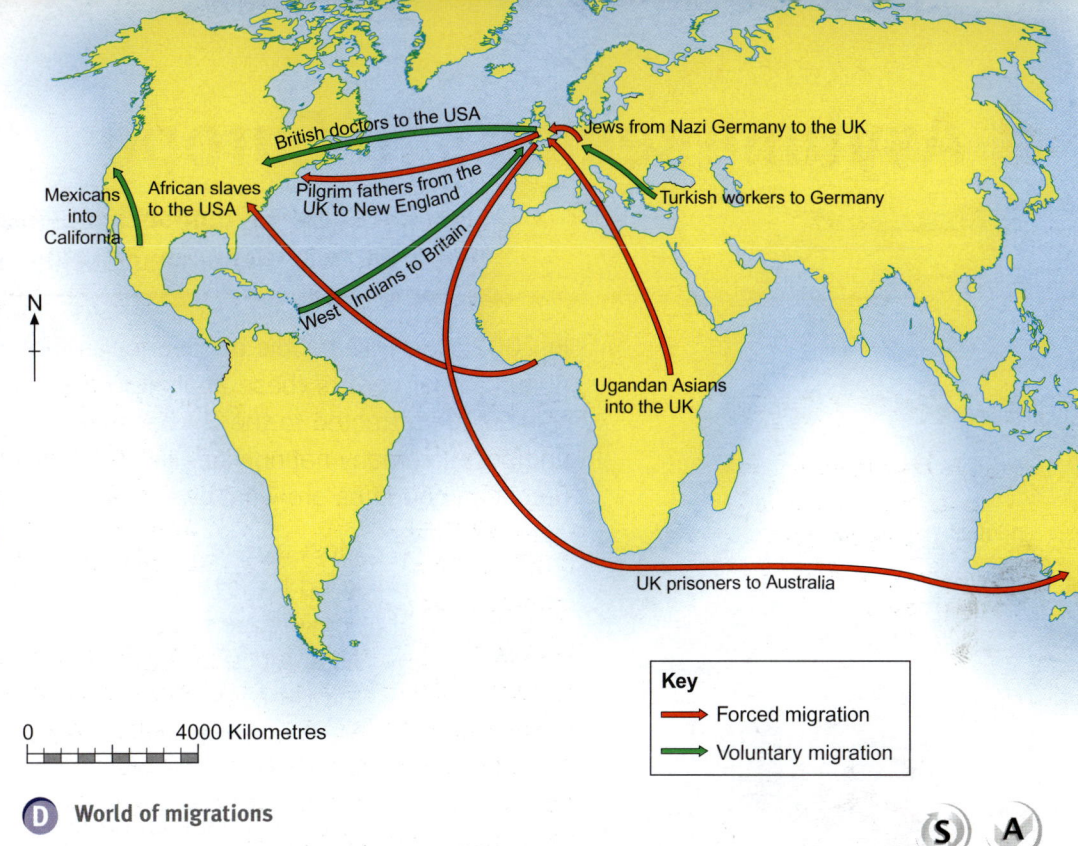

Map labels:
- British doctors to the USA
- Jews from Nazi Germany to the UK
- Mexicans into California
- African slaves to the USA
- Pilgrim fathers from the UK to New England
- Turkish workers to Germany
- West Indians to Britain
- Ugandan Asians into the UK
- UK prisoners to Australia

Key
- → Forced migration
- → Voluntary migration

D World of migrations

Activities

1. Look at photo **C**. Have you or your family ever moved? How far did you move? Why did you move? Produce a class survey of everyone's answers.
   a) Can you spot any patterns? For example, do most people move short or long distances?
   b) What are the main reasons why people have moved?

2. **Tops and tails**

   Match the words on the left with the correct definitions.

Word	Definition
Immigration	Something that attracts people to a place
Push factor	People moving out of a country
Migration	People moving into a country
Pull factor	The movement of people
Emigration	Something that makes people move away from a place

3. Study source **A**. Rearrange the push and pull factors into a copy of the table below.

Likely to lead to forced migration	Likely to lead to voluntary migration

4. Choose *one* of the migrations marked on map **D**.
   a) Research the migration by using the Hotlinks site (see page 2). Create a fact file that includes the following information:
   - When did the migration take place?
   - How many people were involved?
   - Where did they emigrate from?
   - Where did they migrate to?
   - Why did they migrate?
   - What were the advantages and disadvantages for the migrant?

   b) Swap your fact file with a partner. Help them to improve their work.
   - What do you like about their work?
   - Have they included all of the information that was asked for?
   - Have they explained why the migration happened?
   - Have they described the advantages and disadvantages to the migrant?

2 Who are the Europeans?

Asylum-seekers in Europe

> Learning about asylum-seekers – facts and figures
> Discussing whether asylum-seekers should be allowed to stay

In 2002, 430 000 people applied for asylum in Europe (see graph **A**). About 25 per cent of these applied for asylum in the UK. A lot of asylum-seekers are attracted to the UK because they can speak some English and because many nationalities live here. Many also believe that western European countries are wealthy.

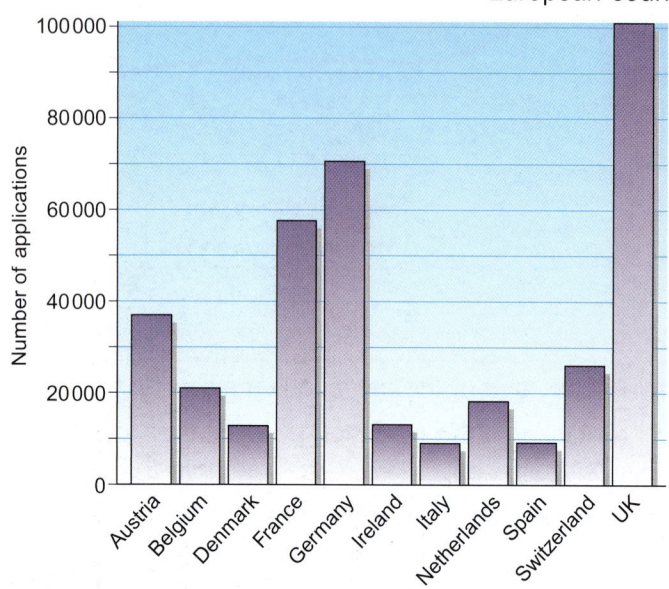

Most people applying for asylum are afraid they will be killed if they stay in their own country. Most asylum-seekers are male, under 30 years old and come from Asia, Africa or the Middle East. Many asylum-seekers to the UK come from Iraq, Afghanistan and Zimbabwe. Most of those hoping to migrate into Europe feel that they have no choice.

In 2002 about 75 per cent of asylum-seekers to the UK were allowed to stay. Glasgow (5665), Birmingham (3555) and Liverpool (1925) took the most people.

People have different views about asylum-seekers. Look at source **B**. Some people are against Europe and the UK accepting them, while others think they should be allowed to stay.

Source: © Crown copyright. Published by the Home Office

A Applications for asylum in Europe, 2002

- A single asylum-seeker claimed £38.26 a week in benefits in 2004.
- Immigration control cost £1.7 billion in 2002–3.
- Asylum-seekers often do the badly paid, dirty and dangerous jobs.
- Asylum-seekers and refugees contribute £2.5 billion to the economy.
- Asylum-seekers cause problems in local communities.
- Some asylum-seekers are doctors, teachers or nurses.
- Asylum-seekers cause housing and job shortages.
- People often don't want detention centres near their homes.

B Should asylum-seekers be allowed to stay?

Activities

1. Study graph **A**.
   a) Which *three* countries received the most asylum-seekers?
   b) Suggest some reasons why these countries were popular.
   c) For what other reasons do asylum-seekers want to migrate?

2. Draw a pie graph chart to show the information in source **D**.
   a) Where do most asylum-seekers come from?
   b) Why do you think there are so many asylum-seekers from Europe?
   (See pages 145–155 of *SKILLS in geography* for more help.)

3. Study the pie graph in **E**.
   a) What percentage of asylum-seekers are under 30 years old?
   b) Why do you think most asylum-seekers are male and under 30?

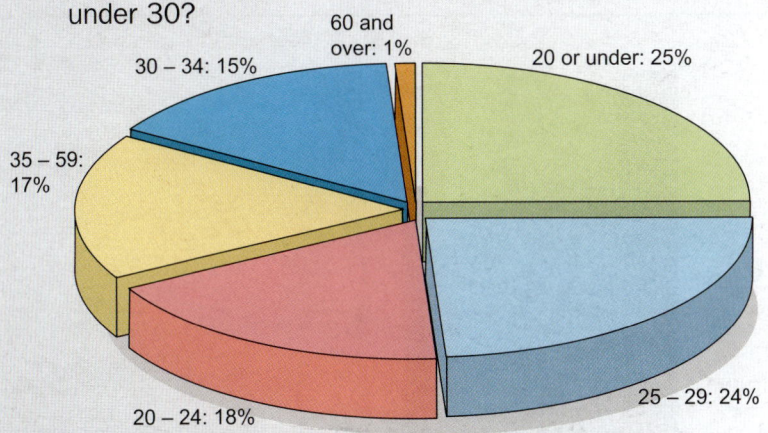

E Asylum-seekers in the UK by age group, 2002
- 20 or under: 25%
- 25 – 29: 24%
- 20 – 24: 18%
- 35 – 59: 17%
- 30 – 34: 15%
- 60 and over: 1%

4. **What are your views about asylum-seekers?**

   Hold a class discussion about whether asylum-seekers should be allowed to stay. Work in small groups; each group should take on one of the roles below.

   - An asylum-seeker – choose your country, making up a name if you like
   - The government of the UK
   - The government of the asylum-seeker's country
   - The asylum-seeker's family left behind
   - A member of the British National Party (BNP), who oppose immigration
   - A charity that supports asylum-seekers
   - Someone who lives near a planned detention unit.

   Research information about asylum using the Hotlinks site (see page 2) and write a short presentation to represent your case.

C Asylum-seekers try to find a way through the Channel Tunnel

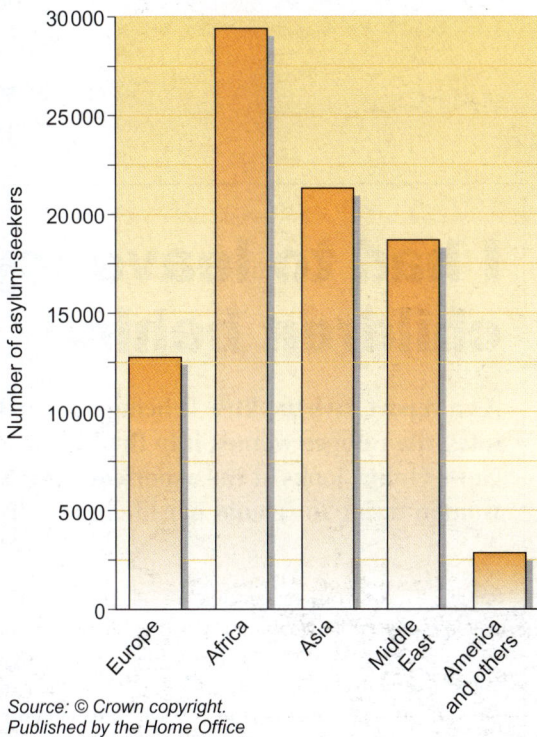

D Where asylum-seekers to the UK came from, 2002

Source: © Crown copyright. Published by the Home Office

Key word

Asylum-seeker – a refugee who applies to stay in another country because they face persecution and possibly death in their home country

2 Who are the Europeans?

Feelings running high!

> Finding out what it is like to be an asylum-seeker
> Exploring the difference between asylum-seekers and economic migrants

Key word

Economic migrant – someone who moves to another country for a better standard of living

Asylum-seekers leave their home country because they face persecution or even death. **Economic migrants** hope to find work and a better quality of life in another country – these migrants are not usually welcome in the UK. The big problem for the authorities is judging whether people are genuine asylum-seekers or economic migrants.

On pages 24–25 you discussed whether asylum-seekers should be allowed to stay in the UK. What are your feelings about asylum-seekers? Sources **A** and **B** show some real-life experiences of asylum-seekers in the UK.

I had to leave my children behind

As a report says too little is being done to help integrate refugee women into British society, BBC News Online looks at the experience of a Somali woman trying to rebuild her life in the UK.

Selima, 27, has not seen her two young sons for three years.

She was forced to leave her home in Somalia because her family belonged to a minority ethnic group. They were being persecuted by a dominant tribe in the country's civil war.

Her father was taken away and murdered, and she had to watch her aunt being raped in the family home.

Her husband was imprisoned before managing to escape and flee to Ethiopia.

Selima initially remained in Somalia where she lived in fear of being raped.

"My mum told me I had to escape because I was a young woman," she said.

"She said it was better for her to die than for me."

"I got very depressed and tried to kill myself" Selima

One day in 1999, fierce fighting broke out in Selima's town, and her people scattered.

"Everyone panicked and I was separated from my family," she said.

"I fled to… Ethiopia, where I stayed with my uncle."

"He found the money to get me to the UK."

After arriving, Selima lived in London for two years, but found it extremely hard to adjust – especially without her children.

"Everything was totally different," she said.

Support network

"I had to ask people to help me do everything, and I spoke very little English so I needed an interpreter to help me.

"It was like being dropped in the ocean and I couldn't bear to live without my children."

Selima consulted her doctor who referred her to a psychologist to help her overcome her depression.

She also found support from a network of Somali friends in Southampton.

She attended college and soon developed excellent English.

She began volunteering as an interpreter with the Refugee Action charity, and through that work found her present job as a bilingual assistant helping Somali schoolchildren.

My dream

She loves her work, but still misses her children – now aged four and six – terribly.

In July, she was told she would be granted refugee status.

She recently managed to contact her mother through a family tracing service and learned that her children are safe and well.

"My dream is that one day soon I will be reunited with my children."

"There are so many women like me out there" Selima said.

Friday, 21 February 2003

A Selima's story. Reproduced from BBC News at bbcnews.co.uk

ASYLUM POLICY SPARKS HIV CONCERN
Doctors are concerned that the UK policy of dispersing asylum-seekers may lead to increased HIV transmission.

MENTOR SCHEME FOR YOUNG REFUGEES
A scheme to help young asylum-seekers in Liverpool to adjust to life in the UK is launched.

JAILING ASYLUM-SEEKERS 'MUST END'
The United Nations' agency for refugees protests over the detention of asylum-seekers in the UK's prisons.

Asylum centre appeal date delayed
Protesters may have to wait another two months for Court of Appeal decision on a new asylum centre.

B UK headlines from news stories about asylum-seekers, 2004. Reproduced from BBC News at bbcnews.co.uk

C Somali asylum-seeker in Islamabad, Pakistan

Activities

1. Read carefully about the experiences of the asylum-seeker in **A**. Use what you have read to contribute to a class discussion about:
   - the push factors that force people to move to the UK
   - the pull factors that attract people to come to the UK
   - the advantages of migration to the asylum-seekers
   - the disadvantages of migration to the asylum-seekers
   - the response of the government, the media and the general public to asylum-seekers
   - your own response to asylum-seekers.

2. Imagine you are a young asylum-seeker who has recently moved into your local area. Either write about your experiences or label a comic strip. You should answer these questions:
   - Why were you forced to leave your home country?
   - Why did you come to the UK?
   - Who did you have leave behind?
   - What has been your experience of living in the UK?
   - What are your feelings and hopes for the future?

Poland – a new entrant to the EU

> Finding out the key facts about Poland's population
> Understanding the similarities and differences between the population in Poland and the UK

Poland (map **A**) is mostly lowland. To the north lies the Baltic Sea and to the south the Carpathian Mountains. There are many lakes, especially in the north east of the country. About 50 per cent of the land area is used to grow crops – the best farmland is in the south west. The capital city of Poland is Warsaw (photo **B**).

Poland is the largest of the ten new countries to join the European Union in 2004. Table **C** shows how some facts about Poland compare with those for the UK.

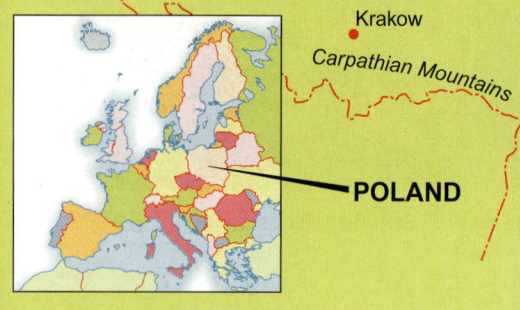

A Poland

B Warsaw

Characteristic	Poland	UK
Total population	38 620 000	60 090 000
Area (km^2)	312 685	244 820
Population density (per km^2)	124	245
Population who live in urban areas	63 per cent	89 per cent
Life expectancy Female Male	 78 years 70 years	 80 years 75 years
Infant mortality rate/1000 births	9	5
Age groups: 0–14 15–59 Over 60	 17 per cent 70 per cent 13 per cent	 8 per cent 66 per cent 16 per cent
Births per thousand people per year	10	11
Deaths per thousand people per year	10	10
Employment: Agriculture Industry Services	 27 per cent 22 per cent 50 per cent	 1 per cent 25 per cent 74 per cent
Average annual income per person (US $)	11 100	27 700
People per doctor	467	300
Adult literacy	99 per cent	99 per cent

C Characteristics of Poland and the UK

As you can see, Poland has a smaller population than the UK but a larger land area. This means that the population density is much less than in the UK. In Poland fewer people live in towns and cities too. Look at **D**. What differences might this mean to the quality of life in the two countries?

Access to clean water

Shelter – a home with bathroom, kitchen, heating

Clean safe jobs in industry and services

Good wages

A holiday abroad

Access to TV and computer

Good education and health services

A healthy and varied diet

D What do people mean by 'quality of life'?

People live only slightly longer (life expectancy) in the UK, even though Poland has far more people per doctor. In Poland the population is younger and there are fewer people over 60. The infant mortality rate is also higher. More people work in agriculture in Poland – perhaps this explains the low average incomes. Will joining the EU help this?

Activities

1. Study a map of Poland in an atlas.
   a) List the countries that border Poland. Which of these are also members of the EU?
   b) Which sea lies to the north of Poland? Which mountains lie to the south?
2. Look at table **C**.
   a) Give *one* similarity between Poland and the UK.
   b) List *three* differences between Poland and the UK.
   c) Explain why Poland has a lower population density than the UK.
   d) Suggest why the average income of people in Poland is so much lower than that in the UK. Hint: think about what jobs they do.
3. In small groups, discuss why you think Poland wanted to be a member of the EU. What benefits do you think it will bring? Why might some countries already in the EU be worried about Poland joining the EU? Contribute your ideas to a class discussion.

Assessing 360°

Who are the Europeans?

A An area with low population density

1. Study photograph **A** and draw a sketch of it (see pages 145–155 of *SKILLS in geography* for more help). Label it to show the reasons why it has a low density of population.

2. Do you think the area in **A** will be in the core or periphery of Europe?

Country	Birth rate	Death rate	Natural increase
France	12	9	12 – 9 = 3
UK	11	10	
Germany	8	10	
Ireland	14	8	

B Population statistics for some European countries, 2004

3. a) Copy and complete table **B** to show the natural increase in each country. The first one has been done for you.
   b) Which countries have a growing population? Which has a falling population?
   c) Suggest *two* reasons why some countries have a falling population.
   d) Read the following statements. Write down the ones that are true of countries with ageing populations.
   - We need to make sure we can pay for all of the pensions that are needed.
   - We need to have more schools and nurseries.
   - We will need more migrant workers as the workforce gets smaller.
   - With more children, larger houses will be needed.
   - We need to close children's wards and open more centres to care for the elderly.
   - We should think about raising family allowances so that birth rates go up.

4. **Tops and tails**
   Explain the differences between each of these pairs of words or phrases.
   - *Emigration* and *immigration*
   - *Population distribution* and *population density*
   - *Push factors* and *pull factors*

»3 Europe's weather and climate

Find the UK on this weather satellite photograph of Europe. What do you think the weather is like? Where would the best place be to see some sunshine?

Learning objectives

What are you going to learn about in this chapter?
- What weather is and how it is measured
- What clouds are and why it rains
- What low and high pressure are
- How and why the weather changes
- Using satellite images
- The difference between weather and climate
- What the European climates are
- How climate affects our everyday lives

What is weather?

> Finding out what weather is
> Learning how people measure the weather

- Heavy rain clouds
- Trees bending show strong winds
- People in waterproof clothes suggest rain and damp surroundings

A Can we tell what the weather is like by looking?

B Weather forecast for the UK, 22 August 2004

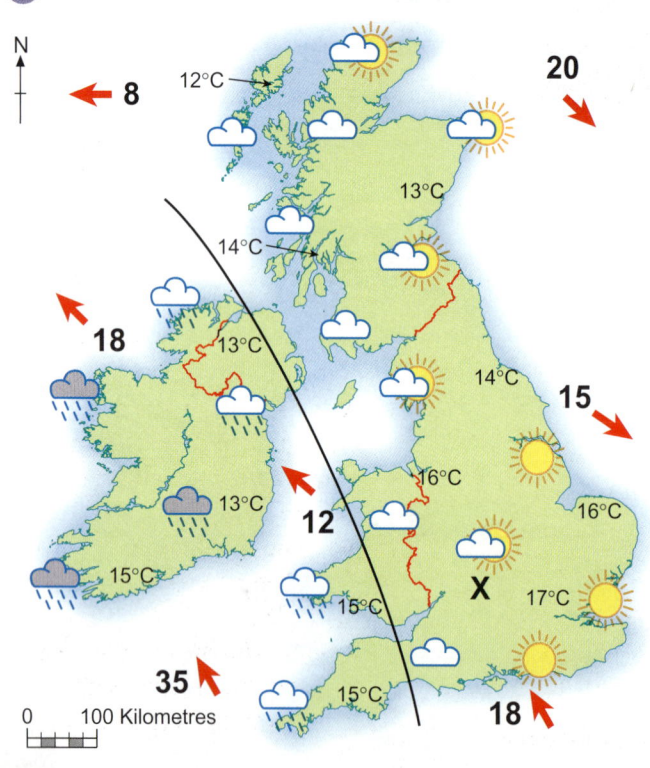

The **weather** is what is happening in the air at any moment; it might be wet or dry, snowing or sunny. Everyone is interested in the weather because it affects their everyday lives so much.

FORECASTING THE WEATHER

You can tell quite a lot about the weather just by looking outside (**A**). You can get more information from a **weather forecast** on TV or in newspapers. Map **B** shows a weather forecast from a newspaper. Most weather forecasts tell you about the temperature, rainfall, cloud and wind. These are all elements of the weather.

People who make weather forecasts need more accurate information about the weather than they can get by simply looking outside! They have to say what the weather is going to be like. To make a weather forecast, a **meteorologist** gets information from:

- instruments collected in one place called a **weather station** (see **C**)
- satellites
- weather ships.

Anemometer and weather vane measuring wind speed in km/h and wind direction. A wind is named by the direction *from* which it blows.

Stevenson Screen holds the thermometer and hygrometer to measure shade temperature and humidity (the amount of moisture in the air).

Sunshine recorder – the sun burns a trace on to a piece of paper. This shows the number of hours the sun shines.

Barometer measures air pressure in millibars. It can be indoors.

Raingauge measures rainfall in millimetres.

C Measuring the weather

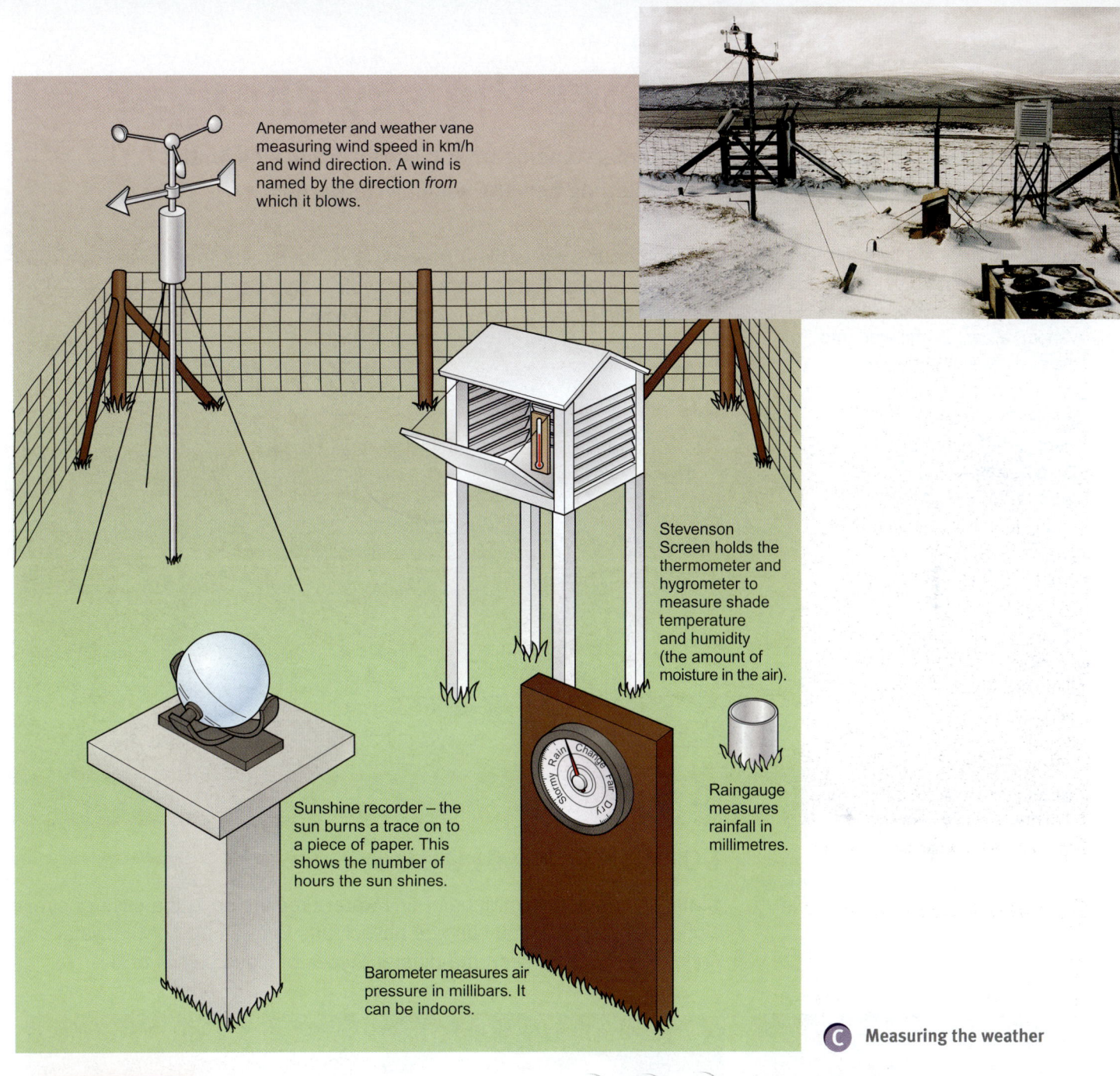

Activities

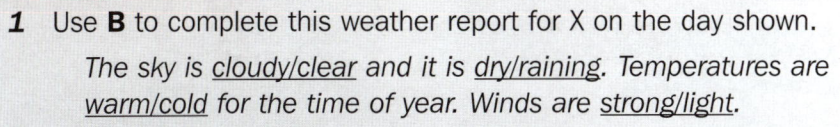

1. Use **B** to complete this weather report for X on the day shown.

   The sky is cloudy/clear and it is dry/raining. Temperatures are warm/cold for the time of year. Winds are strong/light.

2. a) Study map **B**. Make a copy of the weather symbols used on the map. Label each one to show what it means.

   b) Look at the weather symbols on **B**. Look outside and draw the correct ones to describe what the weather is like where you are.

   c) Compare this with what is written in your local paper or use the Hotlinks site (see page 2) to find the forecast on the BBC website.

3. What would someone need to wear for the weather where you are today? Do they need an umbrella or a sunhat?

4. Write your own definitions for these terms: weather, weather forecast.

Key words

Meteorologist – a person who studies the weather

Weather – the state of the atmosphere at any one time: whether it is sunny or raining, cloudy, hot, cold, etc.

Weather forecast – a prediction of what the weather will be like

Weather station – a place used to record the weather with meteorological instruments

3 Europe's weather and climate

How and why does the sky change?

> Understanding what clouds are and why it rains
> Learning how the water cycle works

Key words

Cloud – millions of tiny water droplets or ice crystals
Condensation – when water vapour, a gas, is changed into water as a liquid in water droplets and clouds by cooling
Convection current – when warm air rises through the air
Evaporation – when water from lakes and seas is changed into water vapour, a gas, by heating
Front – the zone where two blocks of air meet
Precipitation – all forms of moisture that reach the ground surface, e.g. snow, rain, sleet, dew
Relief – the height and shape of the land
Water cycle – the movement of water between the air, the oceans and the ground

One minute the sky is blue, the next it is cloudy and then it may rain…but why? The answer lies in the **water cycle** – the way water is moved between the ground, the air and the sea (**A**).

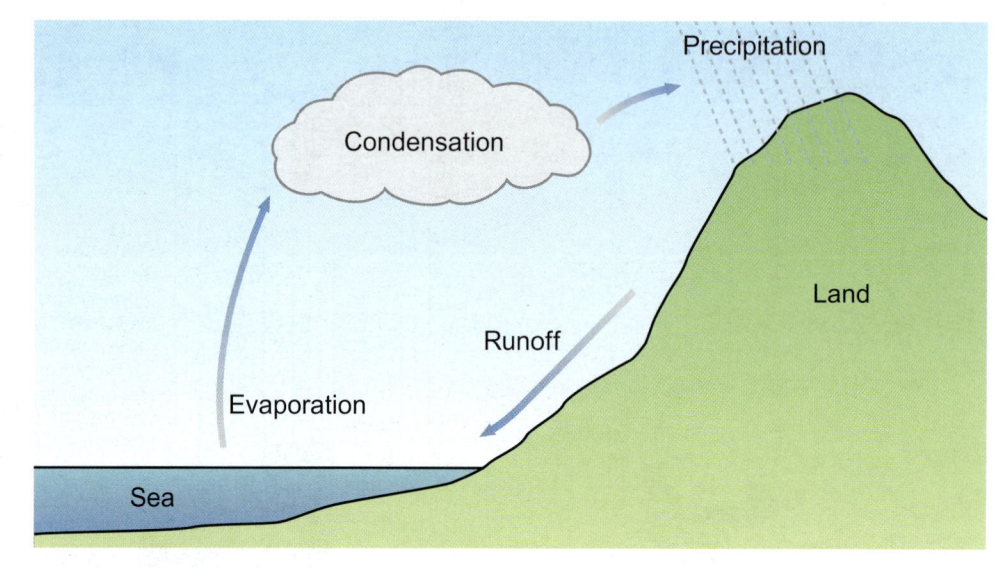

A The water cycle

LOOKING AT CLOUDS

Clouds are made of millions of tiny water droplets or, in the case of cirrus clouds, ice crystals. You can see how clouds form as part of the water cycle, but have you seen the different types of cloud shown in **B**?

B The three cloud types

Cirrus clouds Thin wispy clouds very high in the sky. Temperatures are freezing so the clouds are made of ice crystals. They often mean bad weather is on the way.

Cumulus clouds Fluffy clouds that often rise quite high in the sky. They can bring showers. Some grow into very tall clouds that bring very heavy rain and thunder and lightning.

Stratus clouds Huge blankets of grey cloud often quite low in the sky. They often bring light drizzle.

WHAT KIND OF RAIN IS IT?

Precipitation is the term used for all water that reaches the ground surface, such as rainfall, snow, sleet and frost. Rainfall comes from clouds made of millions of tiny water droplets. Clouds are formed by air rising. Air can be forced to rise in three main ways, so geographers give rain three different names depending on what has caused the air to rise (**C**).

> **Key words**
>
> **Water vapour** – water as a gas in the atmosphere
>
> **Wind** – moving air from an area of high pressure to an area of low pressure

1 Relief rainfall

Winds that blow over the sea pick up moisture. When this moist air reaches high land it can only do one thing: it has to go up. As the air rises it cools and the water vapour it is carrying **condenses**, forming clouds and rainfall. The rain is forced to rise because of the **relief** of the land, so this type of rainfall is called *relief rainfall*.

2 Convectional rainfall

On very warm days, the sun heats the ground, which heats the air above. The warm air rises as a **convection current**. As the air rises it cools, and the moisture condenses to form clouds and rainfall. Sometimes the convection currents are very strong and they produce very tall clouds and heavy rainfall with thunder and lightning.

3 Frontal rainfall

Great blocks of air at different temperatures move around the Earth over sea and land. When warm air and cold air meet, they do not mix. The zone where they meet is called a **front**. At the front the lighter warm air is forced to rise over the colder denser air. The rising air cools and eventually clouds form and rain falls. We call this *frontal rainfall*. The symbols in **D** are used on weather maps. They show fronts where the different blocks of air meet.

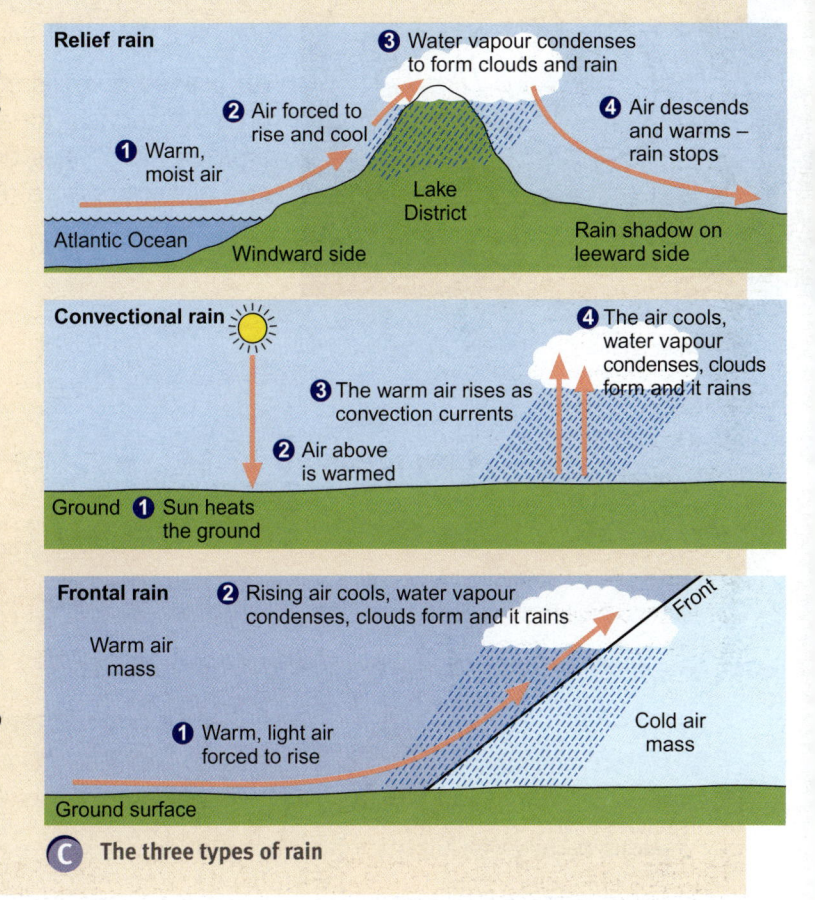

C The three types of rain

D Symbols for warm and cold fronts

Activities

1. Rearrange these sentences so that they are in the correct order to describe what is happening in the water cycle.

   A Some of the rain flows into rivers, and some soaks into the land.
   B As the air rises, it cools.
   C The sun's energy makes water evaporate from the oceans and become water vapour.
   D Clouds form and it rains.
   E The water vapour in the air condenses.
   F The rivers eventually flow back into the oceans.
   G The warm air carrying the water vapour rises.

2. In pairs or small groups, produce an illustrated poster to show the life of a water droplet suitable to give to a pupil in primary school. Think about what words they will understand and what they will find difficult. How can you make it clear for them?

3. Look out of your classroom window at the clouds. See if you can name the type of cloud you can see. Give reasons for your answer.

3 Europe's weather and climate

Feeling the pressure?

> Understanding air pressure and how it is linked to the weather
> Learning the key facts about anticyclones

The air is pressing down on the Earth's surface, although we cannot feel it. This is **air pressure**. People measure air pressure in **millibars** using a **barometer** (**A**). Pressure is shown on a weather map by **isobars**. An isobar joins together places with the same air pressure. It is like a contour line on a map that joins together places with the same height.

Air pressure varies from place to place and from time to time. Air resting on a hot surface, for example a hot desert, tends to rise to give low pressure. Air resting on a cold surface, for example ice, tends to sink and give higher pressure (**B**).

A A barometer

Low pressure

Air cannot rise for ever! So it moves away and eventually...

❶ Warm air rising...
❷ So the pressure is low
❸ But rising air means cloud and rain

Low pressure brings clouds and rain. The lower the pressure, the worse the weather will be.

High pressure

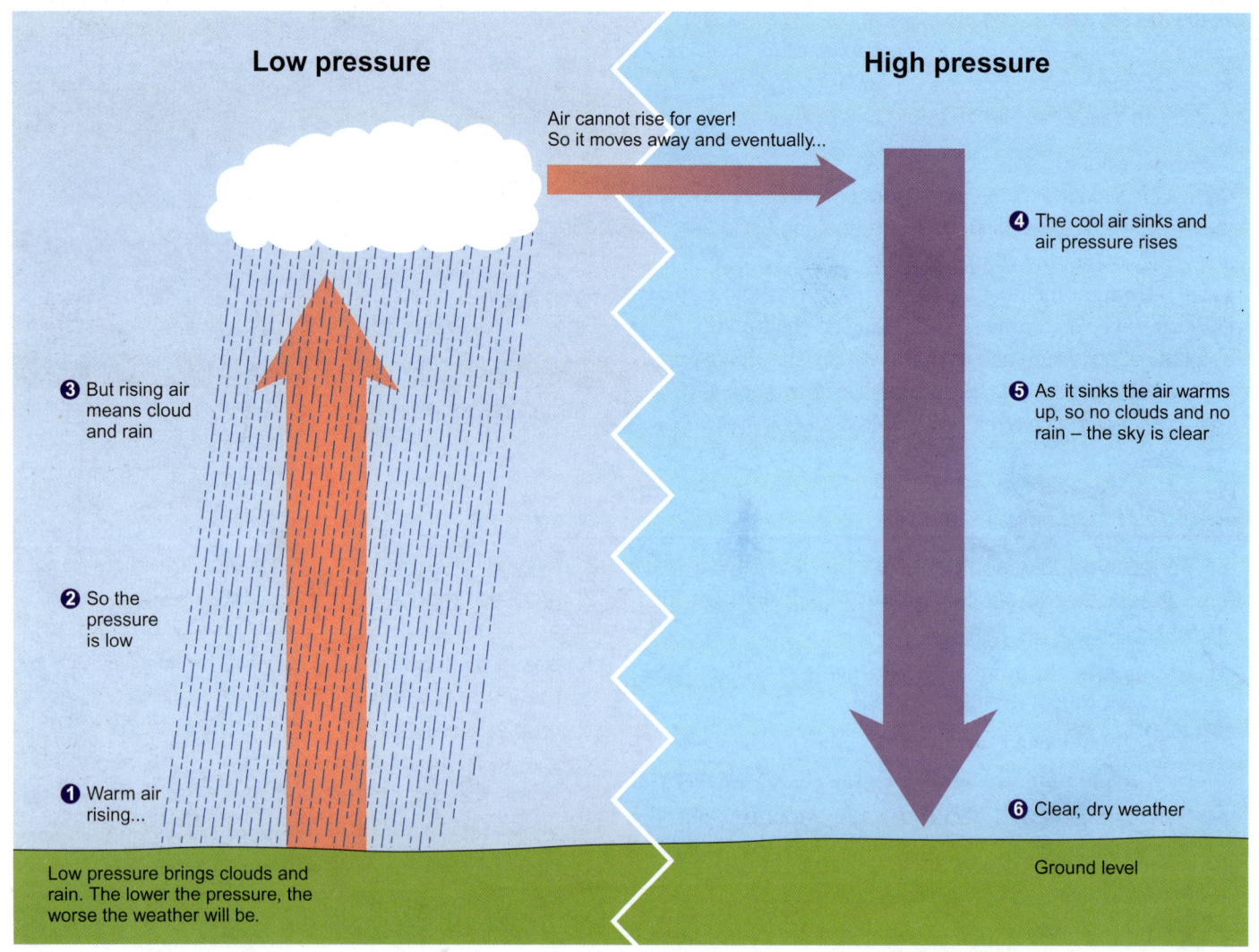

❹ The cool air sinks and air pressure rises
❺ As it sinks the air warms up, so no clouds and no rain – the sky is clear
❻ Clear, dry weather

Ground level

B High and low pressure

FACT FILE: ANTICYCLONES

Areas of low pressure often bring cloudy and wet weather. An area of low pressure often has a front where air of different temperatures comes together. This is called a **depression**. Areas of high pressure are called **anticyclones**; here the air is sinking and so they bring clear skies and dry weather.

Key facts: Anticyclones
- Areas of high pressure
- Air is sinking and warming
- Isobars are far apart so winds are light
- Winds blow clockwise away from the centre
- Skies are usually clear
- Heatwaves in summer
- Cold and frosty in winter, or fog if air is moist

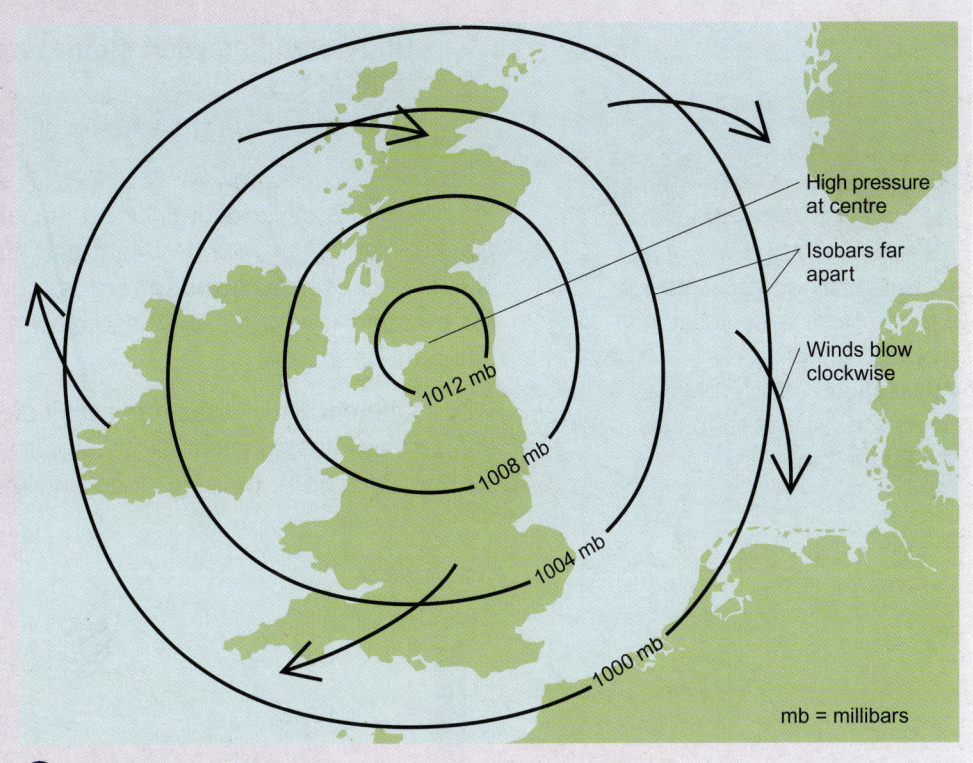

Labels on map: High pressure at centre; Isobars far apart; Winds blow clockwise. Isobars: 1012 mb, 1008 mb, 1004 mb, 1000 mb. mb = millibars

C The closer together the isobars are, the stronger the winds

Activities

1. True or false? Write out the statements that are true.
   A. Air pressure is measured by a barometer.
   B. Contour lines show pressure on a weather map.
   C. High-pressure areas are called anticyclones.
   D. High-pressure areas have rising air and rainfall.

2. Look at **B**. With a partner, draw a labelled sketch to show what happens *either* when warm air rises *or* when cold air sinks. What type of pressure is this? Collect the class findings and discuss them.

3. Using **C**, complete a table like the one below. Choose the correct words so that your table is true for anticyclones.

Feature	Anticyclones
Pressure at the centre	High or low?
Wind direction	Clockwise or anticlockwise?
Wind strength	Gentle or strong?
Weather in the summer	Cold and damp or heatwaves?
Weather in the winter	Cold and frosty or very wet?

Key words

Air pressure – the 'weight' of the air pressing down on the Earth's surface
Anticyclone – an area of high pressure where winds blow outwards
Barometer – instrument used to measure air pressure
Depression – a swirling system with low pressure at the centre and fronts
Isobar – a line on a weather map that joins together places with the same air pressure
Millibars – units used to measure air pressure

3 Europe's weather and climate

Why does the weather change?

> Understanding what air masses are and how they can be different
> Finding out what happens when a depression passes

Key words

Air mass – a huge block of air, thousands of kilometres across, with the same temperature and moisture content

Atmosphere – the 'envelope' of air masses that surrounds the Earth

In some parts of Europe, such as the UK, the weather can change quickly. One day it may be bright and sunny and the next cool and wet. This is because the **atmosphere** is made up of huge blocks of air called **air masses** (see map **A**). These air masses cross Europe and bring different weather.

When different air masses meet they do not mix. The area where the two different air masses meet is called a front (**B**) (see also **D** on page 35). Air rises at a front, causing cloud and rainfall.

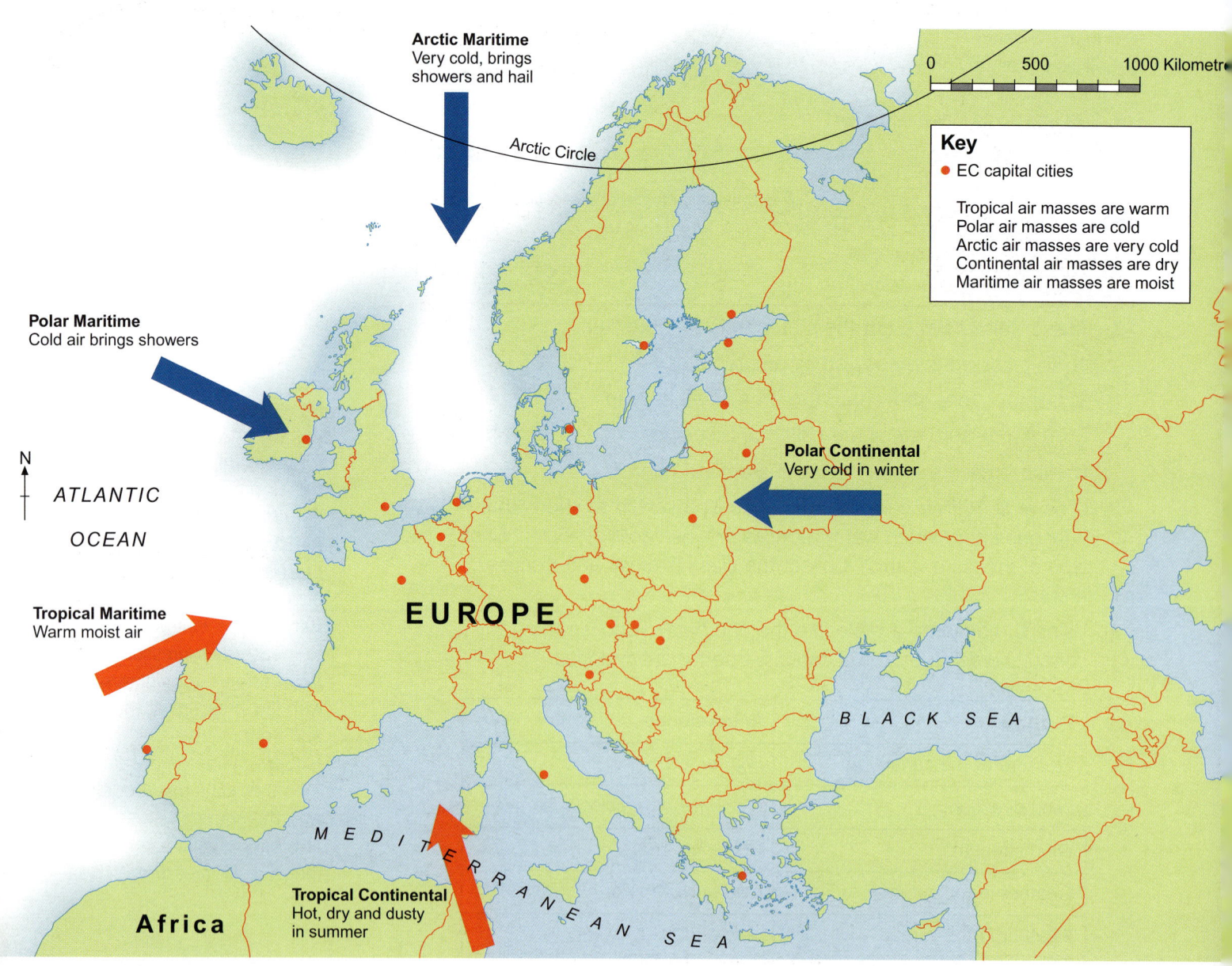

Arctic Maritime
Very cold, brings showers and hail

Polar Maritime
Cold air brings showers

Polar Continental
Very cold in winter

Tropical Maritime
Warm moist air

Tropical Continental
Hot, dry and dusty in summer

Key
- EC capital cities

Tropical air masses are warm
Polar air masses are cold
Arctic air masses are very cold
Continental air masses are dry
Maritime air masses are moist

A Air masses that affect Europe

WHAT'S A DEPRESSION?

A depression is a swirling mass of cloud. At the centre the air is rising so there is low pressure. Depressions have fronts that bring wet and cloudy weather. At the fronts the warm air rises, causing cloud and rainfall. Figures **C** and **D** shows what happens when a depression crosses the UK.

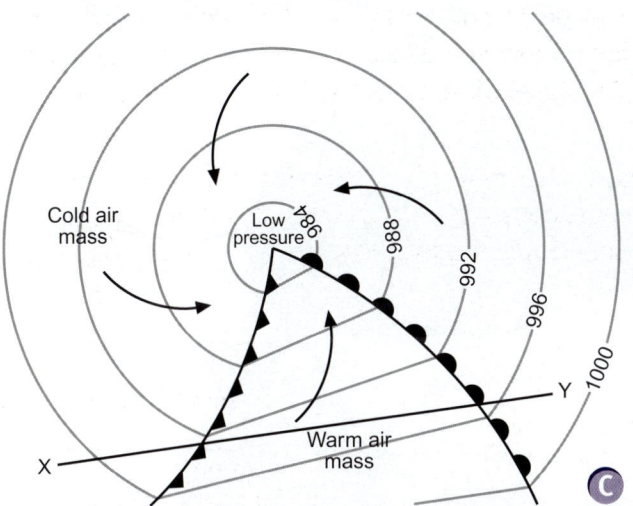

B Different types of front

Where a warmer air mass is behind a colder air mass...

Warmer air mass | Colder air mass

...on a weather map this is shown by a warm front

Where a colder air mass is behind a warmer air mass...

Colder air mass | Warmer air mass

...on a weather map this is shown by a cold front

Fact file: A depression
- Isobars close together, so strong winds
- Winds blow anticlockwise towards the centre
- Two fronts, a warm and a cold one
- Pressure low at the centre
- Two air masses
- Cloud and rain at the fronts
- Move from west to east across Europe

C Weather map of a depression

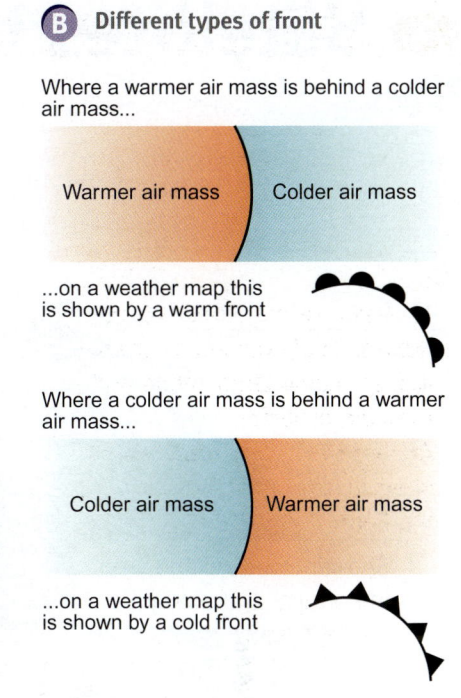

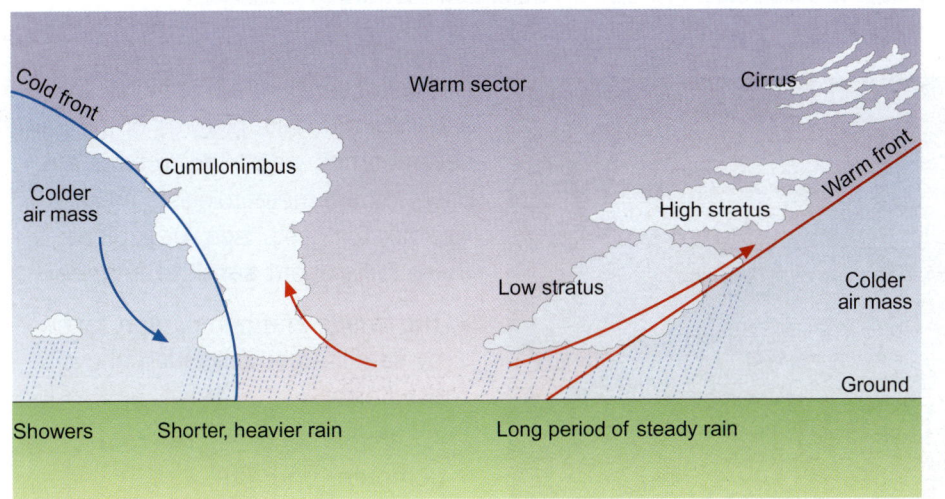

D Cross-section from X to Y through the depression shown in source C

Activities

1. Use map **A** to write out and complete these sentences about air masses.

   The _____ air mass will bring the coldest weather to Europe because it comes from the north/south. The air mass that brings the warmest weather to Europe is the _____ because it comes from the north/south. Three air masses carry a lot of moisture because they have travelled over the land/sea. One example is _____. The others are quite dry because they have formed over sea/land.

2. Draw and label the symbols for a warm and cold front.

3. Would a depression or an anticyclone bring the right weather for these activities?
   a) Hanging out your washing.
   b) Walking in the rain.
   c) Swimming in the local outdoor pool.
   d) Playing cricket.

3 Europe's weather and climate

Satellites help forecast the weather

> Finding out how a satellite works
> Looking at how people use satellite images

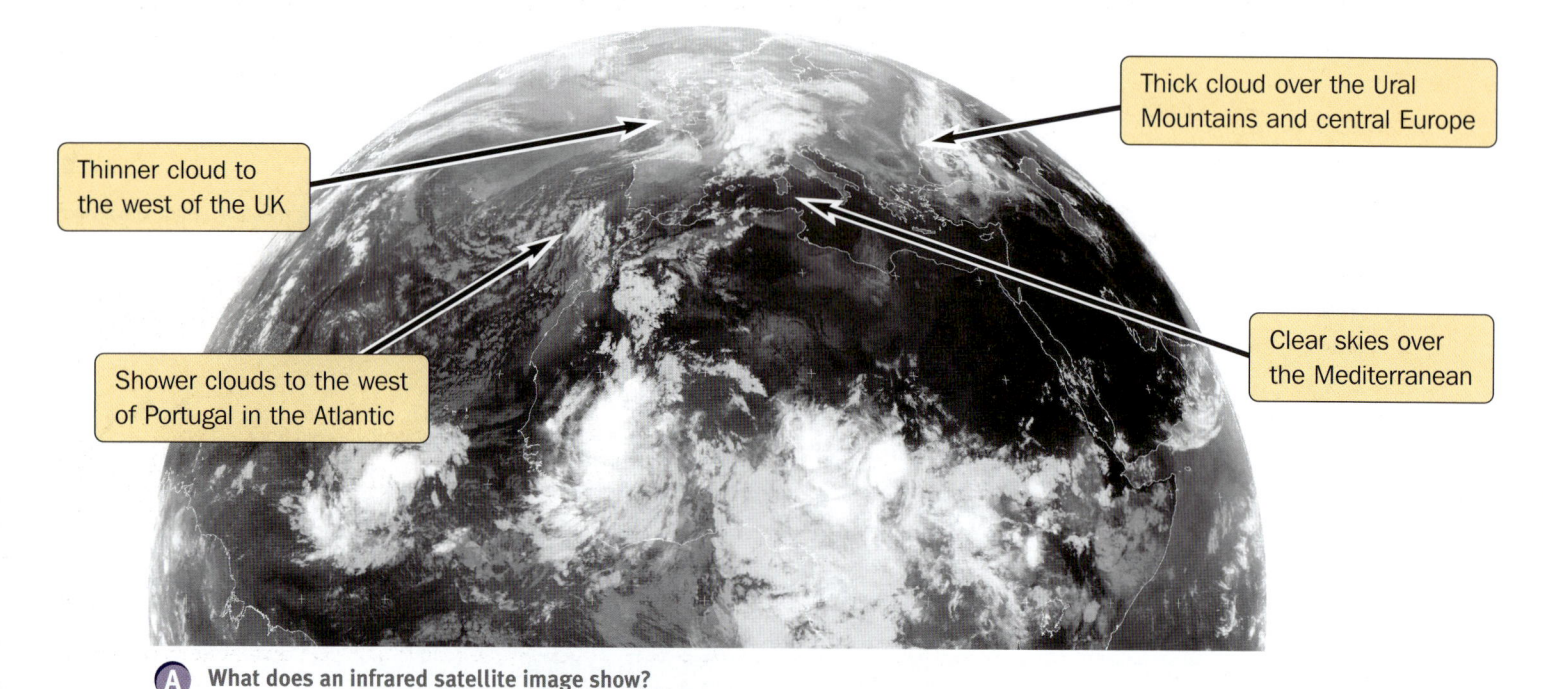

Thinner cloud to the west of the UK

Thick cloud over the Ural Mountains and central Europe

Shower clouds to the west of Portugal in the Atlantic

Clear skies over the Mediterranean

A What does an infrared satellite image show?

Out in space there are artificial satellites that take pictures of the Earth several times a day. The pictures are used to help meteorologists prepare weather forecasts (see **A**). Look at these facts about **satellite images**.

- The image is a photograph taken by satellite cameras high above the Earth.
- A camera sends signals to a computer on Earth.
- The computer adds coastlines, lines of longitude and latitude and sometimes colour.
- The image shows the cloud cover at a particular moment.
- On an **infrared** image, areas with no cloud cover appear black, and white areas are dense cloud.
- Infrared images can be taken at any time of day or night because they use heat, not light.
- Visible images can only be taken during daylight hours.

B Infrared satellite image for 6am on 27 October 2000

geography 360° Foundation Book 2

THE STORMS OF OCTOBER 2000

Meteorologists were able to forecast the severe weather that was to hit Britain, but that didn't seem to stop the chaos that followed (see **B** and **C**)!

Image **B** shows a deep depression in the north-west Atlantic. The depression moved westwards and swept over the UK. It brought heavy rain, strong winds and **tornadoes**. Areas were flooded and buildings damaged. Trees were brought down, blocking roads and railways. The article in **C** tells some of the story.

STORMS LASH BRITAIN

The worst storms in a decade have battered southern Britain, killing three people and flooding roads and towns

Winds reaching almost 100mph brought travel chaos, prompting Railtrack to close stations across the region and bringing a warning to motorists to stay at home.

Hundreds of houses have been evacuated and fallen trees have caused damage to power lines.

The port of Dover was closed for several hours, but most services had resumed by Monday afternoon. Thousands of passengers had been stranded mid-Channel waiting for the winds to die down.

Huge waves burst over the promenade at Dover

C Newspaper report, 30 October 2000. Reproduced from BBC News at bbcnews.co.uk

Activities

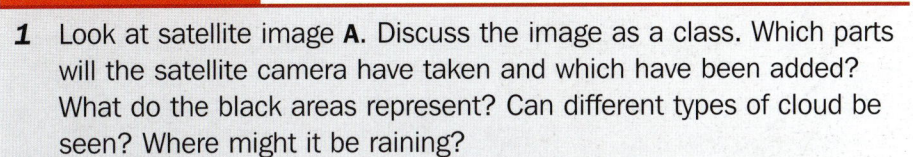

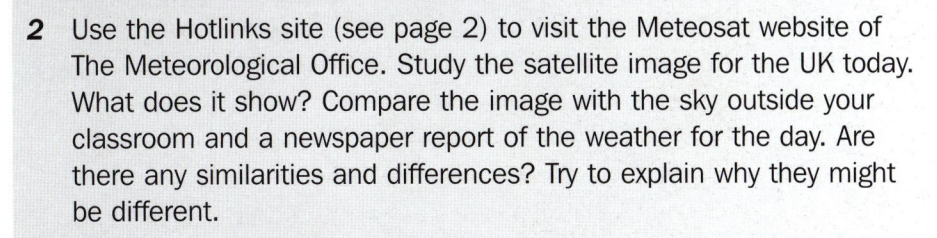

1. Look at satellite image **A**. Discuss the image as a class. Which parts will the satellite camera have taken and which have been added? What do the black areas represent? Can different types of cloud be seen? Where might it be raining?

2. Use the Hotlinks site (see page 2) to visit the Meteosat website of The Meteorological Office. Study the satellite image for the UK today. What does it show? Compare the image with the sky outside your classroom and a newspaper report of the weather for the day. Are there any similarities and differences? Try to explain why they might be different.

3. **The storms of October 2000**

   How was your region affected by the storms of October 2000? Look at the BBC News website for 31 October 2000 via Hotlinks to find out. On a map of your local region, add labels to show the damage caused by the storm. You could draw some small pictures to show the damage caused.

Key words

Infrared – radiation that is similar to light but invisible to humans; it can be used in photography

Satellite image – a photograph taken by a satellite camera high above the Earth's surface

Tornado – a rapidly moving and vicious spiral of air that is smaller than a hurricane

3 Europe's weather and climate

Europe's climates

> Understanding the difference between weather and climate
> Finding out about the different climates in Europe

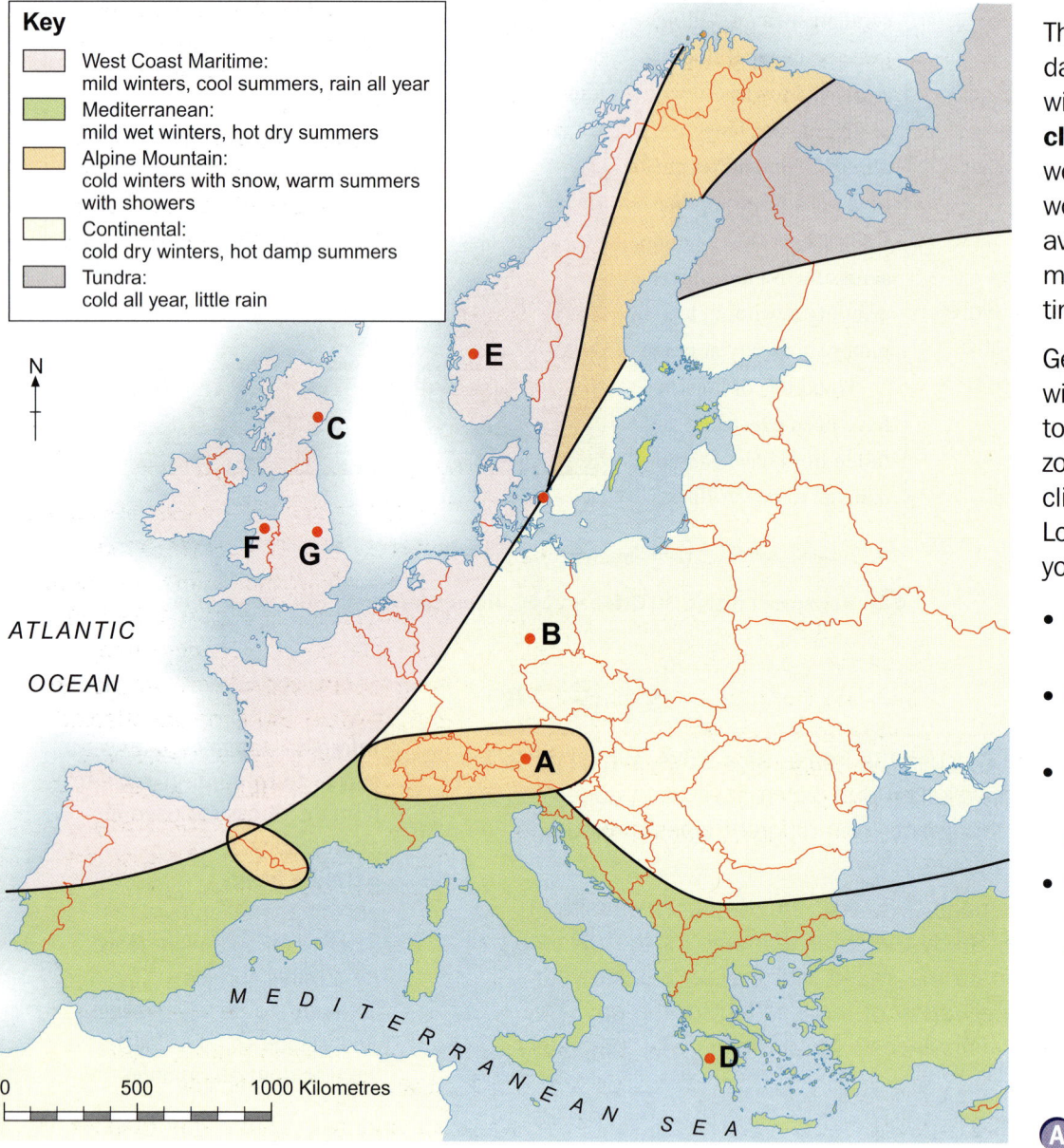

Key
- West Coast Maritime: mild winters, cool summers, rain all year
- Mediterranean: mild wet winters, hot dry summers
- Alpine Mountain: cold winters with snow, warm summers with showers
- Continental: cold dry winters, hot damp summers
- Tundra: cold all year, little rain

The **weather** is the day-to-day, hour-by-hour rainfall, wind and temperature. The **climate** is the average weather of a place. It is worked out by taking the average of weather measurements over a long time, often over 30 years.

Geographers group places with similar climates together into climate zones. Map **A** shows the climate zones in Europe. Look carefully at map **A**; you can see that:

- in the north it is colder than in the south
- it is wetter in the west than in the east
- upland areas, e.g. the Alps, are colder than lowland areas
- the Mediterranean region has the hottest and driest weather in Europe.

A Europe's climate zones

WHY DO DIFFERENT CLIMATES EXIST?

The effect of latitude

The further north you travel in Europe, the further from the Equator and the heating effect of the sun you go. So countries further north are cooler than those further south because they receive less energy from the sun. The sun's rays have to travel further through the atmosphere and heat a larger land area.

geography 360° Foundation Book 2

The effect of land and sea

In summer, coastal areas are cooler than those inland. This is because the sea is cooler than the land in summer and onshore winds cool the land down. The reverse happens in the winter because the sea is warmer than the land so coastal areas are often warmer. In western Europe this is helped by the warm ocean current – the North Atlantic Drift.

Key words

Altitude – the height in metres above sea level
Climate – an area's average weather over a period of time
Latitude – the distances north or south of the Equator; lines of latitude are parallel to the Equator
North Atlantic Drift – a warm ocean current
Onshore wind – when a wind blows from the sea to the land

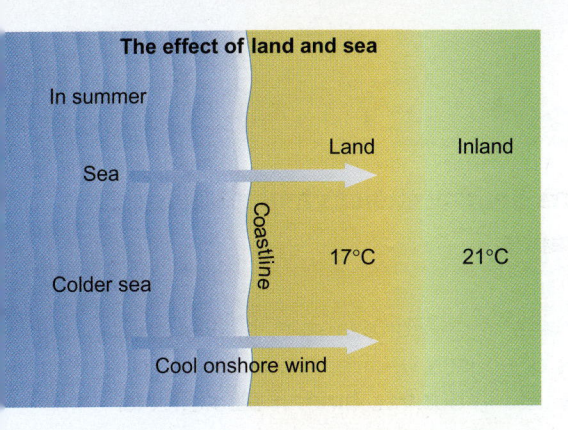

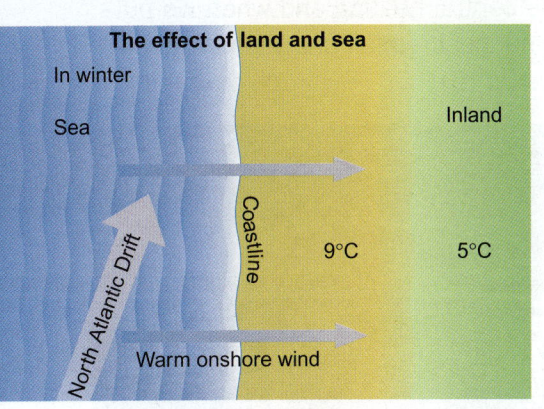

The effect of altitude (height above sea level)

As you climb up a mountain it often feels colder. This is because temperature falls as altitude increases. The temperature falls by about 1.6°C for every 100 metres.

The effect of winds

Winds that have blown over land are dry and bring dry weather to the area they blow over. Winds that have blown over the sea have picked up water and are moist. They often bring rain to areas they blow over. In Europe some countries are affected by the westerly winds. These have blown over the Atlantic Ocean and are moist. This explains why countries in the west of Europe are often wetter than those in the east.

Activities

1. What is the difference between weather and climate?

2. Decide whether each of the following statements describes the climate or the weather of an area.

   A The match was cancelled because of heavy rain on Saturday.
   B It is usually very hot and dry in Greece in the summer.
   C We always ski in Switzerland in the winter when it is cold enough for snow.
   D In August 2004 Boscastle was badly flooded by a terrible rainstorm.

3. Look at places A–G on map **A**. In small groups decide on the answers to these questions.

   a) Which place is further south but cooler than B?
   b) Which place is the coldest of all the places shown?
   c) Which place receives high rainfall, higher than G?
   d) Which place is warmer than G in winter but colder than G in summer?
   e) Which place is very hot and dry in summer?
   f) Which place is cooler than G at all times of the year?

   Choose *one* of the places shown and try to give reasons for the climate.

3 Europe's weather and climate

How does the climate affect us?

> Exploring how climate affects holiday choices and farming
> Learning to draw climate graphs

The climate affects the lives of every one of us. For example, it affects what we wear, what we eat, the sorts of houses we live in, where we go on holiday (see **A** and **B**) and what we do in our free time. It also affects us in other ways – when we put on the central heating and when we put an extra duvet on the bed. Look at the annual rainfall and temperatures for London and Bergen in northern Europe (**C**).

A Where in Europe would you expect to find this scene?

B What kind of holiday would you expect here?

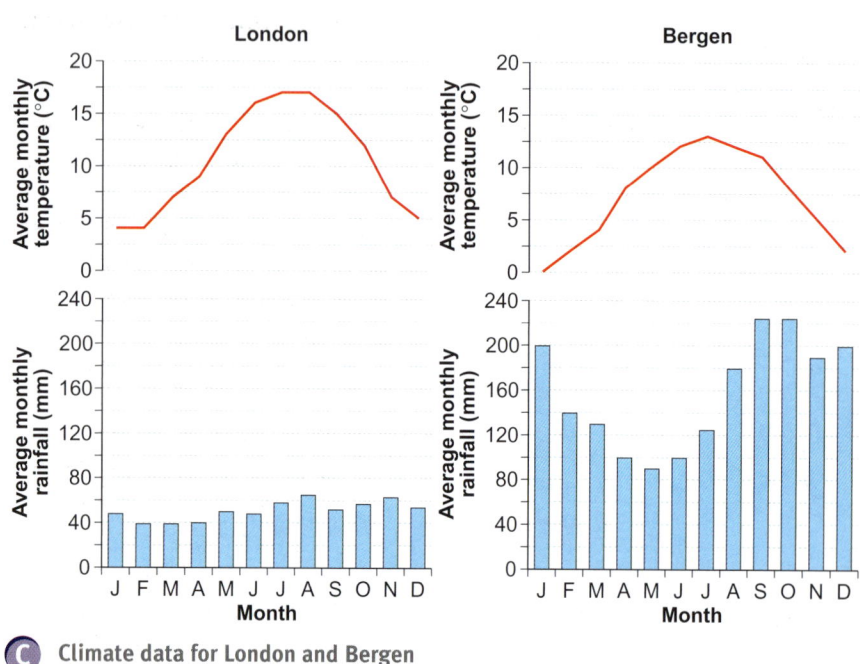

C Climate data for London and Bergen

D A crop of oranges, ready for picking

All kinds of activities are influenced by climate. Farmers have to think about what grows best in their local climate as well.

- Orange trees grow best where there are hot, dry summers and mild, wet winters (see **D**). Spring frosts can ruin the blossom.

44 geography 360° Foundation Book 2

- Hay can grow in a wide variety of climates, including quite cold and wet climates.
- Wheat can survive in a variety of climates but grows best where summers are hot to ripen the grain and there are showers of rain.

Activities

1. a) Look at photos **A** and **B**. Match each house to one of the numbered locations marked on map **A** on page 42.

   b) Complete the table below to show the different features of each house. Write 'A' or 'B' In the second column. In the third column, choose from one of these:
   - To get rid of smoke from heating
   - No need to let rain or snow fall off
   - To reflect the sun and keep cool
   - To allow rain and snow to fall off
   - To keep heat in.

Feature of the house	Which house: A or B	Reason
Flat roof		
Sloping roof		
Painted white		
Has chimneys		
Small windows		

2. Look at photo **D** and map **A** (page 42). Where in Europe would you expect oranges to be grown? Give reasons for your choices.

3. a) Look at the *SKILLS* box. Now draw a climate graph for Athens.

Athens	J	F	M	A	M	J	J	A	S	O	N	D
Temperature (°C)	8	11	16	23	27	31	30	24	17	11	9	7
Rainfall (mm)	48	39	30	25	25	15	10	12	13	43	70	70

   b) Read Alexis's story below. Make your graph into a living graph by adding labels at the correct times of the year (see pages 145–155) of *SKILLS in geography*.

   > I live in Athens – the climate certainly affects what I do at different times of the year.
   >
   > A Temperature has fallen below 10°C. Time to get out my long trousers and sweatshirts.
   >
   > B A really hot weekend – time to go to the beach for a swim.
   >
   > C Temperatures are getting high – over 20°C – need to stock up on anti-mosquito cream and suntan lotion.
   >
   > D Temperatures are below 10°C – time to holiday somewhere hot, perhaps Malaysia or South Africa this year.

4. Complete a calendar of your activities during the year to show how climate affects your life. Try to include the foods you eat, your activities, the clothes you wear and holidays you might go on at different times of the year. You could record your ideas on a table.

SKILLS

How to draw a climate graph
1. Draw graph axes like those in C.
2. Allow 12 cm on the horizontal axis for twelve months. Label these J, F, M, etc.
3. Put a scale for rainfall on the lower part of the vertical axis.
4. Above this put a scale for temperature.
5. Plot the monthly rainfall figures as a bar graph.
6. Plot the monthly temperature figures as a line graph. Place each cross or dot in the middle of the column because it is the average temperature for the month.
7. Add a title and label the axes.

For more help see page 148 of *SKILLS in geography*

Assessing 360°

Choosing where to go on holiday

It's January, and the Carter family are deciding what to do about their family holiday this year.

Capital city	July		November	
	Temp. (°C)	Weather	Temp. (°C)	Weather
London	14	Thunderstorms	7	Cloudy
Dublin	12	Rain	8	Rain
Paris	15	Cloudy	4	Rain
Amsterdam	15	Thunderstorms	6	Cloudy
Brussels	15	Cloudy	6	Cloudy
Luxembourg City	13	Fair	5	Cloudy
Madrid	23	Sunny	8	Cloudy
Lisbon	25	Sunny	14	Sunny
Rome	25	Fair	13	Fair
Athens	30	Sunny	18	Fair
Berlin	15	Sunny	2	Sleet
Copenhagen	13	Showers	−1	Snow

A What's the weather like in Europe?

Mr Carter
I don't like it too hot, I come out in a rash. I would like to do some walking in nice scenery and play golf. I like to go somewhere where there are places of interest to visit. I like Italian food.

Mrs Carter
I want to relax in some sunshine. I don't mind the odd day trip to see the sights and do some shopping. The shorter the flight is, the better. I enjoy good food and wine.

Michael Carter (14 years)
We'll have to go in the school holidays, anyway it's hotter then. I would like to go where there is a beach and lots of water sports – I'd like to learn to scuba dive and I like theme parks. I don't like foreign food and I hate sightseeing and shopping.

Helen Carter (17 years)
I am doing Art A level and I'd like to visit one of Europe's big art galleries. I also want to have a good time – somewhere with a nice beach would be good.

B The Carter family

1. Make a key for the different weather symbols needed to show the weather in table **A**.

2. Look at **B** and the map that your teacher will give you showing the capital cities of Europe. Where should the Carter family go on holiday?

   Work in a group of four. Each person takes the part of one of the Carter family. In role, discuss where is best for your holiday and come to a decision in your group about where and when to go. Present your decision to the rest of the class. Where should the family go, when and why? Did the climate for your choice influence your decision?
   - Who will be happy with your choice of the holiday, and why?
   - Who will be least happy about the holiday choice, and why?

4 Tourism – good or bad?

Why do people like visiting places like this?

How do the people who live here feel about tourism?

Learning objectives

What are you going to learn about in this chapter?
- What a tourist is
- How and why tourism is important
- What changes are taking place in the tourist industry
- Different types of holidays
- Whether tourism is good or bad
- How tourism can be managed

A Costa Blanca, Spain

What is tourism?

> Finding out what tourists and tourism are
> Understanding the growth of tourism

When was the last time you were a **tourist**? Most people would think of their summer holidays. But tourists are not just people who are on holiday. Tourists are people who stay away from home for a short time for business, to visit relatives or for other reasons (see **A**). Hotels, airports, coach drivers and souvenir sellers are all part of what is called the **tourism** industry.

Speech bubbles in image:
- Fieldwork abroad – brilliant! I hope the assignment goes well.
- The shopping is supposed to be fantastic!
- I am so looking forward to meeting my grandson for the first time.
- I've an important business meeting tomorrow.
- Looking forward to visiting all of those historic sites!
- Can't wait to be on that beach!
- I hope my presentation goes down well at the conference.

A What is a tourist?

Tourism is the fastest growing industry in the world (**B**). Tourism has grown so much because:

- people have more days of paid holiday
- people take more holidays during the year
- transport has improved, e.g. long-distance flights, cheap airlines
- large multinational companies require more national and international business travel
- there is more information about different countries and cultures on TV and the Internet
- people are wealthier and can afford to travel
- pensioners are younger and better off
- **package holidays** have made travelling abroad easier.

But not all parts of the world benefit equally. Table **C** shows the top ten destinations for tourists.

Key words

Package holiday – an all-inclusive deal from a travel agent; the package usually includes travel, accommodation, food and some entertainment

Tourism – the industry that caters for visitors

Tourist – a person who travels away from home for a short time and intends to return home afterwards

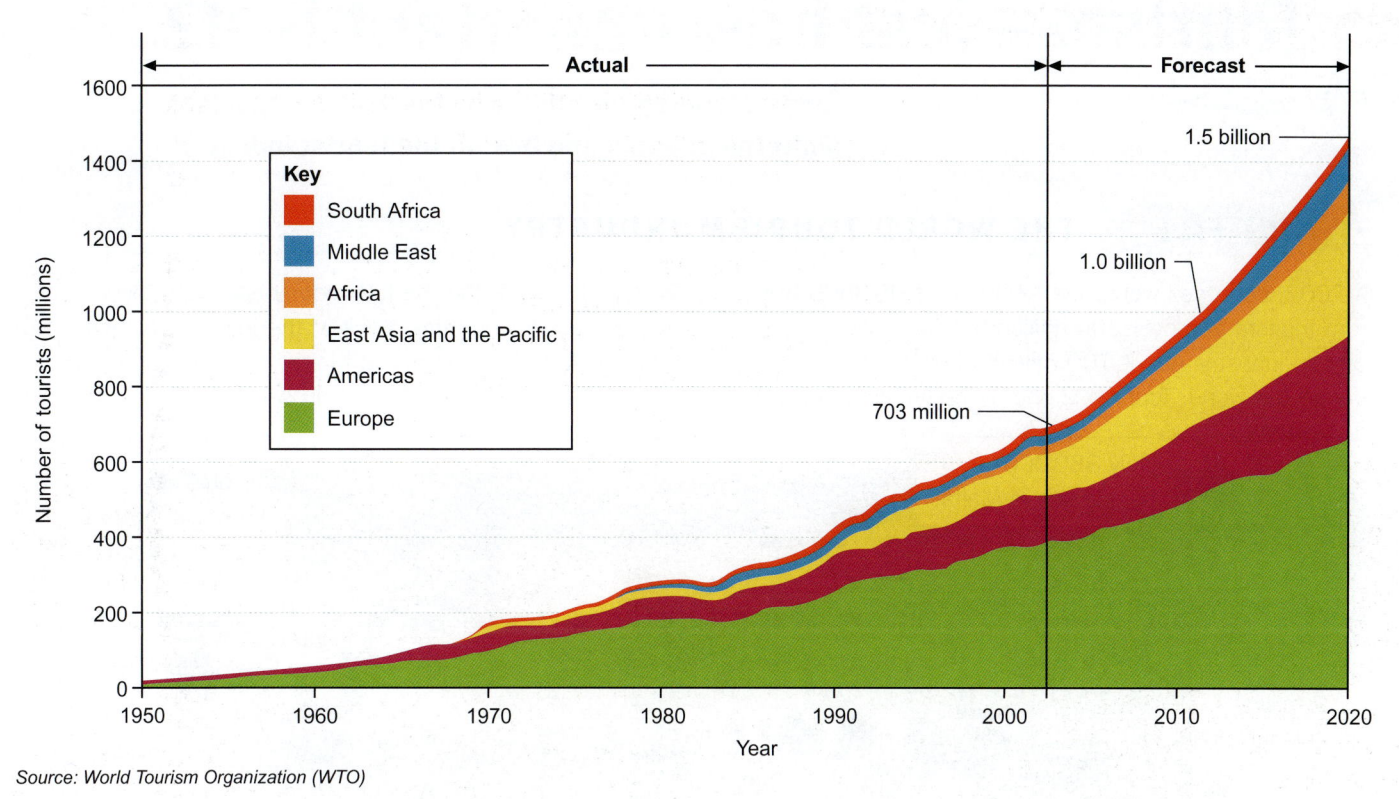

B How has global tourism changed?

Key
- South Africa
- Middle East
- Africa
- East Asia and the Pacific
- Americas
- Europe

Actual / Forecast

1.5 billion
1.0 billion
703 million

Number of tourists (millions) vs Year (1950–2020)

Source: World Tourism Organization (WTO)

Rank	Country	Millions of tourists
1	France	75.0
2	Spain	52.5
3	United States	40.4
4	Italy	39.6
5	China	33.0
6	United Kingdom	24.8
7	Austria	19.1
8	Mexico	18.7
9	Germany	18.4
10	Canada	17.5

C The top ten destinations for tourists (2003)

Source: World Tourism Organization (WTO)

Activities

1 a) In pairs, list all the types of holiday you can think of. Think of the holidays and trips that you, your families and friends have been on. These definitions of holidays may help you:

package   independent   sports
short break   activity

b) As a class, put your lists together. How many different kinds of holidays did you think of? What makes each of these trips seem like a holiday?

2 Study **B**.

a) How many tourists were there in 1950, 1980 and 2004?

b) How many tourists are predicted for 2020?

c) Describe what has happened to the numbers of tourists over time.

d) In pairs, discuss why you think some regions get more tourists than others. Complete two lists with the following titles:

- Why some places have many tourists
- Why some places don't have many tourists

3 Study **C**.

a) Draw a bar graph to show the figures in **C** (see pages 145–155 of *SKILLS in geography*).

b) Colour in the countries according to the region they are in. For example, you could colour all those countries in Europe in the same colour.

4 Tourism – good or bad?

Tourism – just how important is it?

> Understanding how and why tourism is important
> Patterns of boom and bust in the tourist industry

FACT FILE — THE WORLD TOURISM INDUSTRY

In 2002, countries worldwide earned over US $500 billion from tourism and over 200 million people worked in the tourism industry. About 700 million tourists were moved around the world. Tourism is one of the largest industries in the world.

Tourism is one of the top five money-earners in over 80 per cent of countries. Look at the information about Malta in **A**. For countries like Malta, it is very important to keep the tourists coming. You can see how these countries earn the money in **B**.

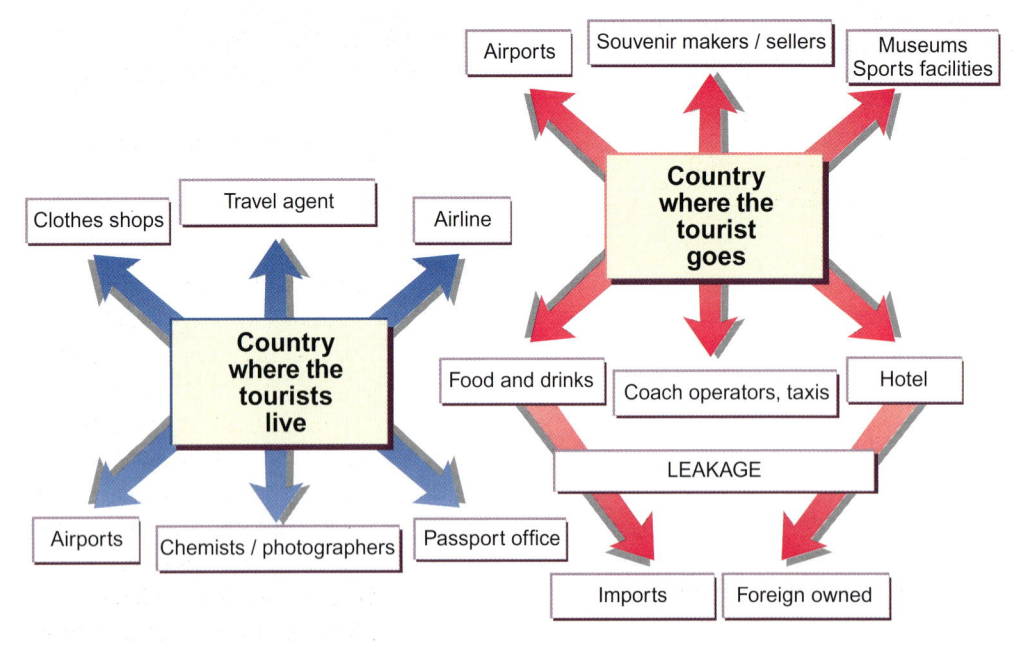

- Only 380 000 people live in Malta.
- There were over 1.2 million tourists in 2004.
- Tourism generated US $650 million.
- Forty per cent of Malta's wealth comes from tourism.
- Malta is very dependent on tourism.
- What will happen if the tourist trade collapses?
- The country only exports a limited number of other products.

A Malta – dependent on tourism

B Who benefits from tourism?

WHO BENEFITS FROM TOURISM?

Tourism is a **service industry** and employs many people in transport, hotels, and catering. But many of these jobs only last for the tourist season. In the winter the people may lose their jobs. This is called **seasonal unemployment**. The people may not get the same job next year and they often have no pension and no training. Seasonal unemployment is a real problem in countries or resorts that have many tourists. So, looking at **B**, who benefits from tourism?

Tourism is especially important in the poorer countries of the world (see table **C**). But not all these countries have a large and successful tourist industry, while others may see a sudden fall in the numbers of tourists to their country.

WHAT ATTRACTS TOURISTS?

Countries with a successful tourist industry have many attractions and facilities for visitors (**D**). There may be **physical attractions**, such as the climate, beaches, rain forests and mountains. There may be **human attractions**, such as historic buildings, theme parks, sporting facilities and events. Countries with few natural and human attractions benefit little from the tourist industry.

Country	% population living on below US $1 a day	% of country's income (GDP) coming from tourism
Nigeria	70	2
The Gambia	54	11
Honduras	41	10.6
Ghana	39	8.4
Nepal	38	7.7

C Tourism earns money in poorer countries

WHAT ARE THE PROBLEMS?

Even successful tourist industries can suddenly see visitor numbers drop. Reasons for this may be:

- Political, e.g. bombing in Israel and the 9/11 disaster in New York
- Natural, e.g. hurricanes in the Caribbean
- Medical, e.g. the SARS outbreak in Nepal
- Fashion: other countries become more fashionable
- Facilities, e.g. in Benidorm the facilities and hotels became out-of-date.

Changes like these can be disastrous, especially for poor countries.

Activities

1. Complete a table like the one here to show the physical and human attractions in **D**.

Physical attractions	Human attractions

2. Investigate your local area. What are the physical and human attractions for tourists where you live? Produce a short ICT presentation to show the attractions a family might enjoy on a visit to your home area.

3. Read the statements below. Which ones would cause a rise in the UK tourist industry and which would cause a fall?

   A London winning the bid for the 2012 Olympic Games

   B A terrorist attack in London

   C The collapse of British Airways

   D The opening of Legoland

   E Climate change – the UK becomes warmer and sunnier.

D A booming tourist industry

Key words

Human attractions – facilities for tourists built by people

Physical attractions – natural features that attract tourists, e.g. climate, rivers, mountains

Seasonal unemployment – when jobs are only available for part of the year, leaving people without work at other times

Service industry – industry where people provide a service instead of making a product

4 Tourism – good or bad?

Europe's tourist attractions

> Looking at different types of holidays in Europe
> Learning how to draw compound bars

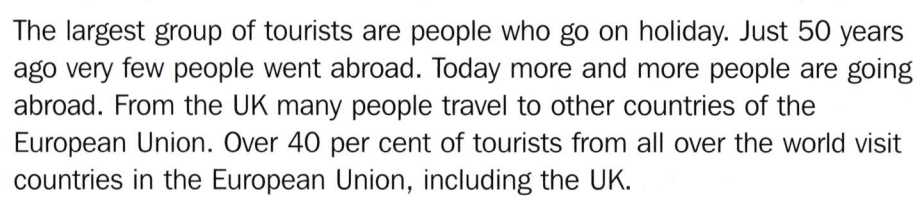

The largest group of tourists are people who go on holiday. Just 50 years ago very few people went abroad. Today more and more people are going abroad. From the UK many people travel to other countries of the European Union. Over 40 per cent of tourists from all over the world visit countries in the European Union, including the UK.

The photographs in **A** show some popular tourist attractions in the European Union. They show the four main types of holiday:

- sun, sand and sea
- scenic – mountains and lakes
- winter sports
- cultural and historic.

Sun, sand and sea

Winter sports

Scenic

Cultural and historic

A Types of holiday destinations in Europe

Key
- Cooler, wetter climate
- Hot, dry summers
- Sandy beaches
- Alps
- Snow in winter
- Cultural / historic

Arrivals / Departures (Millions)

B Arrivals and departures of tourists in some EU countries

geography 360° Foundation Book 2

The map in **B** shows some different types of holidays in the European Union. In the north the climate is colder and wetter. What sort of holiday could you have there? Around the Mediterranean Sea summers are hot and dry and there are many beaches around the coast. Many people visit this area for 'sun, sand and sea' holidays. Mountains, such as the Alps, are popular for winter sports but people also visit them in the summer to enjoy the mountains and lakes. Most European countries also have some historic attractions, such as the Tower of London. The map also shows the relative number of people who arrive and depart for holidays within the EU. Notice how some countries have more people who leave, such as France, while others have more people who arrive, such as Spain and Greece.

SKILLS

How to draw a block bar graph
1. Draw vertical and horizontal axes.
2. Draw bars for one set of values.
3. Above them draw bars for the second set of values, and so on.
4. Colour in each of the divisions and add a key.
5. Label the axes and add a title.

For more help see page 150 of *SKILLS in geography*

Activities

1. Conduct a survey to find out your class's main holiday destinations last year. Into which categories of holiday do they fit?

   a) Complete a table like the one below to show the results. You can add other countries to the lists.

Country	Holiday type			
	Sea and sand	Cultural	Winter sports	Scenic
UK				
Other EU countries:				
France				
Non-EU countries:				
USA				

   b) On an outline map of the world, plot block bar graphs (see the *SKILLS* box) to show the number of people who visited each country and the type of holiday. Add a key for the colours used.

   c) Complete these sentences:

   The most popular destination of people in my class for holidays was _____.
   This could be because _____.

   The least popular destination for holidays was _____.
   This was probably because _____.

   The most popular type of holiday was _____ because _____.

   The least popular type of holiday was _____.

2. Study the photographs in **A**. In small groups, choose one of the photographs.

   a) Describe what the photograph shows.
   b) What type of holiday is being shown?
   c) Suggest a possible location in the EU for the scene in the photograph.

3. a) What do the bars showing the arrivals and departures on map **B** mean?

   b) Using map **B**, produce two lists: countries with more arrivals than departures and those with fewer arrivals than departures.

   c) In small groups, discuss why some countries have more arrivals than departures while others have more departures than arrivals. Contribute your ideas to a class discussion.

   d) Produce two spider diagrams to summarise the results of the discussion. Look at pages 145–155 of *SKILLS in geography* for help.

4 Tourism – good or bad?

UK tourism

> Finding out how tourism has changed in the UK
> Understanding why patterns of tourism change in the UK

More and more people are going on holiday every year from the UK. Where they are going has changed, too. Fewer people take holidays in the UK and more are choosing to travel abroad.

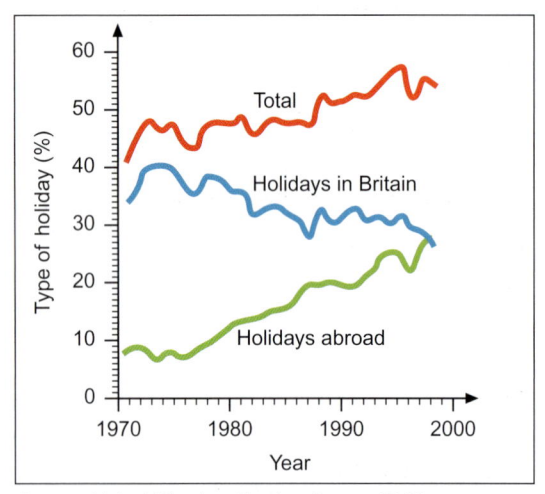

Source: United Kingdom Tourism Survey 2003

A Holidays taken by UK residents

Speech bubbles:
- I've looked in the brochures but everywhere is so expensive – especially when there are five of us.
- You won't get me on a plane, not with all those terrorists about.
- I lost my job and can't afford a holiday.
- Interest rates have gone up, so the mortgage costs more. It will take me longer to save up for a holiday.
- Last year the summer was really hot – I'll try staying at home this year.

B Going abroad? Not this year...

Country	People who stayed four nights or more (%)
Spain	27.5
France	20.2
USA	7.0
Greece	5.3
Italy	4.0
Portugal	3.6
Irish Republic	3.5
Turkey	3.0
Netherlands	2.7
Cyprus	2.6
Belgium	2.3
Germany	1.8
Malta	1.3
Austria	1.3
Other countries	13.9

Source: United Kingdom Tourism Survey 2003

C Where UK residents took their foreign holidays

Notice how the lines on graph **A** go up and down. Some years the numbers of holidays go down. Look at **B** – this shows there are lots of different reasons.

Although holidays are on the increase, there were still 34 per cent of people who took no holiday in 2003. The increase seems to be people who are taking more than one holiday abroad each year.

Europe is still very popular for UK holidaymakers, but people are also beginning to travel further, often to more exotic places (see **C**). Modern aircraft can travel long distances and competition has made air fares cheaper, so long-haul travel is more attractive.

However, UK holidays are still popular. Look at the data for 2003 in **D–F**. This shows some of the characteristics of UK tourism.

Purpose of trip	Millions of trips
Holiday, pleasure/leisure	70.5
Visiting friends and relatives, mainly as a holiday	20.5
Business	22.3
Visiting friends and relatives	34.3
Other	3.4
All purposes	151.0

Source: United Kingdom Tourism Survey 2003

D Purpose of tourism in the UK in 2003 for UK residents

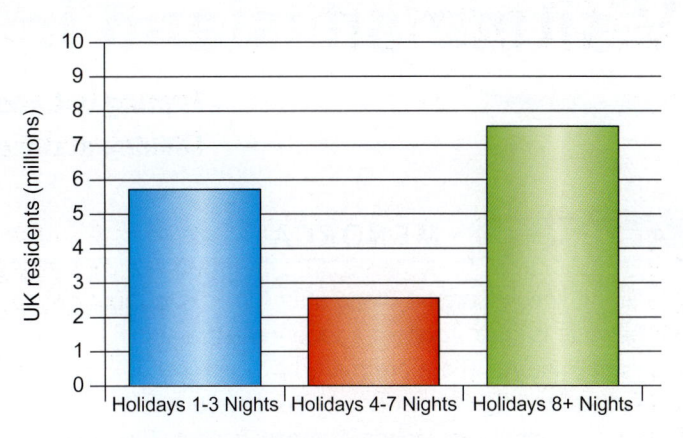

E How long UK residents stay

Source: United Kingdom Tourism Survey 2003

Activities

1. Look at **A**.
   a) How have holidays in Britain changed?
   b) How has the number of holidays abroad changed?
   c) In pairs or small groups, try to think of reasons why:
      - the total number of holidays has increased
      - the number of holidays abroad has increased
      - the lines are not straight but go up and down.

2. Look at **C**.
   a) List the countries that are not part of Europe.
   b) Why are Spain and France very popular with UK tourists? Why are they more popular than Greece or Belgium? Look at the reasons below and choose the three most likely answers.

   A Spain and France offer more package holidays for families.

   B Spain and France are closer to the UK than Greece and therefore cheaper to get to.

   C Belgium cannot offer beach holidays.

   D Spain and France offer a greater variety of holidays because they are larger countries.

   E You can drive to Spain and France for camping/caravan holidays.

3. Look at **D–F**.
   a) What is the most important purpose of tourism in the UK?
   b) What is the most popular length of stay and the most popular mode of travel?

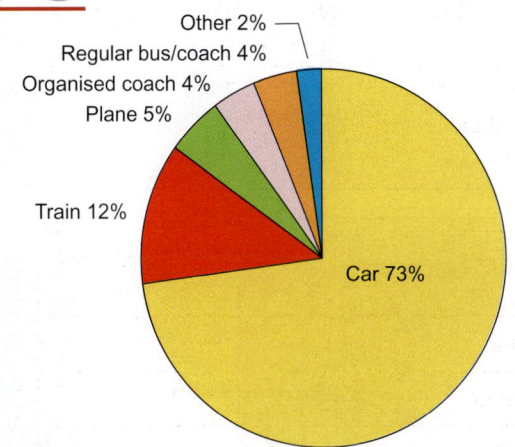

Other 2%
Regular bus/coach 4%
Organised coach 4%
Plane 5%
Train 12%
Car 73%

Source: United Kingdom Tourism Survey 2003

F How UK tourists travelled

4 Tourism – good or bad?

Visiting an island in Europe: Menorca

> Finding out about Menorca's attractions for the tourist
> Looking at the problems and future of Menorca's tourist industry

FACT FILE   MENORCA

Menorca is the second largest island after Majorca in the Spanish Balearic Islands. It offers a variety of attractions for the tourist (map **A**). There are many bays with sandy beaches (photo **B**). There are two main towns: Cuitadella, the island's old capital and Mahon, the new capital. The island is famous for its cheese, wine and leather articles. Inland the landscape is quite hilly with farmland, pine forests and small market towns. The island also has its share of human attractions such as fiestas (**C**), golf courses, a water park, and shops, hotels and restaurants.

B A cove in Menorca

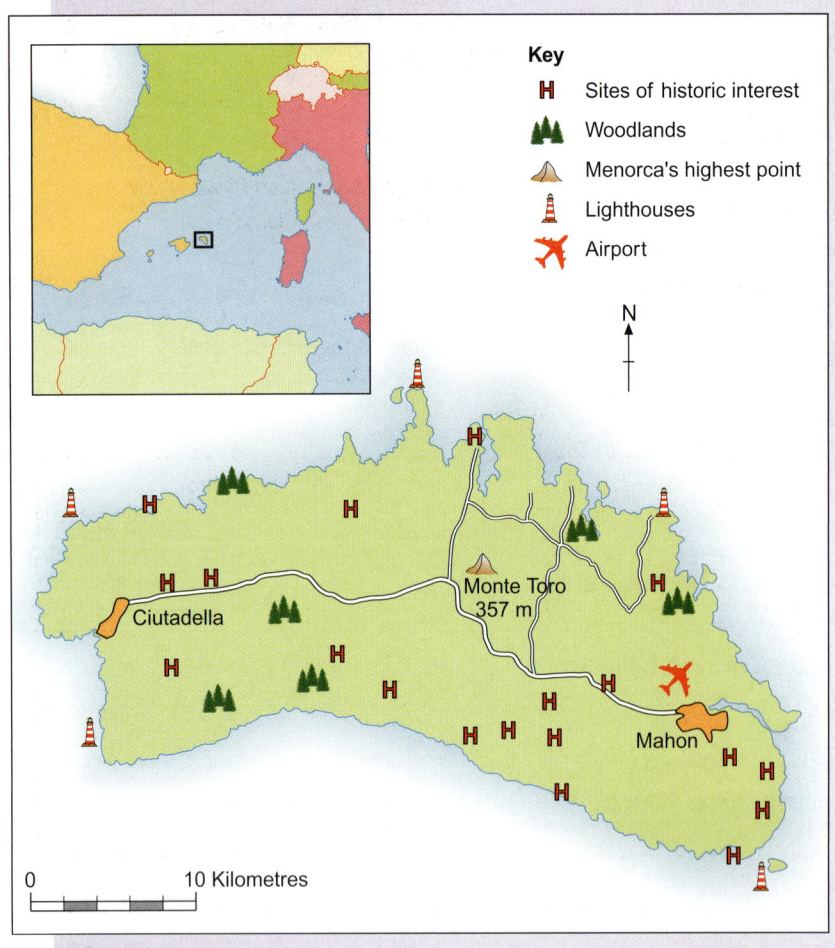

C Fiesta horses in Alayor

Menorca is fairly unspoiled. The local authorities have tried hard to avoid mass tourism, with its high-rise hotels and concrete jungles. But tourism is going through a difficult time. The number of tourists visiting the island is falling because of:

- International terrorism
- Economic problems in Germany and Italy
- Cheap flights making short-stay holidays attractive
- Improving weather in other parts of Europe – people stay at home
- Low prices in other countries, especially poorer ones, make them cheaper to visit.

Key
- H Sites of historic interest
- 🌲 Woodlands
- ⛰ Menorca's highest point
- 🗼 Lighthouses
- ✈ Airport

A Menorca

WHAT CAN BE DONE?

There are plans in Menorca to:

- enlarge the airport at a cost of 66 million Euros
- make the one main road across the island into a dual carriageway at a cost of 234 million Euros
- build more golf courses.

But these changes are not welcomed by everyone. Look at the comments in **D**.

> A bigger airport will mean more planes, more people and more traffic – disturbing the peace and causing more pollution.

> Golf courses won't attract that many more tourists, and they eat up huge areas of land. They also need huge amounts of water – one thing Menorca has not got.

> The larger road will be ugly – there are already three accidents a day on it.

D Views on development in Menorca

Menorca has no energy resources of its own, although a few wind turbines have been built. Tourism puts pressure on the water and energy resources of the island. In recent years visitors have demanded air-conditioning – another drain on electricity supplies. In Menorca the season is very short and many locals suffer seasonal unemployment (**E**).

> Until this year I worked in the airport, driving the tourist buses from the aircraft to the terminal building. I hated it – it was so hot and the shifts were tiring. The really hard thing was that the tourists only come from April to October. After that there was no job. I tried to get a job as a postman. But this year I have a new job. I'm still driving but at one of the holiday complexes. I drive the free bus to the beach and the shops. It is much better. You can speak to people and get to know them. I have had some nice tips. I am also hoping that they will keep me on in the winter to help with maintenance jobs, painting the chalets and so on.

E Santiago was born and lives in Menorca – he tells you about his work

Activities

1. Should Menorca try to increase its numbers of tourists? Complete a table like the one here to show the advantages and disadvantages of tourism in Menorca. The first ones have been done for you.

	Advantages	Disadvantages
Build more golf courses	More tourists will visit	Use large areas of land. Need a lot of water
Build more wind farms to increase the electricity supply		
Widen the main road to form a dual carriageway		
Expand the airport		
Build high-rise hotels		

2. Look at **E**.
   a) What are the disadvantages of the jobs Santiago has had?
   b) Why would being a postman be better?

4 Tourism – good or bad?

Visiting a poorer country: Jamaica

> Finding out why tourism is so important to Jamaica
> Learning about eco-tourism in Jamaica

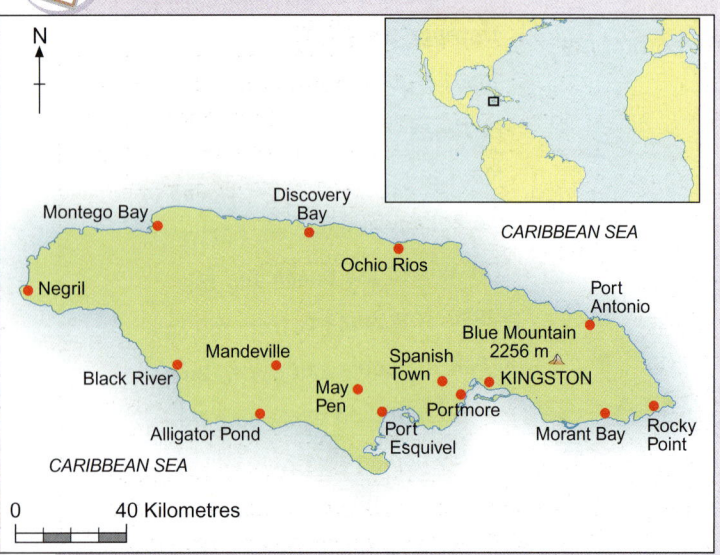

FACT FILE JAMAICA

Jamaica is an island in the Caribbean Sea (**A**). The island is mountainous: the highest point, the Blue Mountain peak, is 2256 metres above sea level. There is a narrow coastal plain with many sandy beaches. The climate is tropical and it is hot all year (**B**). There is also the threat of hurricanes, although very few hit. The island is popular for its beaches and water sports. It also attracts bird-watchers. Kingston is the capital of Jamaica.

Jamaica is home to 2.7 million people, many of them very poor. Most of its money comes from tourism and the export of **bauxite**. The tourist industry provides almost a quarter of all jobs in the country. Over 1 million tourists visit Jamaica every year, mostly from North America and Europe. The number of tourists fell sharply after 11 September 2001. There are other problems for tourists too.

A Jamaica – a tropical paradise

- Some areas have lots of crime and drugs.
- Tourists on the beaches can be harassed by lots of people selling food, drinks and souvenirs.
- The large **shanty towns** in Kingston can be upsetting.

	J	F	M	A	M	J	J	A	S	O	N	D
Rainfall (mm)	29	24	23	39	104	96	46	107	126	181	95	40
Temp (°C)	30	30	31	31	32	32	33	32	32	32	31	31

Source: www.wordtravels.com

B Jamaica's climate

FACT FILE HOW HAVE JAMAICANS DEVELOPED THEIR TOURISM?

Since 1999 there has been a new master plan for tourism in Jamaica which aims to develop more **eco-tourism** (**D**).

Eco Lodge lies in an eighteen-acre tropical nature reserve resort with vast stretches of coastline. The area has no huge hotels or crowds of tourists. The resort has cabins and camping for up to 30 people. The activities include:

- Meeting Jamaican families
- Spiritual and traditional music
- Prayer and meditation
- Massage and exercise
- Traditional meals, such as curried goat
- Nature trails, boat trips and river gorge hiking
- Farm tour to see an orchid house and papaya farm
- Blue Mountain cycle tour.

C Eco Lodge in Jamaica

WHY DO TOURISTS COME BACK TO JAMAICA?

Kingston – Jamaica's capital city – here you can visit Rockfort, a seventeenth-century fortress, the Church of St Thomas and the eighteenth-century Headquarters House.

Ocho Rios – the first tourist here was Christopher Columbus. Many more since have enjoyed the spectacular scenery. You can also enjoy the shopping, the food and the nightlife with its reggae music.

Negril, at the far western tip, is famous for the fantastic sunsets and a seven-mile stretch of white beach.

Montego Bay Harbour Street market – braiding and beading your hair and visiting the Rose Hall with its resident ghost are 'musts'.

The Blue Mountains, which lie to the north of Kingston, appear blue when the mist hovers over them. Famous for their coffee-growing areas, they are also full of trails, rivers, waterfalls, birdlife and fruit.

The South Coast is largely untouched and is a wildlife haven for crocodiles and birds such as ostriches. There are also famous waterfalls and caves. Eco-tourism is being developed in this area (see **C**).

D The attractions of Jamaica

Activities

1. Draw a sketch map of the island of Jamaica (turn to pages 145–155 of *SKILLS in geography* if you need help). Add symbols and labels to show the attractions for the tourists. Add a title and a key to your map.

2. a) Using **B**, draw a climate graph for Jamaica (see pages 145–155 of *SKILLS in geography*).

   b) Which would be the best month to visit Jamaica? Give reasons for your answer.

3. In pairs, look at the fact file on eco-tourism and use Hotlinks (see page 2) to look at the Eco Lodge website. In what ways is Eco Lodge a good example of eco-tourism? In what ways may it be a poor example? Could anything be done to improve it?

Key words

Bauxite – a mineral from which aluminium is made
Eco-tourism – allows tourists to have a good holiday but conserves the environment and involves the local people (also called *green tourism*)
Shanty town – area of slums with hand-built shacks where the poorest people live

4 Tourism – good or bad?

Managing tourism

> Finding out what 'leaky tourism' is
> Understanding how to be a sustainable tourist

Key words

Leakage – when much of the money paid for a holiday goes to companies based in richer countries instead of the country visited

Sustainable tourism – tourism that does not damage the environment or the way of life of the local people

Vicious cycle – where one thing leads to another, which leads to another so that the situation gets worse and worse

Tourism has to be managed carefully. Countries like Jamaica earn a lot of money from tourism, and tourism provides much-needed jobs. But Jamaica gets very little of the money that tourists pay. This is called **leakage**. Money leaks out to all sorts of people and places. Look at what happens when a UK family books their package holiday to Jamaica.

- Some of the money goes direct to the travel agent.
- Some goes to the tour operator whose package they buy.
- Some goes to the airline, usually British.
- Some goes to the hotel-owners in America.
- A lot of the food and drink is also imported from abroad.
- The hotel manager and some of the other top staff are American, so their incomes are paid into bank accounts in their home country.
- Jamaicans are employed as waiters, cooks, cleaners, taxi drivers, etc. They earn very little, and some are not employed all year round.

Imagine how much more money Jamaica could make from tourism if this leakage did not take place.

Tourism also brings with it conflicting viewpoints (see **A** and **B**).

A 'Been here nearly a week and haven't left the hotel – just relaxing! I'm avoiding the souvenir-sellers and their demands for money.'

B 'These rich tourists can be so greedy and rude – they make the beaches so crowded and make us short of water. They don't eat our home-grown food – it's all imported for them and we don't benefit at all. My friend works as a waiter and he sometimes earns less than me. They don't care about the people or the culture, or that most of their money goes to other countries.'

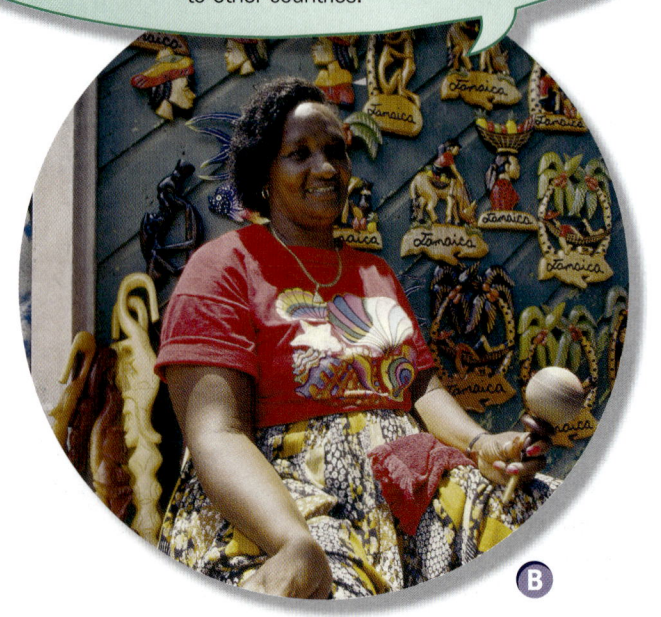

FACT FILE — MISMANAGING TOURISM

The chart in **C** shows what can happen if tourism is not carefully managed. This is often called a **vicious cycle**. Imagine the impact this would have on countries like Jamaica where the people are already poor and 45 per cent of their foreign income comes from tourism.

```
Tour operators offer cheap packages
  ↓
More people book to go because it is so cheap
  ↓
So developers build new hotels and facilities
  ↓
But development is not managed or controlled
  ↓
So the resort's natural attractions are ruined
  ↓
Now many tourists are put off
  ↓
So prices have to be cut further
  ↓
IN THE END NO ONE WANTS TO GO – the industry declines
```

C The vicious cycle of tourism – tourism can ruin a place

How can we manage tourism?
Holidays are fun, and tourism can bring many benefits to the country that tourists visit and its people. But it can also do real harm: to the environment, to the people and to their culture. Today many countries have a tourism development plan and they hope to make tourism more sustainable. But what does this mean? **Sustainable tourism** means that the tourist can still have a good time but without damaging the environment or the culture. The local people can also have a say in how the tourism is planned and earn a fair share of the profits that are made.

Sustainable tourism is important for all countries. It is especially important for poor countries because the effect of a drop in tourism is much greater. Also a thriving tourist industry can help millions of people have a better standard of living.

How to be a sustainable tourist
- Remember you are a guest in another person's country.
- Get to know the people and their culture.
- Dress and behave correctly – away from your resort, try to dress and behave like local people do.
- Pack environmentally friendly products, e.g. shampoo, suntan lotion, cosmetics.
- Support the local economy: buy local food, drinks, souvenirs and visit local attractions.
- Stay in eco-friendly, locally owned accommodation.
- Don't waste energy – have showers rather than baths, and switch off lights and air-conditioning when they aren't needed.
- Don't waste water or drop litter.
- Use public transport to visit places.
- Ask permission before taking photographs.

Activities

1. a) Look at the bulleted list on page 60. Write a list of all the ways money goes to the richer countries where people buy their package holidays.
   b) In what ways do the local people benefit from tourism?

2. Look at photos **A** and **B** – in what other ways can tourism cause problems?

3. Look at **C**. It shows a possible vicious cycle. But countries like Jamaica can't afford to lose their tourist industry. What would happen if the Jamaican government:
   a) banned all high-rise development?
   b) stopped all development beyond the edges of resorts?
   c) started its own airline, and funded the building of all new hotels and other developments?

4. Think about a holiday or day trip that you went on recently. Was it a package tour or was it more environmentally sustainable? Use the fact file to think about your holiday. What did you do that was sustainable? What can you do to make your holidays more sustainable in the future?

Assessing 360°

Tourism – good or bad?

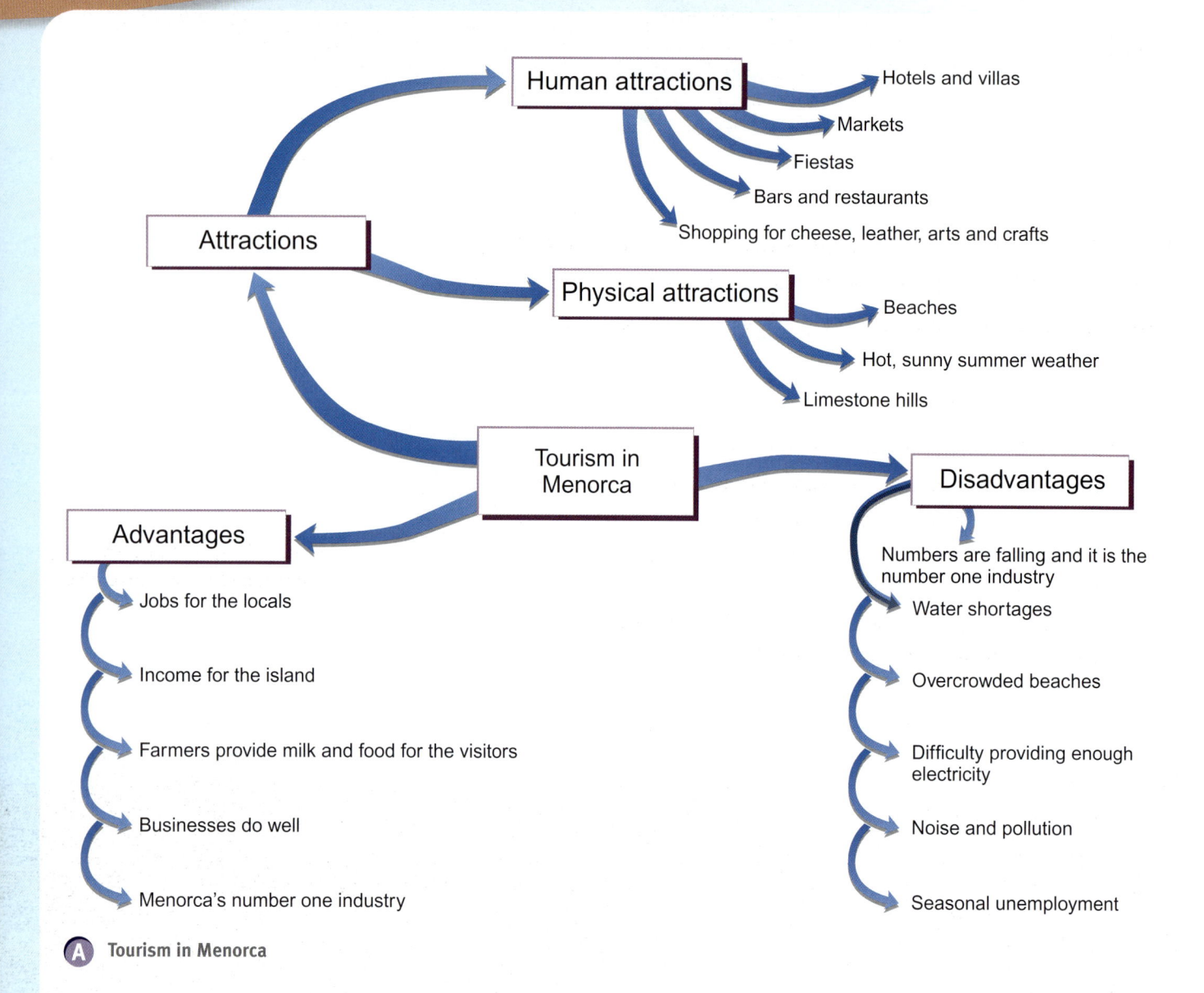

Tourism in Menorca

- **Attractions**
  - **Human attractions**
    - Hotels and villas
    - Markets
    - Fiestas
    - Bars and restaurants
    - Shopping for cheese, leather, arts and crafts
  - **Physical attractions**
    - Beaches
    - Hot, sunny summer weather
    - Limestone hills

- **Advantages**
  - Jobs for the locals
  - Income for the island
  - Farmers provide milk and food for the visitors
  - Businesses do well
  - Menorca's number one industry

- **Disadvantages**
  - Numbers are falling and it is the number one industry
  - Water shortages
  - Overcrowded beaches
  - Difficulty providing enough electricity
  - Noise and pollution
  - Seasonal unemployment

A Tourism in Menorca

1. Use **A** as a base to draw a pictorial map for Jamaica or another holiday resort or country. Look at pages 145–155 of *SKILLS in geography* for help.

2. Imagine you work for the Tourism Development Ministry in Jamaica. In pairs or small groups, design and present a six-point plan for the future development of tourism in Jamaica. Write a brief summary at the end to explain the advantages of your plan. Think about:

   - Planning – should more hotels be built? What kinds of hotels?
   - Taxes – should tourists who visit the country be taxed?
   - Laws – should there be laws to restrict the beach sellers?
   - Minimum wages – should locals have a minimum wage?
   - Imports – should these cost the tourist more to buy?
   - Food – should the government pay local farmers to grow crops for the hotels? Should the hotels be made to buy local produce?

›› 5 Rivers and floods

Have you seen waterfalls as large as these? These falls are in Brazil, one of the world's most water-rich countries. Can you think of any benefits and disadvantages of large rivers and waterfalls?

Learning objectives

What are you going to learn about in this chapter?
> How the water cycle operates both above and below the ground
> The importance to people of both natural and human stores of fresh water
> River landforms in both upland and lowland areas
> Why rivers flood
> Whether or not people can prevent rivers from flooding
> How to investigate rivers using fieldwork

A Igacu Falls, on the border between Brazil and Argentina

Water cycle – processes

> Finding out how rivers fit into the water cycle
> Learning about how people use rivers

What happens to the water that falls on the land as rain? It goes back into the atmosphere as water vapour (page 34) to make more rain.

PROCESSES

Precipitation is all types of moisture that falls from the atmosphere. One type is shown in **A**. Can you name three more types of precipitation?

Three things can happen to water that reaches the ground.

1 It goes back into the atmosphere in three different ways:
- Evaporation is when water from lakes and seas is changed into water vapour by heating.
- Transpiration is the loss of water from plants into the atmosphere.
- Evapo-transpiration is the name for all water losses into the atmosphere.

High temperatures and strong winds increase rates of water loss into the atmosphere.

2 It moves over the surface as runoff, leading to the formation of rivers.
- Runoff is fast on steep slopes, over impermeable rocks and in areas with little or no cover of trees.

A Winter morning in the Lake District. Night cooling has led to condensation and precipitation. What shows this?

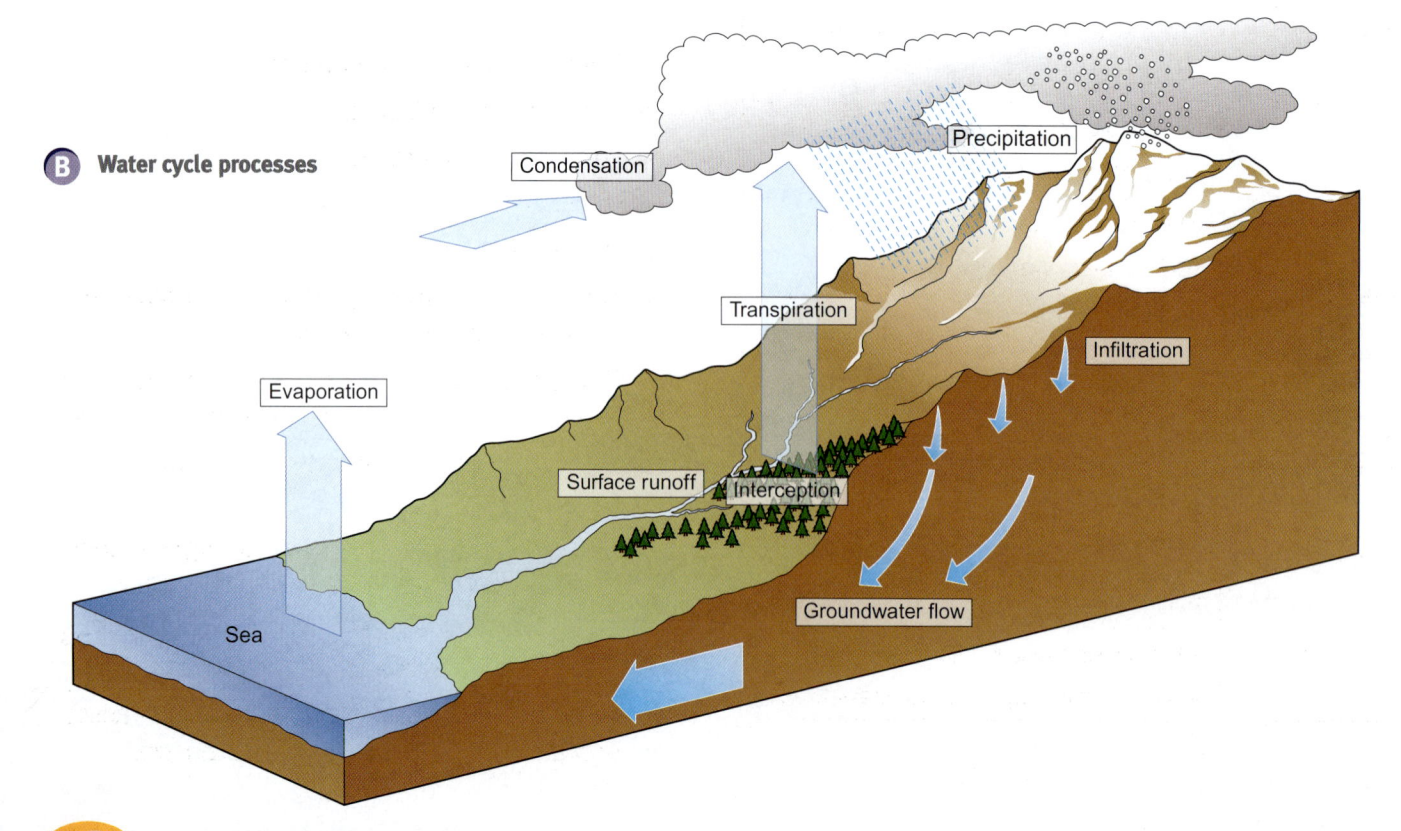

B Water cycle processes

- Runoff is slow in woodland, because rainwater is intercepted by branches and leaves.

3 It seeps into the soil and down into the ground by infiltration.
- Permeable rocks (rocks with many holes and spaces in them) allow water to infiltrate. Water moves through holes in rocks like limestone and sandstone as groundwater flow.

RIVERS

Rivers are a vital part of the Earth's water cycle. Rivers carry rainwater from land to sea. Most rivers start in upland areas as very small streams. As they flow towards the sea, they get larger because smaller rivers supply them with more water.

What is the name of the river that flows through your nearest city or town? Many settlements in the UK are located in river valleys and near rivers. This is because rivers have many uses (see **C**).

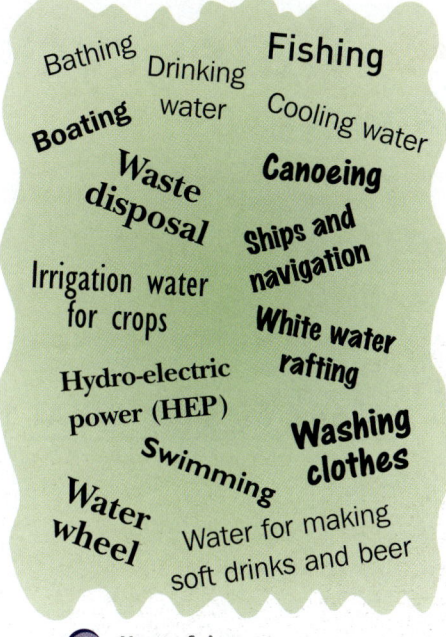

Bathing, Drinking water, Fishing, Boating, Cooling water, Waste disposal, Canoeing, Ships and navigation, Irrigation water for crops, White water rafting, Hydro-electric power (HEP), Swimming, Washing clothes, Water wheel, Water for making soft drinks and beer

C Uses of rivers

Activities

Key words	Definition
Precipitation	downward movement of water into soil
Interception	loss of water from plants into the atmosphere
Runoff	rock with spaces and holes that allow water to pass through it
Infiltration	loss of water into the atmosphere from all surface sources
Permeable rock	water from lakes and seas is changed into water vapour, a gas, by heating
Groundwater flow	movement of water over the ground surface after precipitation
Evaporation	water vapour, a gas, is changed into water as a liquid in water droplets and clouds by cooling
Transpiration	when rain is prevented from reaching the ground by trees
Evapo-transpiration	movement of water through spaces and holes in rock
Condensation	all forms of moisture that reach the ground surface e.g. snow, rain, sleet, dew

1 **Key words – mix and match**

First copy the list of key words. Then write the correct definition next to each key word.

2 a) Name a type of precipitation shown in **A**.
   b) Why do you get it on winter mornings in the UK?
   c) State *two* problems it causes for people.

3 Rearrange the uses of rivers in **C** under these headings.
   a) Domestic (uses in the home)
   b) Factories and industries
   c) Leisure and recreation
   d) Transport
   e) Power and energy

4 **Group activity – Investigation of the river or stream nearest your school**
   a) Find out basic information, e.g. where it starts and ends, names of places it passes through.
   b) State its main uses, e.g. for recreation, water supply.
   c) Does it have any disadvantages, e.g. for roads crossing over it, used for dumping waste?
   d) Draw a map or sketches to show how the river and land around are used.
   e) Would you say that your local river is an asset or a problem? Try to explain your answer.

5 Rivers and floods

Water cycle – stores and water supply

> Learning about water stores
> Finding out about water as a natural resource

Water is a **natural resource**. Fresh water is *the most valuable* of all the Earth's natural resources. Human life on Earth would be impossible without it.

FACT FILE — WHAT IS A WATER STORE?

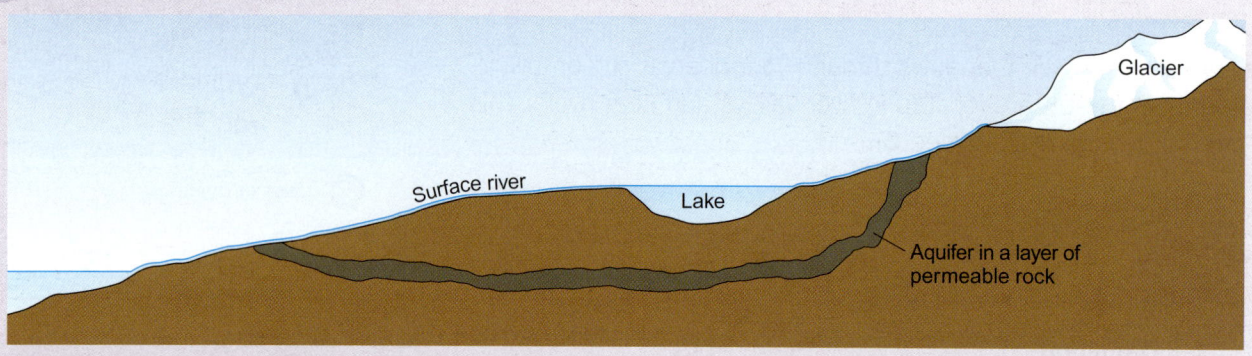

A Natural stores of fresh water

There are three main places where freshwater is stored on land (see **A**).

- As ice in glaciers
- On the surface in lakes and rivers
- Underground in layers of permeable rock.

Where is the largest amount of fresh water on Earth stored? You can see the answer in **B**.

The natural stores of fresh water shown in **A** are vital sources of water supply for people. However, there are two problems.

1. Only 13 per cent of the water on Earth is fresh water. The rest is salt water.
2. The biggest fresh water store is in Antarctica, but no one lives there.

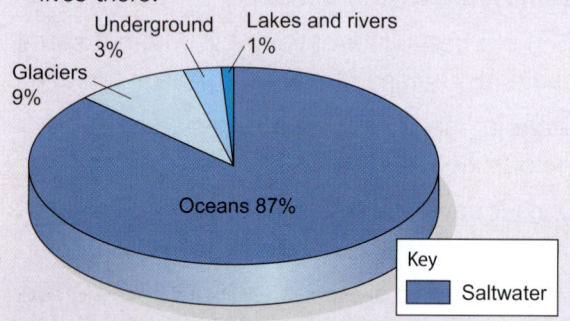

B Water stores on the Earth's surface

- Oceans 87%
- Glaciers 9%
- Underground 3%
- Lakes and rivers 1%

Key: Saltwater

To increase water supplies, people build dams across rivers. Water is stored in **reservoirs** behind them.

Where does it come from?

Do you know where the water that flows from your taps at home comes from?

- In most parts of the UK, tap water comes from lakes and reservoirs in the uplands. These are filled up by rivers.
- In East Anglia and South East England, some tap water comes from **aquifers** – underground stores in permeable rocks, especially chalk. Tap water also comes directly from large rivers, such as the Thames, without any storage. However, it does pass through the water treatment works before reaching your taps!

C Summer users of the River Thames at Reading

The UK has many rivers. It also has a wet climate. Despite this, the UK is not 'water-rich' by world standards (see **D**). This is because the UK has a high population density. Even 'dry' Australia is fifteen times better off for water per head than the UK.

There is another big problem for water supply in the UK. Many people live in London and the South East where rainfall is lowest. Here the government has plans for building more houses.

	Water per head (m^3)
UK	1 219
World average	6 918
Europe average	8 547
Australia	18 596

D Water resources

London 'could be without water inside ten years'

London could run out of water within a decade if it does not spend more on replacing leaking mains built in Victorian times or on building reservoirs, Thames Water said yesterday.

The company has warned that the population of London is now expected to grow by 800 000 by 2016. Demand for water will be greater than existing supplies. Population growth and new housing will place severe pressure on the capital's water supplies.

Thames Water has already announced its intention to build a desalination plant (to extract fresh water from sea water) within three years to provide drinking water for 900 000 people.

Dry summers already cause problems for the company. 'We have nothing up our sleeves to keep things running in a dry summer,' said the managing director.

E Adapted from a newspaper report by Charlie Clover, Environment editor, *Daily Telegraph,* 23 October 2004.
© Telegraph Group Limited (2004)

Activities

1. Draw a labelled diagram to show the natural stores of water.
2. a) (i) What % of water on Earth is saltwater?
      (ii) What % is stored as ice and snow?
      (iii) Why are both of these of little use for water supply for people?
   b) (i) What % of water on Earth is stored in rivers and lakes?
      (ii) Why are rivers and lakes the most important stores of water for people?
3. Draw a bar graph to show the values in **D**.
4. a) Write down *two* reasons why water supply for London is a great problem.
   b) Describe *one* way Thames Water is trying to reduce the problem.
5. Work in groups.
   a) Name the Water Authority that provides water in your home region.
   b) Visit its website to discover where your tap water comes from.
   c) Do you have problems with water supply during dry summers in your area?

Key words
Aquifer – underground store of water in permeable rock
Natural resource – something that occurs naturally that people can use
Reservoir – artificial lake used to store water for human use

5 Rivers and floods

Rivers in the uplands

> Understanding the work of rivers in the uplands
> Finding out about the common upland river landforms

Each river has its own **drainage basin** (see **A**). The **source** is where the river starts in the uplands. The **mouth** is where the river meets the sea. Between the two, the main river is fed by smaller rivers and rivers called **tributaries** that increase its size.

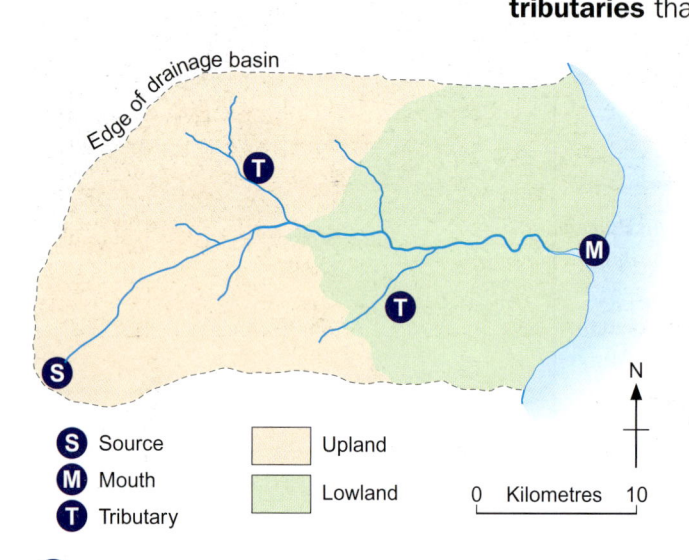

S Source
M Mouth
T Tributary

Upland
Lowland

0 Kilometres 10

A River drainage basin

B River Tees in its upper course: notice the rocky bed and steep gradient typical of a river in the uplands

FACT FILE — THE WORK OF RIVERS IN THE UPLANDS

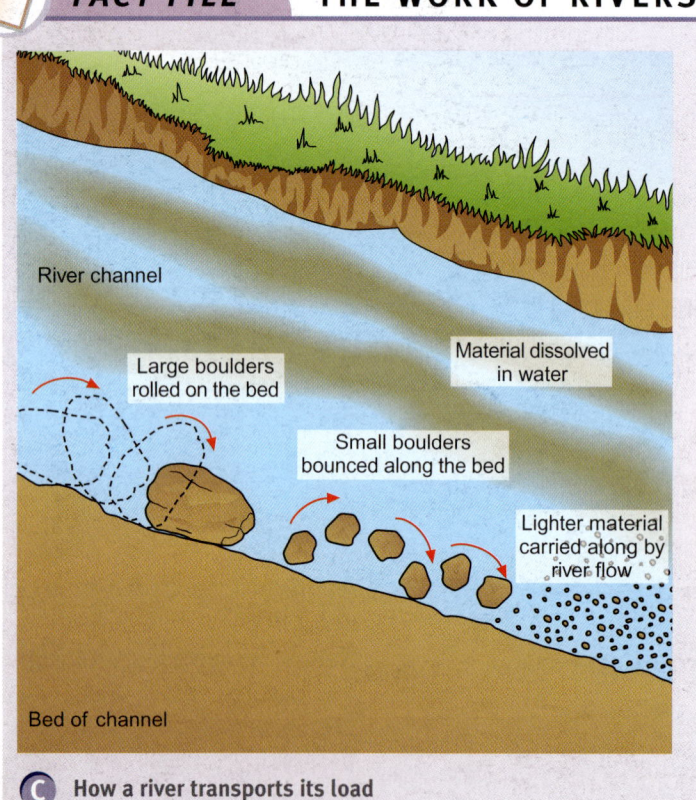

When a river has spare energy, it does two types of work.

1 Transportation

Boulders, stones, sand and silt are moved down-stream. The total amount carried by a river is its **load**. Ways of transporting this load are shown in **C**.

2 Erosion

The bed and sides of the **channel** are worn away by abrasion and hydraulic action (see **D**). (The same terms were used for wave erosion at the coast.)

Abrasion
Boulders, bounced along the bed, break off pieces of rock as they are moved.

Hydraulic action
Water washes against the bed and banks, dislodges and removes materials.

C How a river transports its load

D How rivers erode

68 geography 360° Foundation Book 2

UPLAND RIVER LANDFORMS

Rivers form **V-shaped valleys** (see **E** and **F**). Why? The river flows in the lowest part of a valley. It is here that the bed and banks are eroded by moving water. Rivers in the uplands cut down into the rock; this is called **vertical erosion**. Sometimes valley sides are high, steep and rocky; this is a **gorge**.

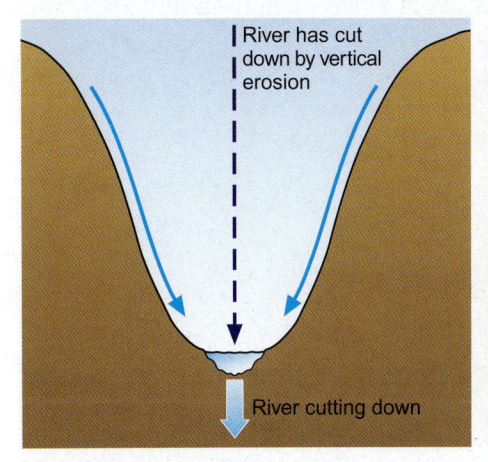

E How a V-shaped valley and gorge are formed

F V-shaped valley

G Gorge

Waterfalls are popular with visitors to upland areas. Look for these three features in any waterfall.

- Hard rock at top (called the *cap rock*) – eroded slowly
- Soft rocks below – eroded fast
- Plunge pool at bottom – formed by the great force of the falling water.

Activities

1. a) Make a frame and draw a sketch of the River Tees from photo **B**.
   b) Add labels to show the river and channel features.
   c) Compare your sketch with those of people near you in the class. Mark your neighbour's sketch out of ten using the following guide to marking;
   - Amount of detail shown – up to four marks
   - Appearance and neatness – up to two marks
   - Number of labels used – up to four marks.
   d) Are any of the others better than yours? How could your own sketch have been improved?

2. Look at **E–G**.
   a) Draw a cross-section of a V-shaped valley (**E, F**).
   b) How is a gorge different (**G**)?
   c) This gorge attracts many visitors. What do they go to see?

3. Draw and label a storyboard for a cartoon to show people in your class how a river transports its load.

Key words

Channel – area between the banks where the river flows
Drainage basin – area of land drained by a river and its tributaries
Gorge – deep, narrow, steep-sided valley
Load – all materials transported by a river
Mouth – point where a river goes into the sea
Source – point where a river starts to flow
Tributary – smaller river that flows into a larger one
Vertical erosion – wearing away land in a downward direction
V-shaped valley – river valley that is lowest in the centre
Waterfall – where the river suddenly drops in height

Rivers in the lowlands

> Understanding the work of rivers in the lowlands
> Finding out about the common lowland river landforms

River channels and valleys change as rivers leave upland areas (see photos **A** and **B**).

- The river becomes wider and deeper.
- There are fewer large boulders in the channel bed.
- Water flow is smoother.
- Bends in the river get larger.
- The sides of the V-shaped valley become less steep.

A River on the edge of the Pennine uplands

B River Cuckmere in Sussex, almost at the sea

FACT FILE — HOW IS THE WORK OF RIVERS DIFFERENT IN THE LOWLANDS?

There are two main differences from rivers in the uplands.

1. The river wears away land on the *sides* of the channel and valley – called **lateral erosion**.
2. The river drops a lot of its load in the channel and on the banks – known as deposition.

Together they greatly affect landforms (see **C**).

- Results of lateral erosion – **meanders** (large bends) and **ox-bow lakes** (semi-circular lakes)
- Results of deposition – **levees** (high river banks) and **floodplains** (flat land mainly built of **silt**).

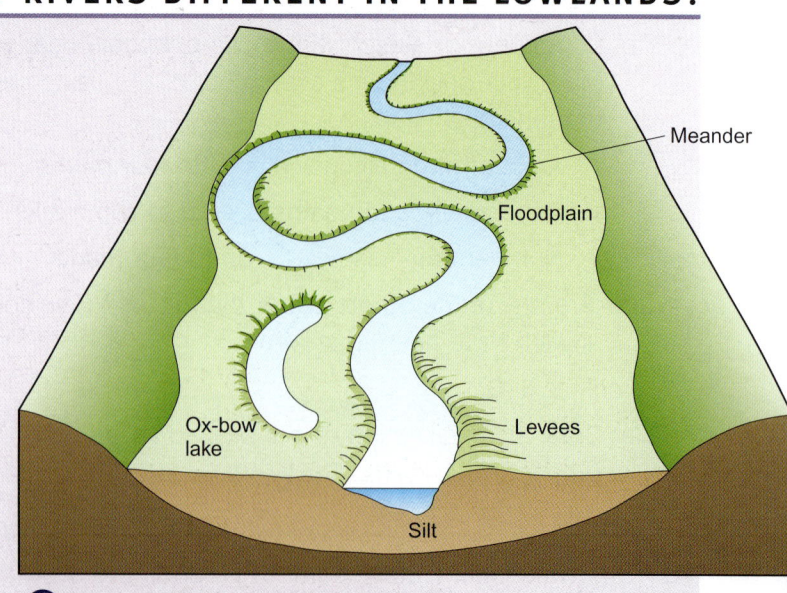

C River landforms in the lowlands

LOWLAND RIVER LANDFORMS

Meanders and ox-bow lakes are mainly formed by erosion, but some deposition takes place on inside bends (see **D**).

- On a bend the main river current swings towards the outside bend.
- The bank on the outside bend is eroded and forms a steep bank.
- On the inside bend water flow is slow.
- Sediment is deposited here to form a gentle bank.
- During a flood the river breaks through the narrow neck between two outside bends and forms an ox-bow lake.

What colour is a river in flood? Most are brown because of the large load of sediment they are carrying. Every time a river floods, the land is covered with a new layer of sediment. Over time, a great thickness of silt is built up, forming the floodplain. Floodplains are widened by lateral erosion on the outside bends of meanders.

During a flood, more silt is deposited on the river banks. This forms the high banks known as levees.

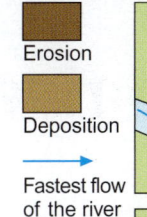

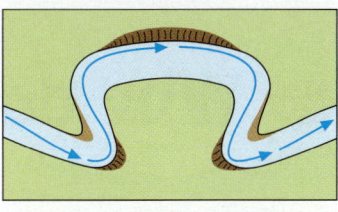

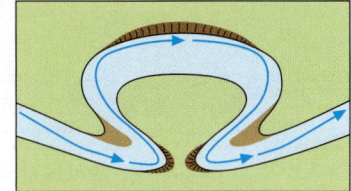

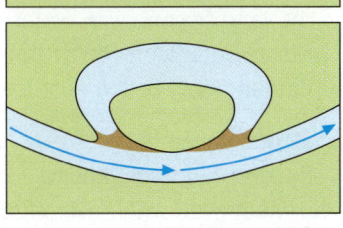

D Formation of a meander and an ox-bow lake

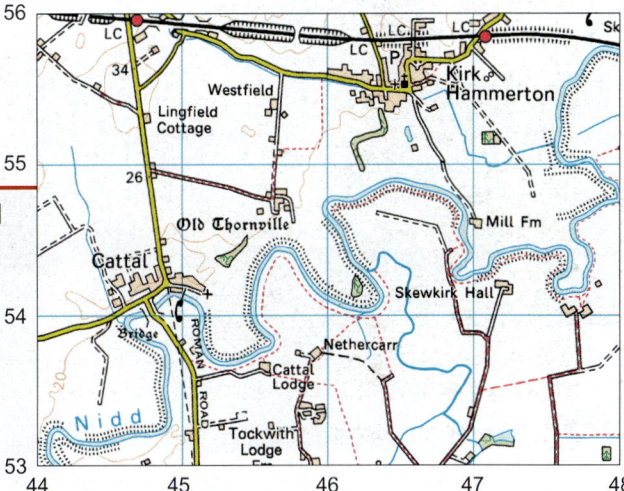

E OS map of part of the valley of the River Nidd between Knaresborough and York, scale 1:50 000.
© Crown copyright, Licence no. 100000230

Activities

1. a) Look at photos **A** and **B**. List *three* differences in river and valley features between them.
   b) Make a frame and draw a labelled sketch of photo **B**.

2. a) Make a frame and draw a grid the same size as OS map **E**.
   b) (i) On your map, mark the course of the River Nidd using the grid lines as a guide.
      (ii) Shade and name Kirk Hammerton.
   c) Find squares 4655 and 4654 on map **E**.
      (i) People live in square 4655. What map evidence shows this?
      (ii) No one lives in square 4654. Why not?

3. **Odd one out**

1 Abrasion	6 Levees	11 Silt
2 Channel	7 Meander	12 Source
3 Floodplain	8 Mouth	13 Vertical erosion
4 Gorge	9 Ox-bow lake	14 V-shaped valley
5 Lateral erosion	10 Plunge pool	15 Waterfall

   a) For each set below, decide which is the odd one out. Give a reason for your choice.
      Set A: 5   11   13   **Set B:** 6   10   15
   b) Make *two* sets of your own. Test them on your neighbour.

Key words

Floodplain – area of flat land on the sides of a river
Lateral erosion – wearing away the sides of the channel and valley
Levees – raised banks on the side of a river forming a natural embankment
Meander – large bend in the river
Ox-bow lake – semi-circular lake on the side of a river
Silt – fine-grained sediment carried and deposited by rivers

5 Rivers and floods

Why do rivers flood?

> Understanding the causes of flooding
> Finding out what happens to the excess water/runoff in urban and rural surfaces

FACT FILE — WHEN DO FLOODS HAPPEN?

A river floods when water overflows its banks and covers the land beyond with water. It is normal for rivers to flood. Most rivers flood two or three times a year. This is why the flat land next to the river is called the floodplain.

Floods cause big problems for people living on or near floodplains. Lives may be lost. A lot of property is damaged or destroyed when rivers flood in towns and cities.

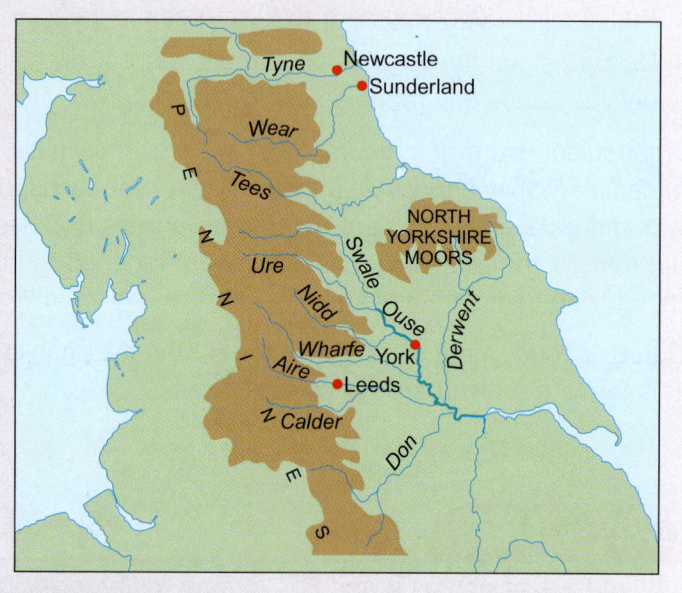

B The main rivers in northern and eastern England. Why does the River Ouse flood more than any of the other rivers?

A River Ouse in flood at York, one of the most flood-prone cities in the UK

Natural causes of flooding

There are three natural causes of flooding.

1. **Rain day after day**
   Water fills all the spaces in soil and rocks. The ground cannot hold any more rainwater. The rest of the rain runs off on the surface into rivers.

2. **Heavy rain (e.g. a thunderstorm)**
   Rain hits the ground so hard that it bounces off. There is no chance of water seeping into the ground (see **C**).

3. **Melting snow and ice**
   Rivers starting in high mountain areas flood in summer. Summer temperatures are high enough to melt the ice and snow on the mountain tops.

C One cause of flooding – a cloudburst

72 geography 360° Foundation Book 2

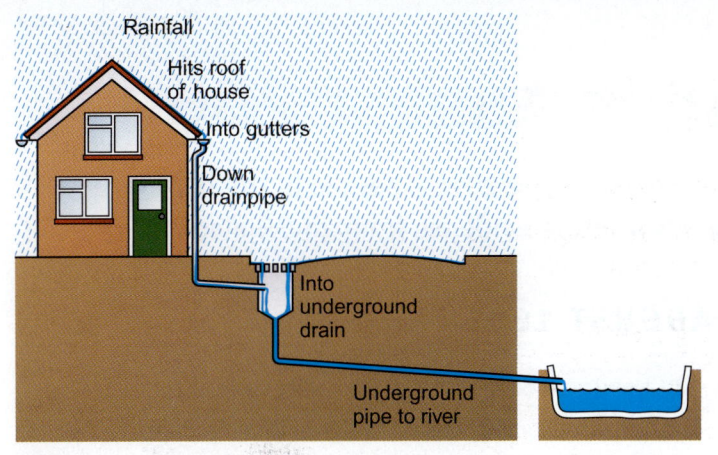

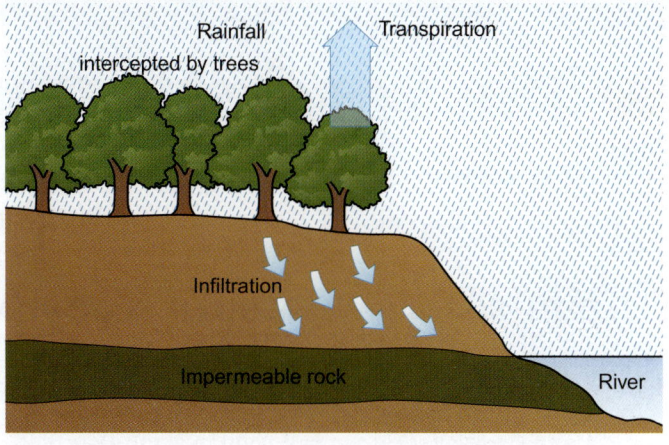

D Water movement in built-up urban areas

E Water movement on vegetation-covered surfaces

HOW PEOPLE INCREASE THE RISK OF FLOODING

You can see in **D** what happens to rain that falls in cities. When it lands on pavements, roads and roofs of buildings, it is led into underground drains. Drains carry the water away into rivers as quickly as possible so that city streets are not flooded.

Now look what happens to rain that falls on woodland in rural areas (see **E**). Tree roots take in some of the water, which is then lost through the leaves by transpiration. Rainwater is delayed from reaching the ground by interception; this gives more time for water to infiltrate underground.

	Forest	Built-up
Evapo-transpiration	40	25
Runoff	10	45
Groundwater	50	30

F What happens to precipitation (100%) in woodland and city areas

FLOODING IS GETTING WORSE

River floods are only a problem when people are affected, but this seems to be happening more often to more people around the world. The estimated number of properties at risk from flooding in the UK in 2004 was 2.2 million.

Activities

1. a) Draw a labelled diagram to show what a river in flood looks like.
   b) State *three* causes of river floods.
   c) Write down *three* problems caused by river floods.

2. a) Look at map **B**. How many rivers flow into the River Ouse north of York? How many rivers flow into the River Ouse south of York?
   b) River flooding is a major problem in York. It is not a big problem in Leeds. Why?

3. What happens to rainwater in woodlands and cities?
   a) Draw *two* pie graphs, side by side, to show the percentages in **F**. Look at *SKILLS in geography* pages 145–155 for help.
   b) Look at **D** and **E**. Write out and finish these sentences.

   (i) Evapo-transpiration in cities is ____ % less than in woodlands, mainly because there are fewer ____ in cities to lose water to the atmosphere through their ____ by transpiration.

   (ii) Runoff is ____ % more in cities than in woodlands, mainly because rainwater in cities falls on hard surfaces such as ____ and flows down ____, which take the water away quickly into ____ .

   (iii) Groundwater is ____ % less in cities than in woodlands, mainly because when rainwater falls on hard surfaces in cities it cannot ____ .

4. Visit the Environment Agency's website via Hotlinks (see page 2). Enter your postcode to check your area for flood risk to your school and home. Can you explain the result shown?

5 Rivers and floods

The Boscastle flood in August 2004

> Finding out how flooding affects people in the UK
> Practising interpreting evidence from an OS map

FACT FILE — LYNMOUTH FLOOD IN AUGUST 1952

There is a high risk of river floods after summer thunderstorms in the steep-sided valleys of North Devon and North Cornwall. One famous flood in North Devon was the Lynmouth flood of 1952.

First two weeks of August
Weather much wetter than usual; ground saturated.

15 August
Rain for 24 hours during which 270 mm fell on Exmoor.

Night of 15–16 August
- Wave of water 4 m high burst into the village at 300 kph (200 mph).
- It carried boulders, trees and telegraph poles.
- Debris collected against bridges, forming dams.
- When these burst, surges of water 10 m high were released.

Morning of 16 August
- In all, 35 people were killed.
- One-quarter of the built-up area was devastated.
- Twenty-eight homes were washed away, sixteen bridges destroyed, 100 vehicles swept out to sea and nineteen boats missing.

BOSCASTLE FLOOD IN 2004

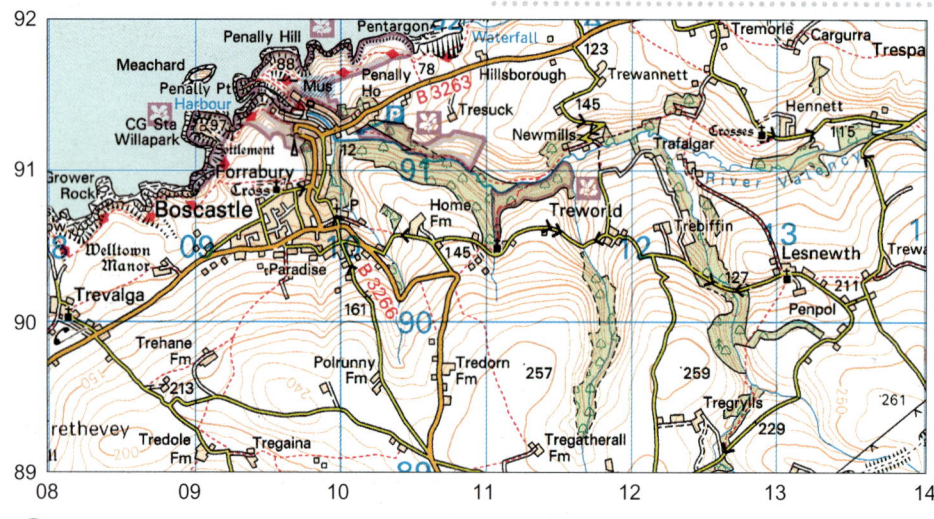

The flood in Boscastle in North Cornwall in August 2004 was similar in many ways. A summer storm dropped 200 mm of rain in four hours, with 90 mm of it falling in just one hour. Rainwater poured down the steep valley sides into the Rivers Valencey and Jordan. These rivers meet in Boscastle and caused the great flood shown in **B**.

A OS map of Boscastle, scale 1:50 000.
© Crown copyright, Licence no. 100000230

A wall of water 3 m high swept through the village.
- Thirty vehicles were washed into the harbour.
- Trees were uprooted and piled up around bridges and houses.
- Two shops on the riverside were destroyed, other properties were badly damaged and one bridge collapsed.
- More than 100 people were rescued by helicopters from roofs and trees.

It was a miracle that no one died. The emergency services came quickly. Because the storm was in the middle of the day, people were awake and could escape. Rescuing people by helicopter was possible in daylight.

83-year-old local man:
'I have never seen it rain as hard as this in all my life.'

House owner:
'It was a normal summer morning, quite peaceful really. In the early afternoon it suddenly turned into a place of mayhem, as water waist-deep swept cars away past our front door. We had to punch holes in the roof of our house to escape the water and await rescue by helicopter.'

Hotel guest:
'One minute the water was ankle-deep. The next minute the water was up to our chests. We ran up the stairs. The water just rose up after us. It was like a horror film.'

Local councillor:
'I do not think anything could have been built to hold back this kind of rainfall.'

Local resident:
'The rain turned the roads into rivers. Cars, wheelie bins and trees went flying past in a torrent of water and disappeared out to sea.'

Tourist:
'When the waters started to rise in the river bed, at first it was more like a tourist attraction. The car park was full of people looking at the water. Then the river banks suddenly burst and people started fleeing for their lives.'

B Floodwater sweeps through the centre of Boscastle

C Comments from witnesses of the flood

Activities

1. Make a large summary chart like the one below for the Lynmouth and Boscastle floods.

	Lynmouth	Boscastle
Time of year		
Weather		
What the flood was like		
Numbers killed		
Damage to property		

2. Write down *two* similarities between the Lynmouth and Boscastle floods.

3. a) Which flood was more serious?
   b) Give reasons for your choice.

4. Imagine that you were a newspaper reporter looking at the scene shown in photo **B**. Write a short newspaper report (about 200–300 words) in two parts.

   Part 1: Describe what you could see (from photo **B**).

   Part 2: Write about what it was like for people caught in the flood (**C**).

5. Look at OS map **A**.

   a) What is the valley of the River Valencey like? (For example, are the valley sides steep or gentle? How many tributaries join the river?)

   b) State *four* things from the OS map which show that this area gets a lot of tourists.

5 Rivers and floods

Flood prevention measures

> Finding out what can be done to prevent floods
> Discovering the advantages and disadvantages of human intervention

Measures to prevent river flooding are shown in **A**. The cost and size of the flood prevention measures increase as you move from left to right in **A**.

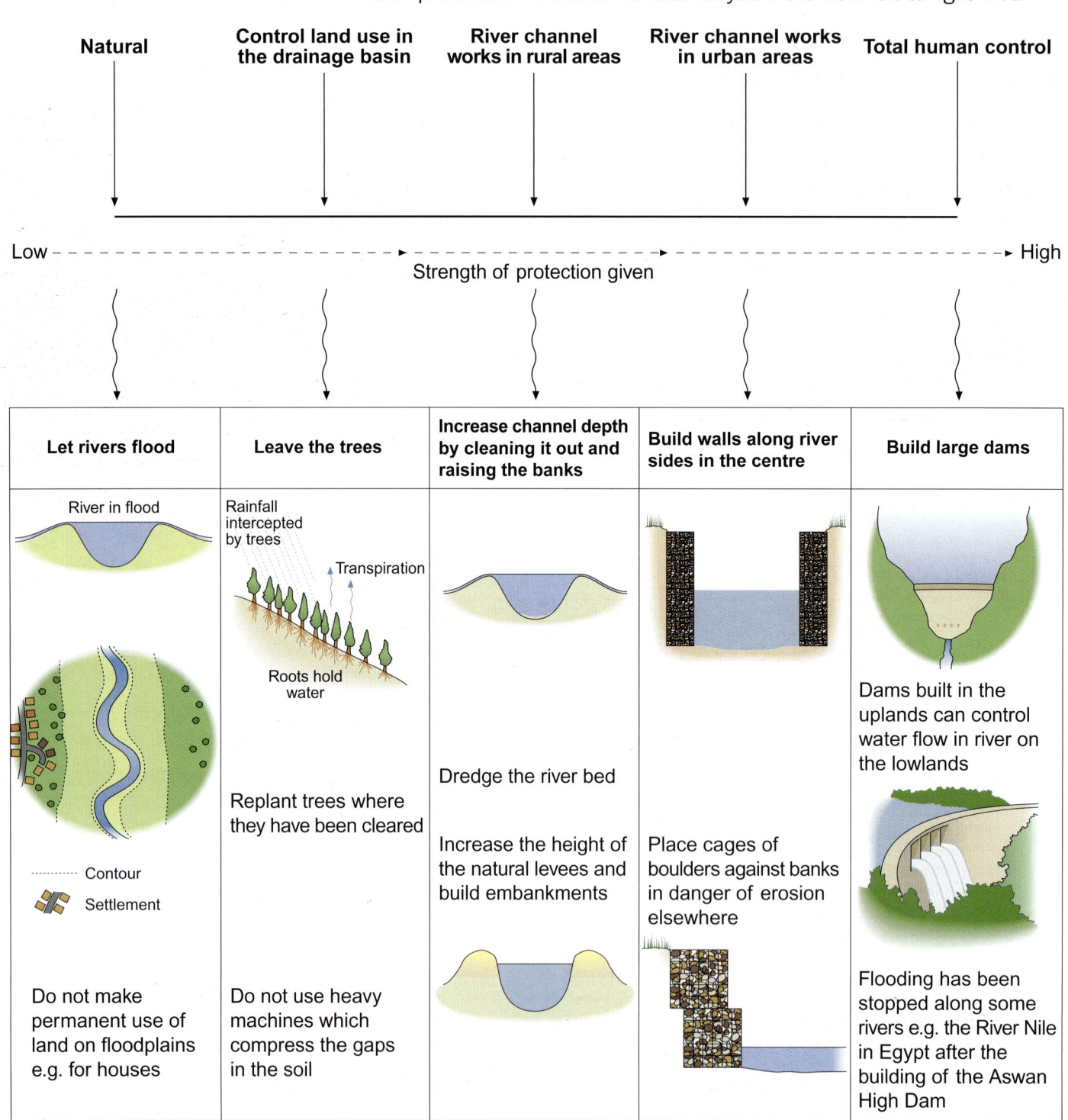

| Natural | Control land use in the drainage basin | River channel works in rural areas | River channel works in urban areas | Total human control |

Low — → High
Strength of protection given

Let rivers flood	Leave the trees	Increase channel depth by cleaning it out and raising the banks	Build walls along river sides in the centre	Build large dams
River in flood	Rainfall intercepted by trees / Transpiration / Roots hold water			
	Replant trees where they have been cleared	Dredge the river bed		Dams built in the uplands can control water flow in river on the lowlands
Contour / Settlement		Increase the height of the natural levees and build embankments	Place cages of boulders against banks in danger of erosion elsewhere	
Do not make permanent use of land on floodplains e.g. for houses	Do not use heavy machines which compress the gaps in the soil			Flooding has been stopped along some rivers e.g. the River Nile in Egypt after the building of the Aswan High Dam

A Different measures to prevent flooding

ADVANTAGES AND DISADVANTAGES OF DIFFERENT MEASURES

In rural areas flood prevention measures are usually small-scale.

- Advantage – they cause little, if any, damage to the environment.
- Disadvantage – they will not stop big floods.

In urban areas stronger flood protection measures are essential. Why?

1 More people live there.
2 There is a lot more property to protect.

Flood prevention measures used include:

- walls along the river banks
- metal gates which can be closed to protect property on the riverside (see **C**).

Even these may not be enough to stop large rivers from flooding in very wet weather (see photo **B**). Building a large dam is the most successful flood prevention measure.

- Advantages – dams hold back all the water after heavy rainfall and stop flooding. They also have other uses, e.g. water supply, irrigation and electricity.
- Disadvantages – large dams are very expensive to build. People have to move out of the valley behind the dam. Wildlife habitats are lost.

B The River Wear in Durham in flood for the second time in the wet year of 2000

C High walls and metal gates protect housing on the banks of the River Tees in Yarm

Activities

1 Make a large chart to show *three* measures of flood prevention, their advantages and disadvantages. One has been done to show you what to do.

Measure of flood prevention	Advantages	Disadvantages
1 Making the embankments higher	River water levels can rise higher without flooding the land behind	Large floods will still go over the top
2		

2 **Group work – Investigation of the river flowing through your nearest town or city**

a) Name the measures of flood prevention in use along the river.

b) Draw labelled field sketches to show what they look like.

c) How far do they extend?

d) Have they been 100 per cent effective so far (i.e. does the river ever flood)?

Investigating rivers using fieldwork

> Learning about safety precautions during river fieldwork
> Finding out what can be investigated in river fieldwork and how to do it

River fieldwork can be great fun. You must work in a group because one or two people are needed to hold the equipment. Others are needed to take measurements and note down the results on a recording sheet.

River fieldwork can be dangerous. Hazards include:

- deep pools of water
- strong river currents
- rapid changes in water level.

Choose a river that is not too deep and wide, like the one in **A**.

A Group of geography students investigating a river

B Safety first

FACT FILE — PLANNING A FIELDWORK INVESTIGATION OF A RIVER

1 Find a title.

Ask yourself: 'What do I want to find out?' One common title for a river study is:

'In what ways and why does the channel of River ... change downstream?'

The most likely changes downstream in a river and its channel will be:

- they will get wider and deeper (because the river is joined by more tributaries)
- water speed will increase (because a larger river can flow more smoothly)
- load size will decrease (because boulders and pebbles are replaced by small stones and sand).

2 Prepare to do the fieldwork.

- Draw a recording sheet (your teacher can give you an example to help).
- Assemble the measuring equipment.

Then you should be ready to start.

WHAT CAN BE INVESTIGATED AND HOW?

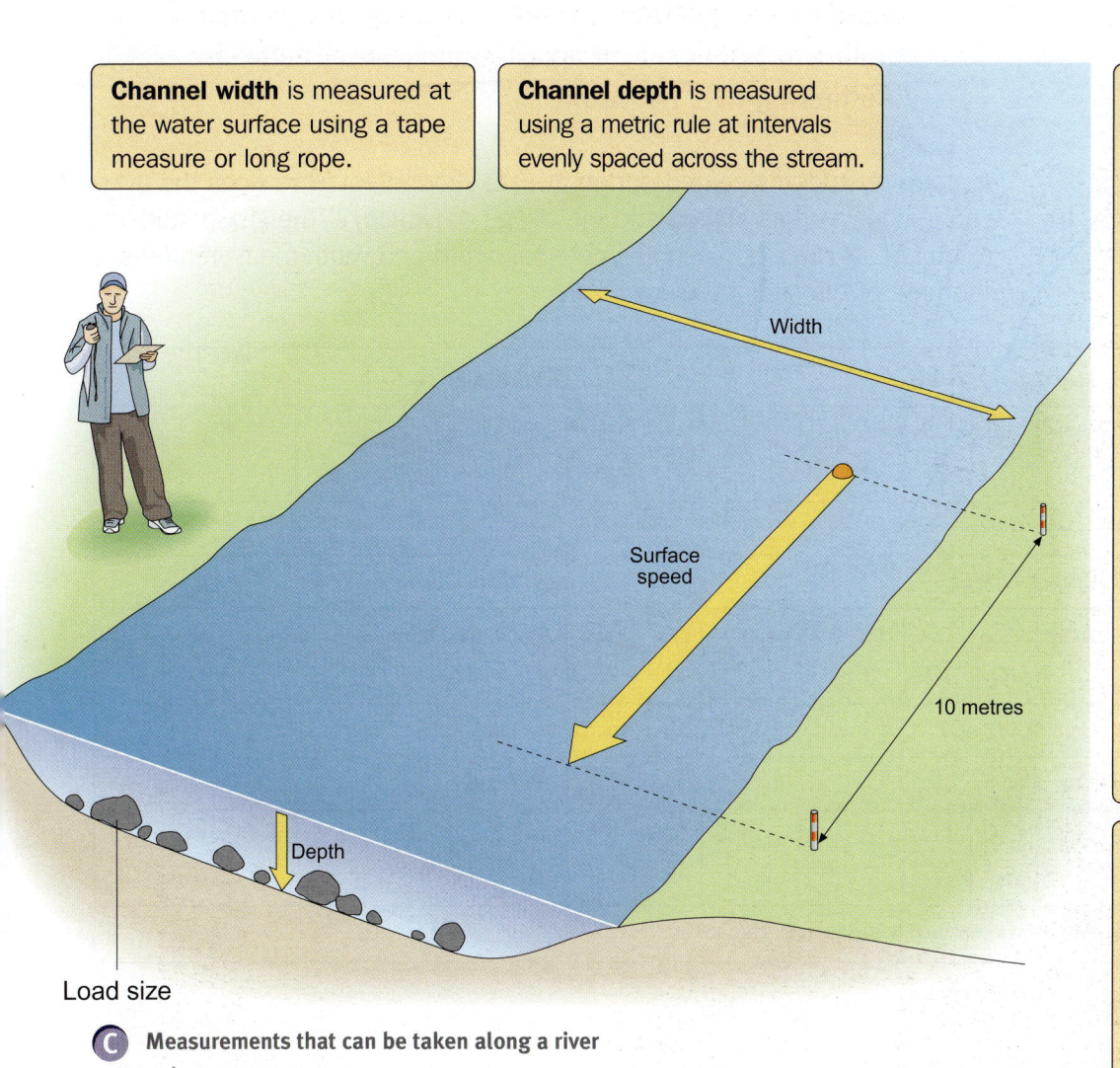

Channel width is measured at the water surface using a tape measure or long rope.

Channel depth is measured using a metric rule at intervals evenly spaced across the stream.

Surface speed can be measured with a flow metre. Not everyone has access to one of these, which is why the method below is used more often. It is also more interesting.
- Measure a 10 metre stretch of river.
- Throw a float into the river at the start. Possible floats include pieces of wood, oranges, onions and dog biscuits.
- Use a stopwatch to time how long it takes the float to go 10 metres.
- Calculate surface speed using this formula:

$$\text{Surface speed} = \frac{\text{Distance}}{\text{Time}}$$

Load size is obtained by measuring pebbles and stones from the stream bed using a ruler. Take a sample of up to ten pebbles from the river bed, measure the longest edges and calculate the average length of pebbles in your sample.

C Measurements that can be taken along a river

Activities

1. Make a list of the equipment for doing river fieldwork mentioned on these two pages.
2. Draw labelled diagrams to show how a) channel width and depth and b) speed of water flow can be measured by fieldwork.
3. a) Why is the river in photo **A** suitable for geography fieldwork?
   b) Draw a labelled sketch of a river that would *not* be suitable for geography fieldwork.
4. Think of reasons why you should do the following.
   a) Take float measurements for river speed more than once at each site (i.e. what might happen to the float to stop it giving an accurate measurement?)
   b) Take measurements of up to ten pebbles at each site for load size.
   c) Make observations of what the river valley is like at each site as well.

How can the results from river fieldwork be used?

> Interpreting river fieldwork

A group of students carried out an investigation titled: 'How does the river change between its source and the village of Langley?' The group studied a total of six sites. You can see channel depth and width measurements for three of the sites in **A**.

	Location: Close to source of stream								Width: 1.7 m					
Site 1	Depth (metres from bank)	0.5	1.0	1.5	–	–	–	–	–	–	–	–	–	–
	depth (cm)	7	10	4										
	Valley observation: Small and narrow													
	Location: Below the road bridge								Width: 5.2 m					
Site 3	Depth (metres from bank)	0.5	1.0	1.5	2.0	2.5	3.0	3.5	4.0	4.5	5.0	–	–	–
	depth (cm)	10	10	11	12	14	15	15	13	12	10			
	Valley observation: Flat land near the river, rising ground further away from river													
	Location: Next to the village								Width: 7.1 m					
Site 6	Depth (metres from bank)	0.5	1.0	1.5	2.0	2.5	3.0	3.5	4.0	4.5	5.0	5.5	6.0	6.5	7.0
	depth (cm)	6	7	7	8	8	8	10	15	17	20	19	19	18	14
	Valley observation: Floodplain on both sides of the river													

A Examples from a recording sheet for river fieldwork at three study sites

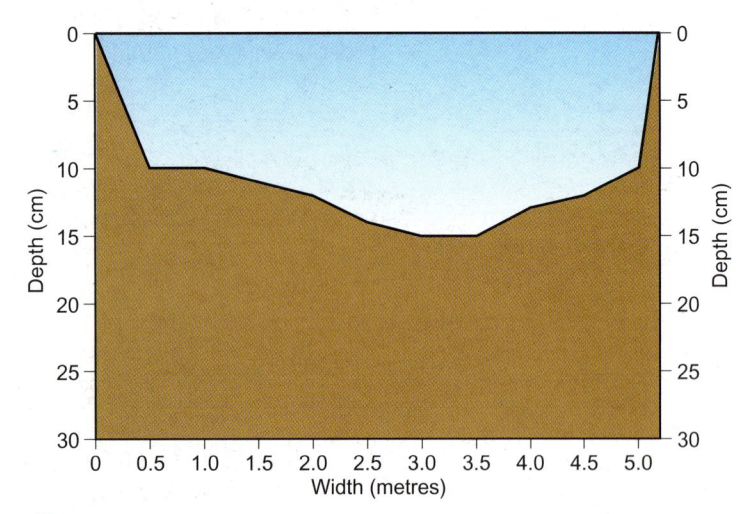

B Channel cross-section at site 3

When you have collected fieldwork data, the next stage is to show the results using graphs, photographs and sketches.

Site 3 as an example
After measuring channel width and depth, a channel cross-section can be drawn (see **B**). This makes it easier to see what the river channel looks like. It shows that water depth was almost the same across the river, just slightly deeper in the middle.

This is the cross-section shape you expect to find where a river is straight. You can see from photo **C** that the river was straight at site 3. In **D** you can see what one of the students wrote about site 3.

C Photograph taken at study site 3

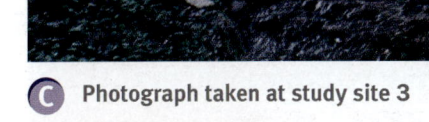

Activities

1. It is always best if photographs used in fieldwork write-ups are labelled.
   a) Make a large frame and draw a sketch of what can be seen in **C**.
   b) Add labels to show some of the channel and valley features that the student refers to in the write-up.

2. a) Using values in **A**, draw a channel cross-section for site 6.
   b) State *two* differences between the cross-sections for sites 3 and 6.

3. Look at recording sheet **A**.
   a) How much wider was the river at site 6 than at site 1?
   b) How much deeper was the river at site 6 than at site 1?
   c) How was the valley different at site 6 from at site 1?
   d) Are these the changes expected as you follow a river downstream? Answer as fully as you can.

> The river channel is now three times wider than it was at the source. It is also deeper. The water in the channel is more than 10 cm deep and deeper still in the middle: up to 15 cm deep. The river is wider and deeper now because two tributaries have joined it.
>
> There are some large stones on the river bed. They are causing ripples as the river flows over them. These can be seen on the photograph. The photograph also shows that the banks of the channel are quite steep and deep. I think that the river must still be cutting downwards by vertical erosion. All of these are features of a river in the uplands.
>
> There is one big difference from site 1. Land beyond the river banks is now flatter. It seems to me that a floodplain is starting to form. You can also see this on the photograph. The land around the river is now lower and flatter than it was.

D Student's write-up for site 3

5 – Rivers and floods

Assessing 360°

Can river flooding in the UK be stopped?

A University lecturer in geography
'Don't people understand why the flat land next to rivers is called the floodplain? River flooding is a natural event – all rivers flood. You could say that it is their own fault if people are having problems with flooding.'

B Director of a house-building company
'Building new houses on flat land is easier than building on slopes. Buying floodplain land off farmers is cheap, because it is only useful for summer pasture. We are making better use of the land.'

C House owner
'We looked around the house on a beautiful summer's day and fell in love with it. It cost us over £200 000. We put all our savings into it and still needed a big mortgage. Last winter the local stream flooded us out, twice. What is our dream house worth now?'

D Shop owner in the flood zone
'I blame the Council for not keeping up with river works to stop these floods. How are they spending all the money I pay them in business rates?'

E Council leader
'The number and size of river floods seem to be increasing because of global warming. With more government money, new protection measures could be built. But even with more government money, I do not think we can remove the risk of flooding altogether.'

A Some views on flooding

1. Who thinks that river flooding can be stopped?
   a) Draw a line like the one below, showing the two extreme views.

Impossible to stop	Can be stopped by spending money

   b) Read the views of the five people in **A**. Put the letters A to E where you think they should go along this line.
   c) (i) What is your own view about stopping river floods? Mark M on the line for 'my own view'.
      (ii) Explain why you placed M on the line where you did.
2. Write a paragraph about: 'Why different people have different views about river flooding and how to stop it'.

›› 6   Italy

Would you like to live somewhere like this? This is the hilltop settlement of Rivello in the south of Italy. What are the difficulties of living on the top of a hill? How is the landscape different from landscapes in the UK?

Learning objectives

What are you going to learn about in this chapter?
> The major features of the physical and human geography of Italy
> How Italy can be divided into a rich North and less wealthy South
> Why the gap in wealth between North and South opened up and why it is difficult to close
> Why Italy is an attractive destination for many different types of tourists
> How Venice is unique and why this causes big problems
> Italy's ageing population and why it is about to cause a pensions crisis

A Rivello, Italy

Physical background

> Understanding the physical geography of Italy
> Learning about Italy's climate

Italy is shaped like a boot. The toe is ready to kick the island of Sicily like a football. It is a peninsula of land surrounded by the Mediterranean Sea. Sicily and Sardinia are the two largest islands (map **A**).

DIVIDING ITALY INTO PHYSICAL REGIONS

A **region** is an area with one or more features that are the same. Look at map **A**. How many physical regions are there in Italy? Some of the possible ways of dividing Italy into physical regions are shown in **C**. They are mainly based on differences in relief (height and shape of the land).

The three physical regions of Italy

1 Alps – high mountain range, with rocky mountain peaks above 3000 metres covered by snow and ice. Large lakes fill the floors of deep, steep-sided mountain valleys.

2 North Italian Plain – lowlands on the sides of the River Po. The River Po, Italy's longest river. It flows across a wide floodplain and forms the largest area of flat land in Italy.

3 Apennines – long mountain range, extending almost the full length of Italy. All peaks are below 3000 metres, which makes them lower than the Alps. In the northern Apennines there are many hills covered by forest, green fields and vineyards. In the south, bare limestone rock outcrops cover more of the land (photo **B**). The highest mountain in the south of Italy is Mount Etna, the active volcano on the island of Sicily.

A Physical map of Italy

Key
- Land over 1000 m
- Land between 500 and 1000 m
- Land under 500 m
- Lake
- Major city
- Volcano

B Apennines in southern Italy

Key word

Region – area of land with one or more similar features

Two regions	Three regions	Four regions
1 Mountains	1 Alps	1 Alps
2 Lowlands	2 North Italian Plain	2 North Italian Plain
	3 Peninsular Italy and islands	3 Apennines
		4 Islands

C How can Italy be divided into physical regions?

CLIMATES OF ITALY

Italy can also be divided up into three climatic regions (see map **E**). Which one covers the largest area?

1 **Alpine** – colder because of greater height, with plenty of snow in winter.
2 **North Italian Plain** – cool in winter, but hot in summer, when most rain falls.
3 **Mediterranean climate** – hot dry summers and warm wet winters.

The Mediterranean climate is different from the others because of the summer drought. On most days in summer the sun shines from clear blue skies, giving hot dry weather.

Region	Area (millions of hectares)
Italy (total)	30.1
Mountain (above 700 m)	10.6
Hill (150 m to 700 m)	12.5
Lowland and plain (below 150 m)	7.0

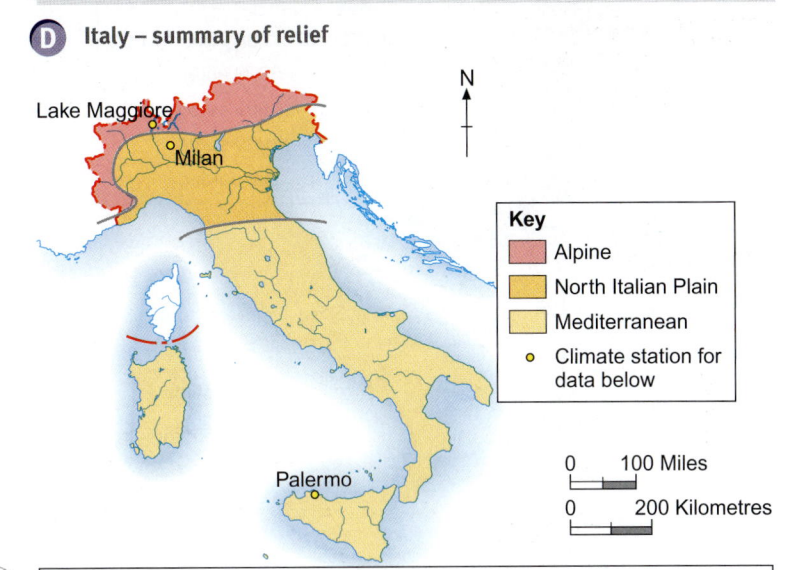

D Italy – summary of relief

E Climatic regions of Italy

	Alpine	North Italian Plain	Mediterranean
Temperature (°C)			
Jan	–1	2	10
July	18	25	26
Sunshine hours per day			
Jan	3	2	4
July	9	9	10
Precipitation (mm)			
Annual total	1745	1017	512
Winter (Dec-Feb)	225	53	176
Summer (Jun-Aug)	589	273	29

Activities

1 **Odd one out.** Look at **A**. Which is the odd one out in each group? Explain your choices.

   a) Alps   Apennines   Etna
   b) Adriatic   Mediterranean   Maggiore
   c) Como   Garda   Po
   d) Sardinia   Sicily   Vesuvius

2 You can find help with graphs in *SKILLS in geography* pages 145–155.

   a) Draw a divided bar graph to show the values in **D**.

   b) The percentages for the values in **D** are:
   - mountain 35 per cent
   - hill 42 per cent
   - lowland and plain 23 per cent.

   Draw a pie graph to show these.

   c) Which of the two graphs do you prefer for showing types of relief in Italy? Give *one* reason.

3 Use or trace an outline map of Italy.

   a) Divide Italy into three physical regions.

   b) Draw sketches and add labels to show the main features of each region. Photo **A** of the Apennines on page 83 may be useful.

4 Make a table to show differences between the Alps and the Apennines. Use these headings: height, relief, drainage (lakes and rivers) and climate.

F Winter in the Alps

Does Italy have a 'North and South'?

> Understanding the human geography of Italy
> Finding out how Italy can be divided into a rich North and less wealthy South

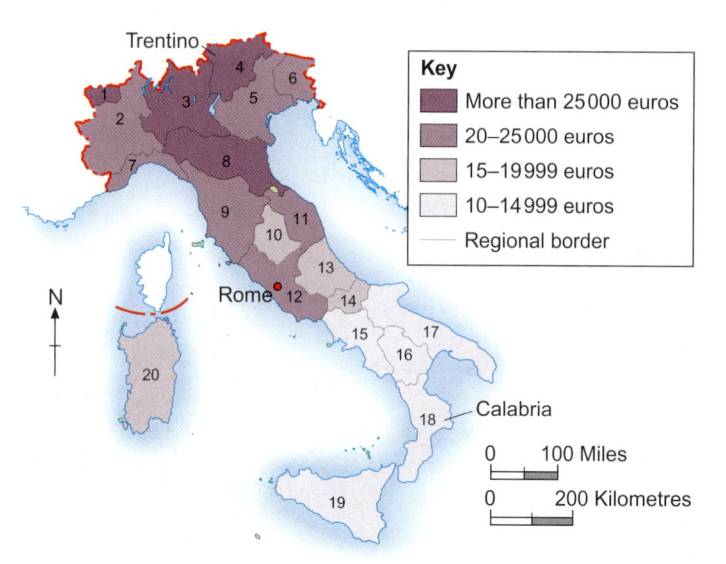

A Income per person

Key:
- More than 25 000 euros
- 20–25 000 euros
- 15–19 999 euros
- 10–14 999 euros
- Regional border

B Percentage unemployed

Key:
- More than 15%
- 10–15%
- 5–9.9%
- Below 5%
- Regional border

Names of administration regions

1. Valle D'Aosta
2. Piedmont
3. Lombardy
4. Trentino
5. Veneto
6. Friuli-Venezia
7. Liguria
8. Emilia-Romagna
9. Tuscany
10. Umbria
11. Marche
12. Lazio
13. Abruzzi
14. Molise
15. Campania
16. Basilicata
17. Puglia
18. Calabria
19. Sicily
20. Sardinia

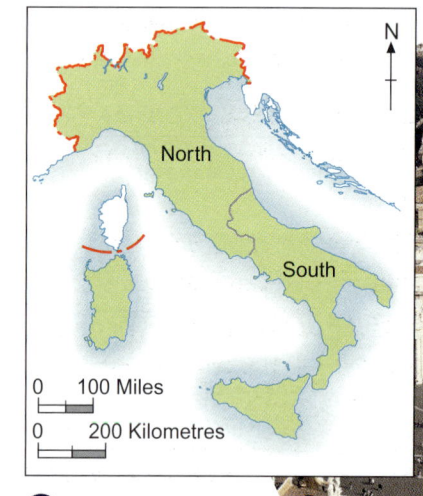

C Line used most to divide North from South

D View over Rome, the capital city, from St Peters in the Vatican. Most consider that the South of Italy begins south of Rome.

The UK is often divided into a rich South and poor North. Does Italy have a North and South as well?

Maps **A** and **B** show differences for income and unemployment within Italy. Where would you draw the dividing line between North and South on these maps?

Out of all the EU countries, the gap between richest and poorest regions is widest in Italy (graph **E**). The gap between rich North and poor South is so wide that the government uses three regions; they are North (the richest), Centre (quite rich) and South (the poorest) (**F**). Check the Italian government statistics website via Hotlinks (see page 2) to find out if there is more up-to-date data.

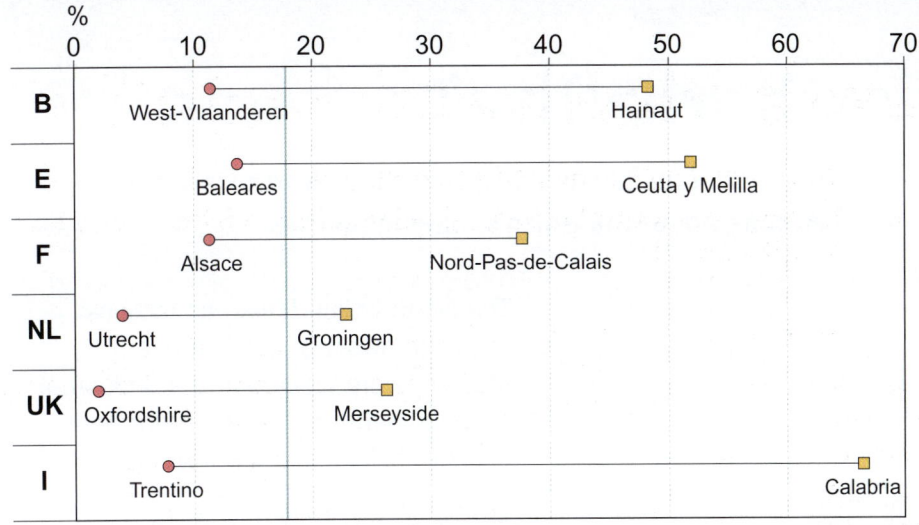

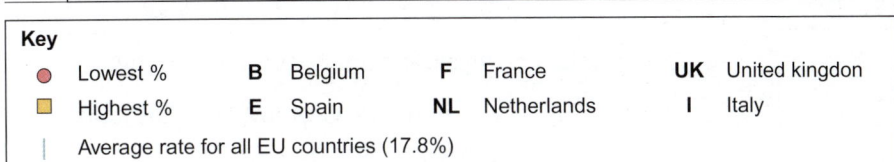

Key
- ● Lowest %
- ■ Highest %
- | Average rate for all EU countries (17.8%)
- **B** Belgium
- **E** Spain
- **F** France
- **NL** Netherlands
- **UK** United kingdon
- **I** Italy

E Best and worst youth unemployment rates inside EU countries (people under 25)

1 Net migration of people in 2000

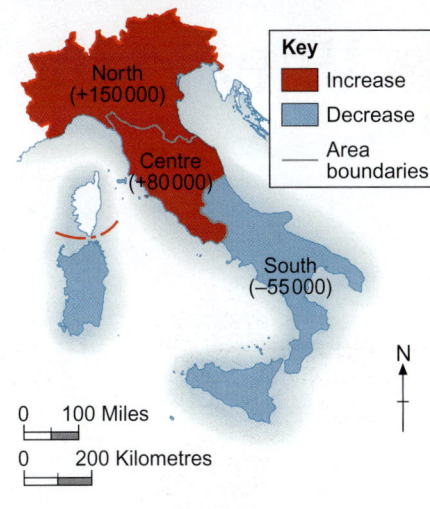

Key:
- Increase (red)
- Decrease (blue)
- Area boundaries

- North (+150 000)
- Centre (+80 000)
- South (−55 000)

2 Percentage unemployed

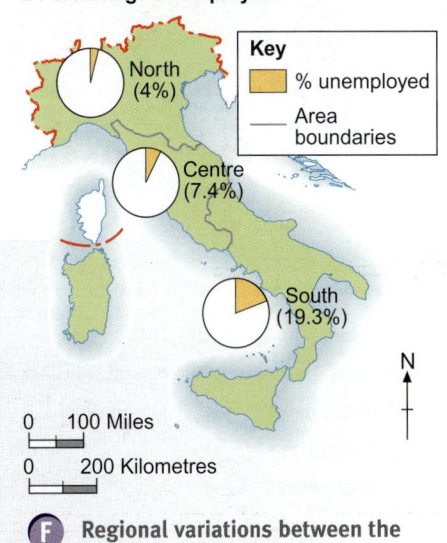

Key:
- % unemployed
- Area boundaries

- North (4%)
- Centre (7.4%)
- South (19.3%)

F Regional variations between the North, Centre and South of Italy

Activities

1 a) Look at **A**. Find incomes per head:
  (i) in Trentino and Calabria
  (ii) in most of the North
  (iii) in most of the South.

  b) Look at **B**. Find unemployment rates:
  (i) in Trentino and Calabria
  (ii) in most of the North
  (iii) in most of the South.

  c) Look at **C**.
  (i) List the differences between areas north and south of the line.
  (ii) Do you think the line is drawn in the best place?

2 Look at **E**.
  a) (i) State the percentage youth unemployment rates in Trentino and Calabria.
  (ii) What is the percentage difference between them?
  b) Work out percentage differences between highest and lowest youth unemployment rates in (i) the UK (ii) Spain.

3 a) Brainstorm with your neighbours.
  (i) Make a list of problems caused by high rates of unemployment.
  (ii) Why is it really bad for people under 25 to be unemployed?
  b) Which *two* problems do you think are worst? Why?

4 a) Write down *one* difference between the South and the other two regions from (i) **F1** (ii) **F2**.
  b) Finish this sentence:
  Figures **F1** and **F2** show that the South is poorer than the rest of Italy because ...

5 Look back at pages 84–87. Draw a large summary chart like the one below showing differences between North and South in Italy.

	North of Italy	South of Italy
Relief (page 84)		
Climate (page 85)		
Income (page 86)		
Unemployment (pages 86, 87)		
Migration (page 87)		

Why is the North wealthy?

> Finding out about the advantages that North Italy has
> Learning about the North's main industries

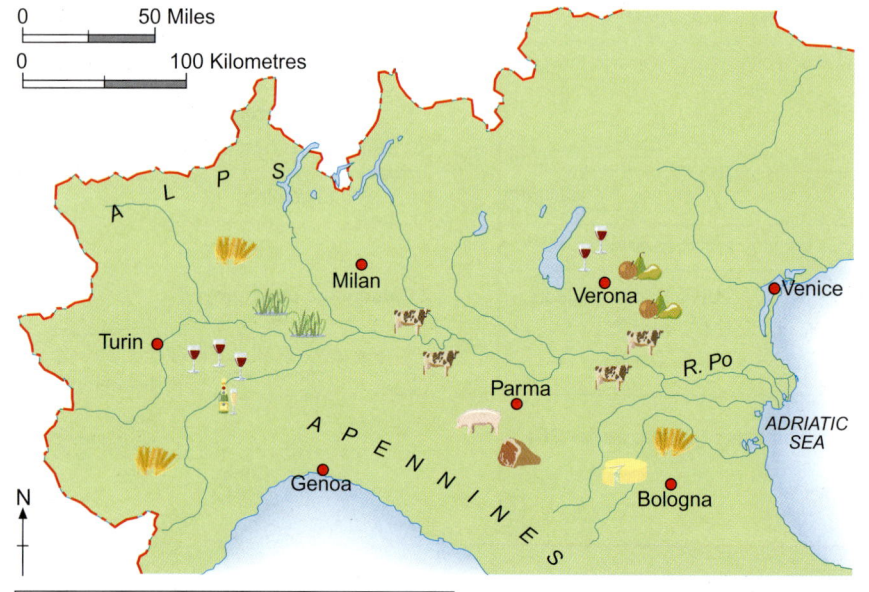

The North Italian Plain has the best farmland. Most of Italy's modern industries are located in the 'Industrial Triangle' between the three northern cities of Milan, Turin and Genoa (see **C**).

BEST FARMLAND

Physical advantages for farming:

- Largest area of low and flat land
- Fertile soils (e.g. silt)
- Hot sunny summers with rainfall
- Plenty of water for irrigation from Alpine rivers and springs.

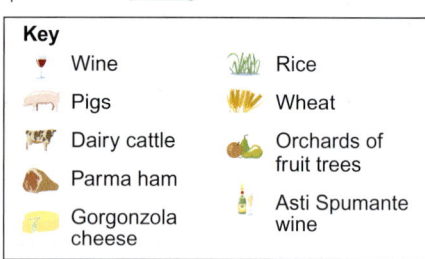

Key
- Wine
- Pigs
- Dairy cattle
- Parma ham
- Gorgonzola cheese
- Rice
- Wheat
- Orchards of fruit trees
- Asti Spumante wine

A Farming on the North Italian Plain

Human advantages for farming:

- Large markets in nearby cities for food produced
- Farmers use modern machinery and methods.

Cereals (wheat, rice and maize), vines (grapes) and fruits (peaches, apples and pears) are the most commonly grown crops. Dairy farming is important on the wetter lands next to the River Po.

Italy is famous for food and drink: pasta, pizza, Parmesan cheese, Parma ham, Asti wines and ice cream. All of these are made from farm products from northern Italy. Pasta is made out of durum wheat, a variety that does not grow as well in the UK's cooler and wetter climate.

MOST INDUSTRY

The North has advantages for manufacturing industry that do not exist in other parts of Italy:

- Raw materials for food-processing factories (**A**)
- Local supplies of power and energy
- Skilled workers because of a long history of industry and trade in northern cities
- Wealthy market in Italy reached by a good network of motorways (autostrade) (**C**).

B View of Milan from the roof of the Cathedral; the sides of the square are lined with shops filled with designer goods. Does it have the look of a wealthy city?

geography 360° Foundation Book 2

Another big advantage is its northern location, close to larger markets in other large EU countries such as Germany and France. There are many road and rail routes through tunnels and passes in the Alps (**C**) to reach markets in these countries.

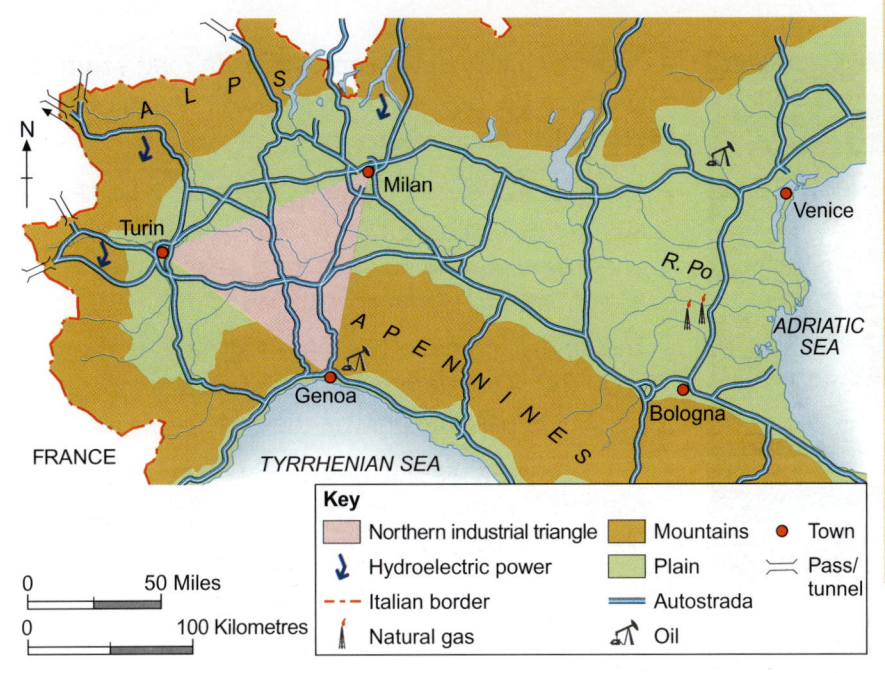

Milan
- Centre of clothing, food processing and light engineering industries
- Famous brands from Milan: Alfa Romeo (cars) and Necchi (sewing machines)

Turin
- Industry dominated by motor vehicles and engineering works making parts for cars
- Home of Fiat (cars) and Olivetti (previously typewriters, now business machines)

Genoa
- Main port importing fuels (crude oil, coal) and raw materials (iron ore, raw cotton)
- Mainly heavy industries (oil refineries, steel works) using imported raw materials

C Manufacturing industry on the North Italian Plain

Activities

1. Area of crops (thousands of hectares) in Italy: Wheat 2200; Fodder crops for animals 1500; Olive trees 1100; Maize 1050; Tomatoes, fruit and vegetables 1000; Vines 700.

    a) Draw a bar graph to show the areas of land covered by these crops. Use *SKILLS in geography* pages 145–155 if you need help.

    b) Name the crop or crops used in each of the following:
    (i) pasta (ii) wine (iii) cooking oil (iv) sweetcorn (v) pizza (vi) spaghetti bolognaise.

2. Write out these sentences. Fill in the gaps and finish the sentences.

    One physical advantage of the North Italian Plain for farming is its relief. The land is _____ and _____ . This makes it easier for farmers to use large tractors and other modern _____. Another physical advantage is climate. Crops grow fast in summer because the weather is _____ and _____ . If crops need more water for good growth, it is easy to get water from _____. Another advantage is the fertile soil made of _____, which was deposited by big rivers such as the River _____. There are large markets for the crops grown in large northern cities such as _____ and _____. In these cities are many food-processing factories; wheat is used to make _____ and milk from dairy cows is used for _____.

3. Make a larger version of **D**. Complete the diagram by filling in the five boxes with information.

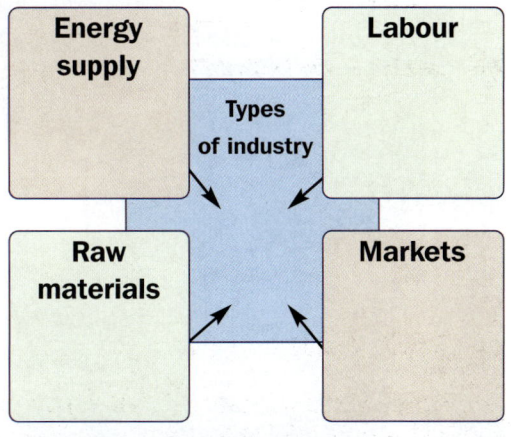

D Favourable factors for industry in the North

6 Italy

Why is the South poor?

> **Discovering the disadvantages of South Italy**
> **Understanding the causes behind the lack of wealth**

As visitors to Italy drive along the main road south, the 'Autostrada del Sole' or 'motorway of the sun', changes can be seen south of Rome.

- The midday heat in summer is greater. A fierce summer sun shines from a clear blue sky. Villages and towns go very quiet as local people take a 'siesta' after a big lunch with wine.
- The landscape becomes more rugged (see **B** on page 84). There are more bare rock outcrops; farming is possible only on the coastal plains.
- More settlements are placed on hilltops (see **A** on page 83). How can people make a good living? Why don't more people live on the flatter lowlands?

The main causes of poverty in the south of Italy are shown in **D**. The causes are both physical and human.

A A close-up view of a hilltop settlement

B Inside a hilltop village. What are the advantages and disadvantages of living along streets like these?

C Hilltop orchard next to the village. Is it being well farmed?

A Old-fashioned farming methods
- Large wheat fields with low yields
- Slopes of hills grazed by sheep and goats

B Climate
- Fierce summer heat
- Outdoor summer temperatures above 40°C
- Summer drought is almost complete

C Drainage
- Lack of surface rivers
- Dry appearance to the landscape
- In summer river beds are dry

D History
- Long history of being invaded
- People lived in hilltop villages for defence
- Marshy lowlands were avoided as places to live because malarial mosquitoes bred there

E Lack of modern industry
- Remote from main EU markets
- Mainly unskilled labour
- No cheap hydro-electric power, unlike the North
- Long history of crime and corruption

G Relief
- Large areas of mountain and hilly land
- Small percentage of plain
- Steep slopes are eroded by heavy winter rain

F Land ownership
- Few farmers own their own land
- Large landowners own big estates (*latifundi*)
- Many landlords live in the cities (not on their farms)
- Little money is invested in improving the land

H Rock type and soils
- The main rock is hard limestone
- It is permeable, leaving dry surfaces
- Thin soils between bare rock outcrops

D Lack of wealth in the South – physical and human causes. Can you separate the human factors from the physical?

Activities

1. A family from Milan is driving to Naples. Draw a table to show some of the differences they will notice between driving:
   a) over the North Italian Plain from Milan to Bologna
   b) through the South between Rome and Naples.

	Milan to Bologna	Rome to Naples
Weather		
Landscape		
Farming		

2. a) Look at **A** and **B**. Draw a labelled sketch to show what the streets are like in a hilltop village.
   b) Write about some of the problems of living in a hilltop village for:
      (i) Old people
      (ii) Young couples with families
      (iii) Delivery van drivers
      (iv) Farmers

3. a) List the eight titles A–H in **D** under two headings – Physical and Human. Four of them go under each heading.
   b) Rank the eight titles A–H in their order of importance, starting with 1 (most important) and ending with 8 (least important).
   c) Explain why you chose the top two.

4. a) Make a recording sheet like the one here. Note down the rank orders from five other people in the class.
   b) Work out the average rank for each of A–H (total divided by 10).
   c) Which one is top? Explain why.

Order of importance								
	Mine	2	3	4	5	6	Total	Average rank
A	4							
B	1							

6 Italy

Can the gap between South and North be closed?

> Finding out what Italy has done to close the gap
> Deciding how successful these measures were

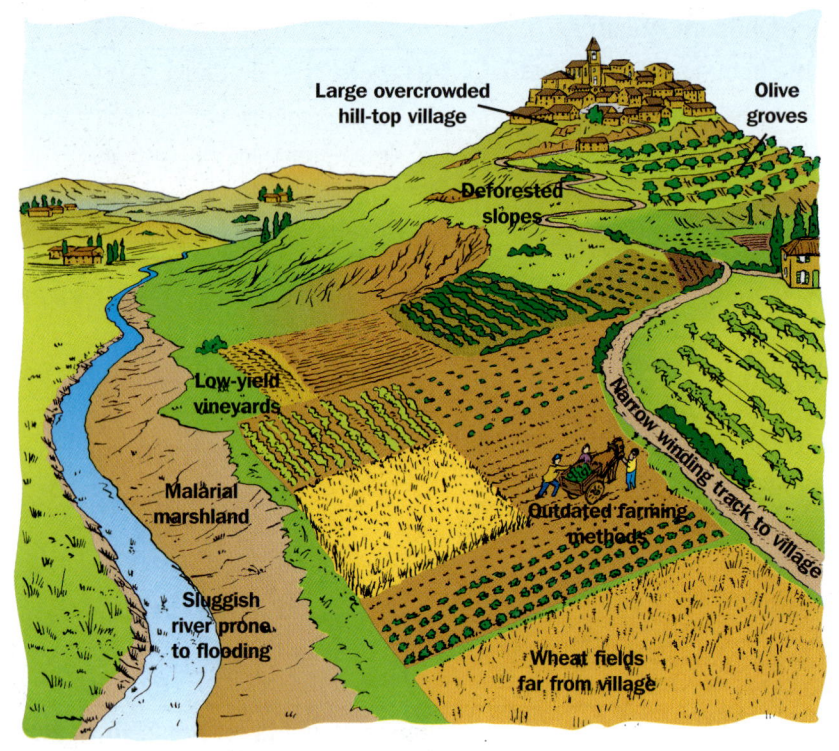

A Landscape in the South of Italy in 1950

(Labels on figure A: Large overcrowded hill-top village; Olive groves; Deforested slopes; Low-yield vineyards; Narrow winding track to village; Malarial marshland; Outdated farming methods; Sluggish river prone to flooding; Wheat fields far from village)

The government has been trying for many years to close the gap. In 1950 it set up the 'Fund for the South'. It began with farming. You can see in **A** some of the farming problems in the South that the government tried to solve.

CHANGES IN FARMING IN THE SOUTH

- Large estates (called *latifundi*) were split up; the land was given to those who farmed the land but did not own it.
- Small dams were built across rivers; water was stored in these to irrigate crops in dry summers.
- Public services were improved; paved roads replaced tracks, villages and farms were connected to mains electricity and telephones.
- Hill slopes were planted with trees; soil erosion was reduced.

Figure **B** shows some of the changes in the South by 1990. The wheat fields and olive groves shown on **A** had gone. In their place on **B** you can see:

- citrus orchards – growing oranges, lemons, limes
- greenhouses – growing salad crops (tomatoes, lettuces, cucumbers).

Which other changes can you spot between **A** and **B**?

NEW MANUFACTURING INDUSTRY

From the 1960s the government supported the growth of industry in the South as well. They hoped that one good thing would lead to another. The hope was this would have a multiplier effect – growth leading to more growth.

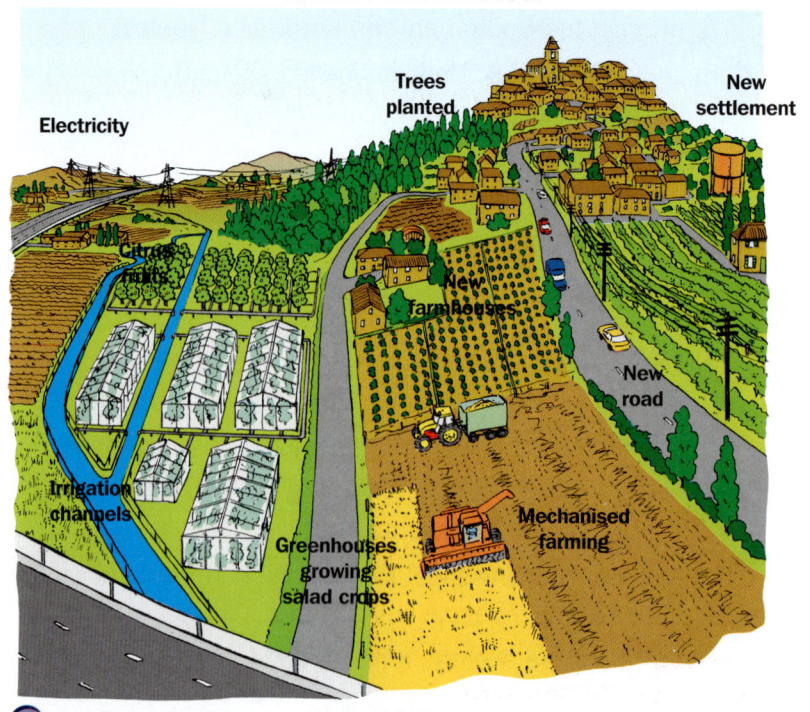

B Landscape in the same area by 1990

(Labels on figure B: Trees planted; New settlement; Electricity; Citrus fruits; New farmhouses; New road; Irrigation channels; Greenhouses growing salad crops; Mechanised farming)

92 geography 360° Foundation Book 2

Steel works and oil refineries were set up in the South. The Autostrada del Sole was built to give a fast motorway link to Rome and Milan. However, too few industries moved into the South to make a real difference.

Some industries failed. When car sales fell, Fiat sacked workers at factories in the South before it reduced numbers in its factories in Turin in the North. Can you think of a reason why?

C View from the top of the castle in a hilltop town in Sardinia. How many of the changes shown in **B** can you see?

A Higher transport costs to markets in Italy and EU

B Difficult to recruit skilled factory workers and office staff

C High rates of absenteeism, especially at harvest time for vines and olives

D Low output from workers not used to factory work

E Workers too tired to work after working on their farms before and after work

D Problems experienced by companies that set up in the South

Activities

1. Make a large chart like the one below. Fill it in using **A** and **B**.

	1950	1990
A Crops grown		
B Farming methods used		
C Public services 　(i) roads 　(ii) other services		
D Settlements 　(i) location 　(ii) types and sizes		

   Changes in landscape and farming in the South of Italy between 1950 and 1990

2. Draw a sketch of **C**. Label the new settlement, farms and orchards.

3. Work in a group. Draw up a list of reasons why farmers find it hard to get used to factory work.

    a) Divide out the work. Start by making a diary of work during the day (from 6am to 6pm) for:
      (i) a farmer keeping animals and growing crops
      (ii) a factory worker (e.g. in a car works), who lives 16 km (ten miles) away from work.

    b) Note down the main differences between working on a farm and working in a factory.

    c) Make a list of reasons why farmers find it hard to change to factory work.

    d) Compare your list with those of other groups.

Italy – a great place to visit

> Learning about Italy as a tourist destination

Italy is in the top ten countries for attracting tourist visitors from other countries. It has a wide range of tourist attractions (see **A**).

1. Italy is a Mediterranean country. Summer sun and warm seas are great for beach holidays.

2. Italy is an Alpine country. The peak tourist season is winter. The steep snow-covered slopes are a winter paradise for skiers and snowboarders. Summer visitors are attracted to the shores of the large lakes.

3. Italy is a country with a long history. There are many Roman remains, great cathedrals and museums full of works of art. Three attractions are unique to Italy:

   - the leaning tower of Pisa (photo **C**)
   - Venice and its canals (see pages 96–97)
   - Pompeii, the Roman town preserved by its covering of ash from the volcano Vesuvius.

4. Italian food and drink are world famous. Italians love their food and take great pride in the quality of their cooking (**D**). Lunch may last at least two hours and will usually be taken with a glass or two of wine (e.g. Chianti).

A Tourism in Italy

B Early morning on the beach; the sunbeds are already out, always arranged in neat rows in Italian resorts

C Leaning tower of Pisa: visitors like to be photographed as if they are stopping the tower from falling over

94 geography 360° Foundation Book 2

When the Italians go on holiday in summer, many make for the beach. More visitors from overseas are attracted to the historical cities with their museums, art galleries and churches (see **E**). In the south there are hot springs and volcanic areas (see **F** and **G**); they show a different type of holiday area in Italy.

Antipasto (Appetiser)
Selection of cold meats and vegetables: Prosciutto (ham), salami, olives, artichoke hearts

Pasta
Spaghetti or macaroni or ravioli

Main course
Veal or chicken in a white wine or tomato sauce

Dessert
Fresh fruit or ice cream

Coffee
Espresso, cappuccino, latte

D Lunch menu in a restaurant

E Types of holidays (percentage in 2001)

Italians: Coast 38%, Historical towns 18%, Mountains 16%, Lakes 3%, Hot springs and volcanic areas 6%, Mixed holidays/other types 19%

Foreign visitors: Coast 28%, Historical towns 30%, Mountains 17%, Lakes 12%, Hot springs and volcanic areas 4%, Mixed holidays/other types 9%

F Mount Etna – a major tourist attraction

G Hot mud pools on the island of Vulcano

Activities

1. Tourist percentages in Italy according to time of year:

   January–March 17 per cent; April–June 23 per cent; July–September 43 per cent; October–December 17 per cent

   Draw a graph or diagram to show these percentages.

2. Write out and finish these sentences. Use **A** and **E** to help you.

   a) One type of holiday area in Italy that is very busy in July to September is _____ because …

   b) One type of holiday area very busy in January to March is _____ because …

   c) ____ % more Italians than foreign visitors took seaside holidays in Italy. I think the reasons for this are …

   d) ____ % more foreigners than Italians took holidays in the historical cities. I think the reasons for this are …

   e) The place in Italy I would most like to visit is _____, because …

   f) The type of holiday in Italy that I would enjoy least is _____, because …

3. Work with a partner. Design a poster with the title: 'Italy – a great place to visit'. Use holiday brochures and websites to help you.

Venice and that sinking feeling

> Understanding the physical geography behind Venice's sinking feeling
> Looking at what human geography can do to help Venice

Venice is built on over 100 islands in the Adriatic Sea (**A**). The Grand Canal forms the 'main street' through the centre of Venice (**B**). Smaller canals lead from it in all directions; these form the 'back streets' (**C**). The easiest way to travel around Venice is by boat, either using the famous gondolas or the *vaporetti* (water buses). Boats in Venice do the jobs of vans in other cities, such as delivering goods and collecting waste.

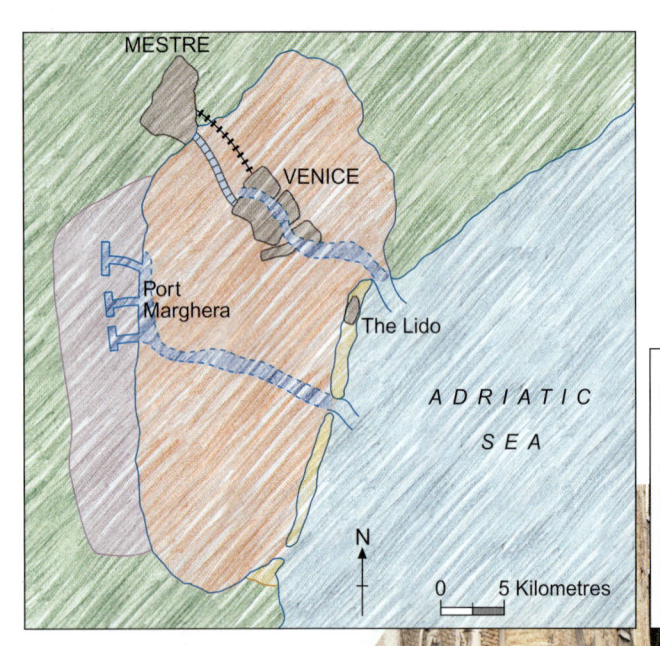

Key
- Built up areas
- Railway
- Causeway
- Deep water channel
- Sand bar
- Reclaimed land
- Mud flats

A Location of Venice

B The Grand Canal, the 'main street' of Venice, busy with water traffic

C One of the 'back streets' in Venice; some of the buildings standing in the water are beginning to show their age

Why was Venice built in the sea? The main reason was for defence. Another reason was for easy trading by sea. Merchants from Venice made great fortunes. How did the rich spend their money 500 years ago? They built fine mansions (called palaces), churches and bridges, and they paid artists to decorate the insides of their new buildings.

96 geography 360° Core Book 2

VENICE'S PROBLEMS

In the past the sea brought wealth to Venice. Today the sea is its main problem, but there are others (see **D**). The organisation Venice in Peril warns that people will no longer be able to live in the city by 2100 unless something is done soon to keep out the sea. You can visit the Venice in Peril website via Hotlinks (see page 2).

SOLUTIONS TO THE PROBLEMS?

Many suggestions have been made, but nothing has been done. One solution is a system of 'floating gates' (see **E**). Three large gates will be built across the three entrances into the lagoon (shown on map **A**); they will lie flat on the sea bed for most of the time. When sea levels rise in winter storms, air will be pumped into each gate so that one end of the gate floats up to block the entrance. The estimated cost is at least £1.6 billion.

Apart from being very expensive, this solution might cause other problems. Where will the sewage go when the gates are closed? Will ships stop using the port if gates block the shipping channels on 100 days a year?

Venice is sinking!
23 cm since 1900:
- 13 cm caused by subsidence
- 10 cm caused by rising sea levels

Current rate 1–1.5 mm per year

Subsidence
Venice is settling into the mudflats
- Cause – weight of buildings on soft foundations

Sea levels are rising!
Rising since the end of the Great Ice Age (about 10 000 years ago)
- Speeding up because of global warming
- Some people are estimating a sea level rise of 60 cm between 2000 and 2100

Flooding
Regular winter floods in central area, e.g. St Mark's Square
- 1900 – 10 floods a year
- 2000 – 100 floods a year

Buildings are crumbling
Stonework rots in the smoggy, acid air and polluted water
- Main cause – chemical works in Port Marghera (see A)
- Other cause – inefficient sewage system

People are leaving
Population 60 per cent lower than 50 years ago
- Ground floors of buildings abandoned as living quarters due to dampness
- One in twelve buildings is empty
- Buildings are rotting away because of rising damp and no repair work

D The problems of Venice and their causes

Activities

1. **Group activity** – prepare a presentation on 'Why Venice must be saved', supported by leaflets and handouts. Pool ideas, share out the work and look at websites for up-to-date information (see Hotlinks page 2). Useful headings for the work include:
   - How Venice is unique/different
   - Problems of Venice
   - Why the problems are getting worse/why urgent action is needed.

2. a) Draw a diagram to show the floating gates.
   b) How will the gates work?
   c) Should the gates be built? Explain what you think.

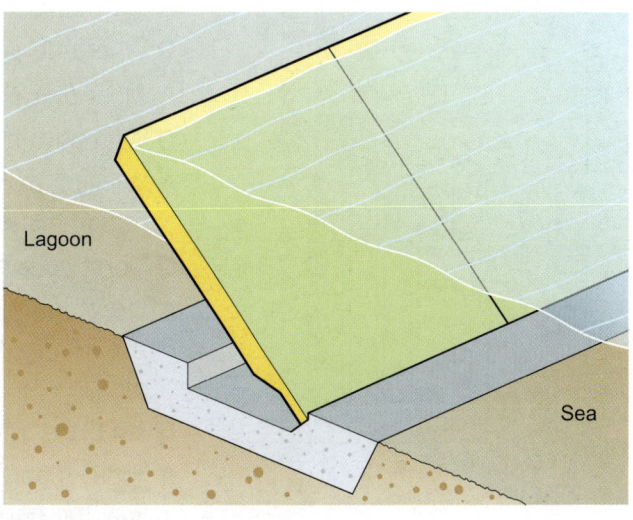

E How floating gates might save Venice from flooding

6 Italy

An ageing population – Italy's economic time bomb

> Finding out why an ageing population is a problem
> Looking at possible economic solutions

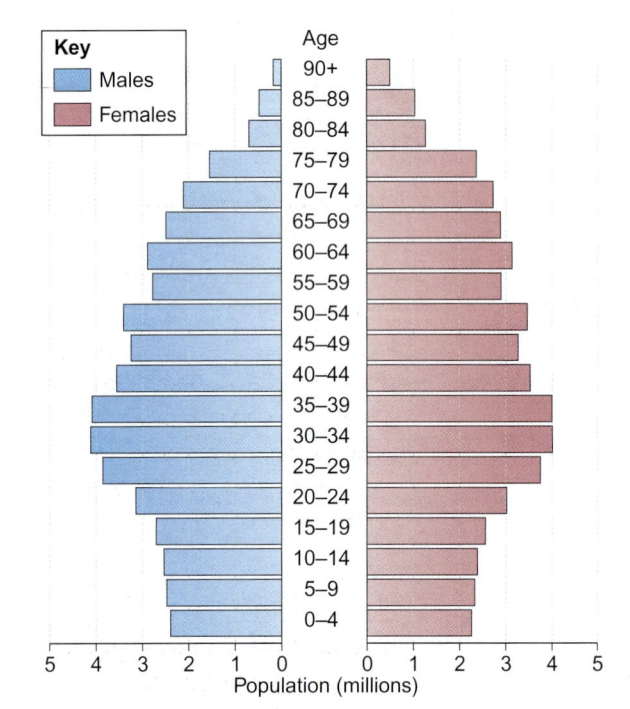

Fertility rates are low in Europe. Fertility rate is the number of children per woman.

- Europe in 1970 – rate 2.4 children per woman
- Europe in 2003 – rate 1.5 children per woman.

The reasons for this decrease are the same in all EU countries.

- Women are better educated and want to have their own careers.
- Women are marrying and having their first babies when they are older.

A fertility rate of 2.1 children per woman is needed if a country is to keep the same total population. In 2003 the fertility rate in Italy was 1.3, joint lowest in the EU with Spain.

Look at the bottom part of the population pyramid for Italy (**A**). What does it show? How large was the percentage of old people aged 65 and above in 2001?

A Population pyramid for Italy (in 2001)

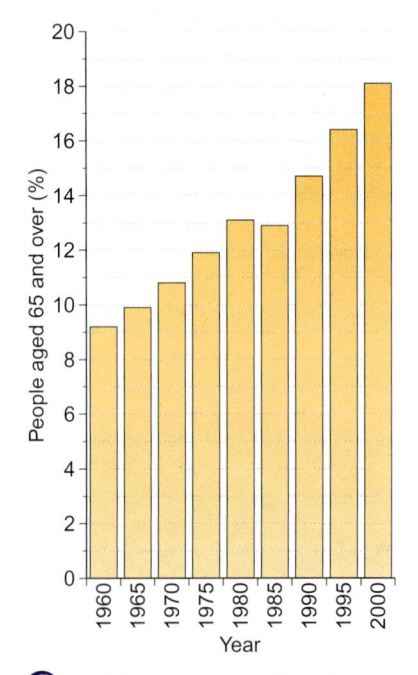

AGEING POPULATION AND PENSIONS

Italy has an **ageing population**. The percentage of old people (aged 65 and above) is increasing (see **B**). Why is this a problem? The government of Italy needs to find more and more money to pay state pensions.

Questions and answers about pensions

Q Where do governments get the money to pay out pensions?

A Most of it comes out of taxes.

Q Who pays most money in tax?

A Working people (mainly those aged 16–64). They pay income tax and national insurance.

Q Don't governments have a 'pot of money' for paying out pensions?

A No. State pensions are paid out on a 'pay-as-you-go' basis. This means the money collected in taxes from working people is paid out to pensioners in the same year.

Q Isn't this system unfair to all the workers?

A Today's pensioners did the same when they were working. This is the way the pension system works.

B Italy – percentage of total population aged 65 and above

The percentage of government income in Italy paid out in pensions is increasing (see **C**).

Year	Number of working age (15–64) for every person 65 years old and older	Estimates for pension costs as a percentage of GDP
2000	4.3	12.6
2010	3.8	13.2
2020	3.3	15.3
2030	2.8	20.3
2040	2.4	21.4

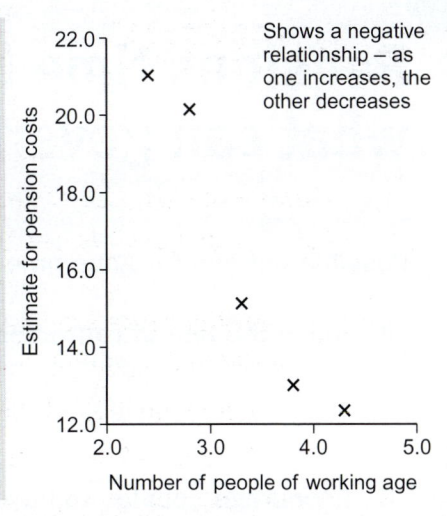

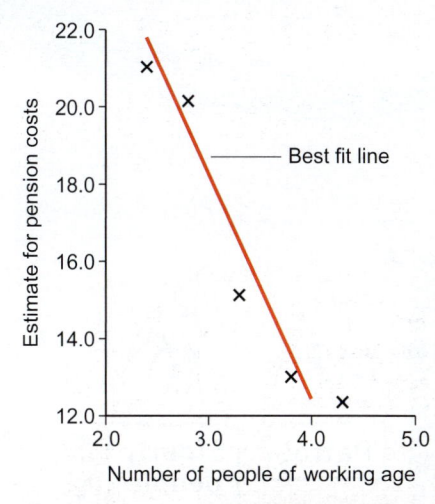

C Future pensions crisis in Italy

Values for the number of working people per pensioner are plotted against likely pension costs in the future in **C**. Pension costs increase as the number of workers per pensioner decreases. This is known as a negative relationship: one value goes up while the other goes down.

Activities

1. Look at **A**.
   a) What percentage are under 15? Is it 7, 14 or 21 per cent?
   b) What percentage are 65 and above? Is it 6, 12 or 18 per cent?
   c) Is the percentage of males and females the same, similar or different for (i) under 15 (ii) 65 and above?

2. a) What is a pension?
   b) Where do governments get the money for pensions?
   c) Why do people in Italy and other EU countries expect a pension when they retire?
   d) Write a short paragraph that starts: 'A big pensions crisis is likely in Italy before 2040 because …'.

3. a) Draw a scatter graph to show the values in **D**.
   b) (i) Does your graph look the same as or different from **C**?
      (ii) Is the relationship shown on your graph positive or negative?

Year	Fertility rate	Percentage aged 65 and over
1960	2.4	9.2
1970	2.3	10.8
1980	1.6	13.1
1990	1.3	14.7
2000	1.3	18.1

D

Key words

Ageing population – increasing percentage of old people (aged 65 and over) in a country
Fertility rate – average number of children born to a woman in her lifetime

SKILLS

How to draw a scatter graph
1. Draw the two axes for the graph.
2. Label the two axes.
3. Choose suitable scales to cover the range of values.
4. Place a cross or dot at the point where the two values meet.
5. Do not join up the dots.
6. If possible, draw a straight line which is the 'best fit' for all the points.

For more help see page 149 of *SKILLS in geography*.

6 Italy

Assessing 360°

Pensions time bomb in the EU – what can governments do?

A Road traffic sign – a warning for motorists. What about for governments?

Possible options for governments

A Raise the age of retirement – from 65 to 70, or even to 75
- Increase the length of time people are working and paying taxes.
- Reduce the number of years that people will draw a state pension.

B Encourage couples to have more children – increase the fertility rate to above 2.1
- Increase length of maternity leave from work with full pay.
- Increase length of paternity leave and make it paid leave as well.
- Improve child care and nursery facilities for the under-fives (more of them and cheaper).

C Allow more immigrants to come in – especially in the age group 20–40
- Issue more visas and work permits to people living in countries outside the EU.
- Fill in gaps in the job market and increase the number paying taxes.

D Reduce state pensions – workers take out private pension plans with insurance companies
- Transfer responsibility for pensions from the state to the workers.
- Money problem for government reduced if pensions go down at the same time as income from taxes.

1 Look at **A**.
   a) Government money is needed for both groups shown on the road sign. For what purposes?
   b) Why do governments like people in the age group in between these two?
2 Governments must do something about the pensions time bomb. They cannot do nothing. Which of the four things A, B, C and D do you think will work best?
   a) Draw a line like the one on the right with a scale of 1 to 10. Place letters A, B, C and D to show what you think about each one.

   Bad idea   Good idea
   1 _____ 10

   b) Explain why you chose the two with the highest and lowest marks.
3 Choose *two* people from the list below.
   - Worker aged 55
   - Owner of a small company with ten workers
   - Manager of a big insurance company
   - Newly married young couple
   a) Draw two more lines. Show what the two are likely to think of A, B, C and D.
   b) Why are their views different?

7 Rich world, poor world

Can you imagine how much a flat costs here? It is the world's greatest concentration of buildings in the world's richest country. Why should there be so much wealth here while other parts of the world are so poor?

Learning objectives

What are you going to learn about in this chapter?
> The differences between a rich country and a poor country
> Where rich and poor countries are located
> Different ways to measure wealth and development
> Physical and human reasons why some countries remain poor
> Why sub-Saharan Africa is the world's poorest region
> How small changes can greatly improve the quality of life for poor people
> Whether poor countries are caught in a trade and poverty trap

A Manhattan, New York

Are you rich or poor?

> Looking at the differences between rich and poor
> Finding out how to use the US dollar to compare wealth

Item	Value
Pay-as-you-go mobile	£65
MiniDisc player	£120
GameBoy Advance	£90
Games, each game	£30
Nike trainers	£75
Bag	£20
Total	£400

A What a typical teenager in the UK carries (approximate UK prices in 2004)

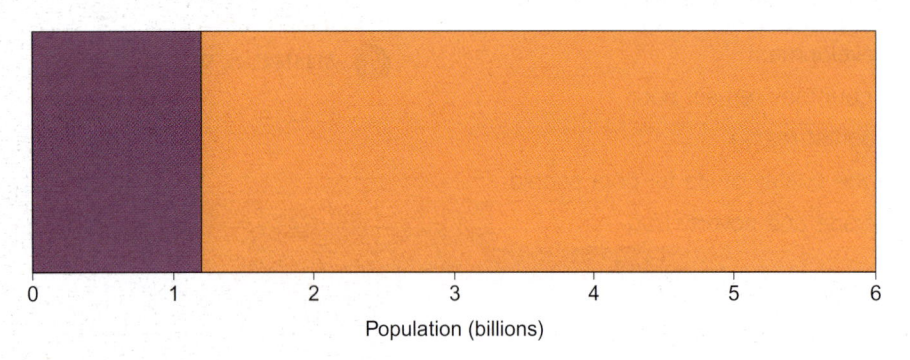

Are you rich or poor? Some of you will give the answer 'poor', probably because you do not have enough money for everything that you would like to buy. Now look at table **A**. How many of those items do you own? Some people say that teenagers in the UK today are the richest ever.

Next look at **B**. The UN (United Nations) estimates that one in every five people in the world lives in great poverty. They live on less than one US dollar per day (see **C**). Could you live on one dollar a day? This must include everything you need for survival – food, clothing and shelter. In English money, one American dollar is worth between 60 and 90 pence. No one in the UK can live on so little.

THE WORLD'S POOREST PEOPLE

Most people living on less than a dollar a day are farmers. They grow all their own food, build their own homes and make their own clothes. All the family collect wood for cooking and heating. It is difficult for people living in a rich country like the UK to imagine how poor some people are in other parts of the world.

Map **D** shows where many poor people live. The poorest region of all is sub-Saharan Africa (below the Sahara Desert), where half the people live on less than a dollar a day. Sub-Saharan Africa includes all the countries in Africa, except for the five next to the Mediterranean Sea in the north.

B People living on less than US $1 per day in 2000

Key
- People living on less than US $1 a day
- People living on more than US $1 a day

THE UNITED STATES OF AMERICA

- The US dollar is the world's major international currency
- People in most countries of the world know what US dollars are worth
- The rate of exchange for the dollar against other currencies goes up and down
- The average exchange rate over the last 10 years was $1.50 = £1 but in 2005 the £ was worth more
- When the rate is $1.50 = £1, take a third off the $ price and you get the approximate price in £
- Buy something for $9 in the USA and you have spent about £6

C US dollars

D People living on less than US $1 per day in 2000 (%)

Map labels:
- Central and Eastern Europe and Russia (CIS) 20.3%
- East Asia 15.6%
- South Asia 36.6%
- Latin America 11.1%
- Sub-Saharan Africa 49%

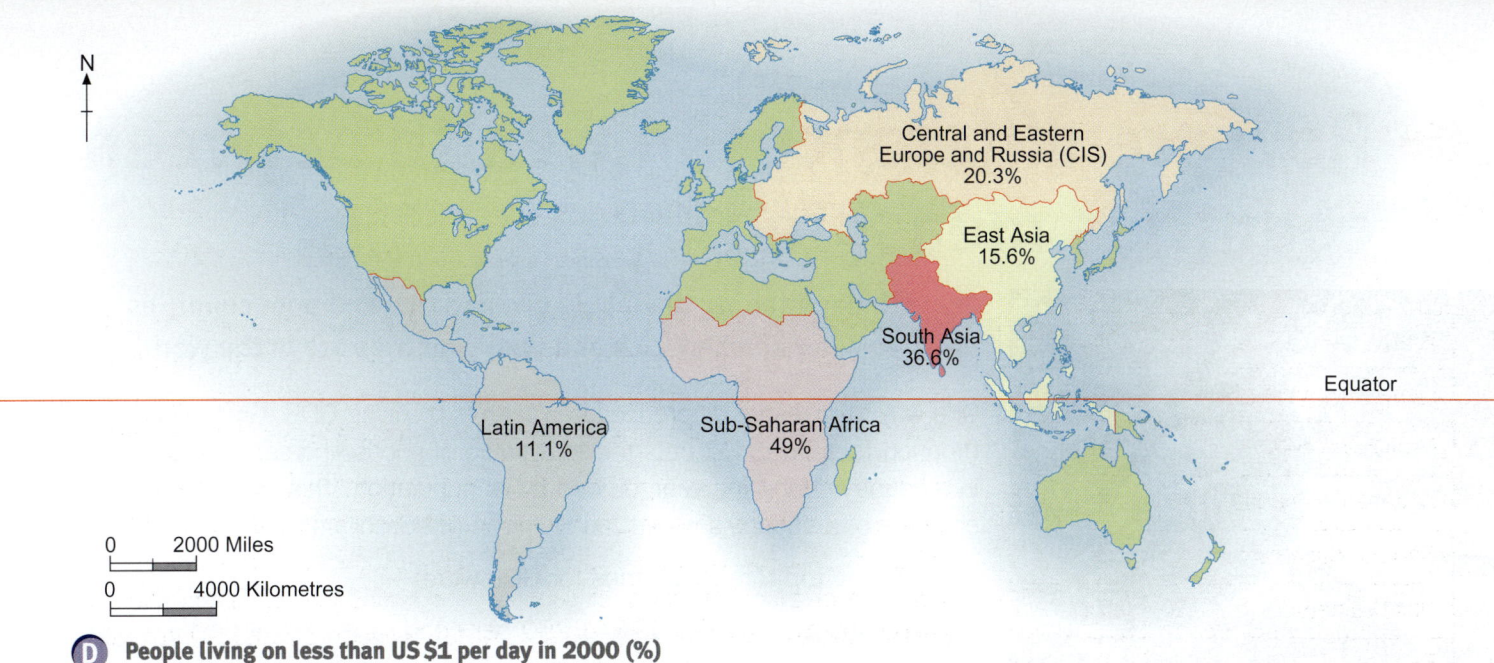

RICH AND POOR

In some places rich and poor people live close to each other. Look at photo **E** taken in Mumbai (Bombay) in India. Notice the home on the beach built by the family living in it. Behind the beach are blocks of flats and hotels for the rich. In other places only rich people can afford to live, such as in Monte Carlo.

Activities

Look at *SKILLS in geography* pages 145–155 for help with these activities.

1. a) Draw a pictograph to show that *one* out of every *five* people in the world lives on less than a dollar a day.

   b) Draw a bar graph to show the percentages given in **D**.

2. a) Trace or sketch an outline map of the continent of Africa.

   b) Shade in and name sub-Saharan Africa.

3. From an atlas, name the *five* African countries not included in sub-Saharan Africa.

4. a) Make a list of all the signs of poverty and wealth shown in photo **E**.

   b) Make a large frame and draw a sketch of photo **E**. Use your list to label your sketch.

5. Some African farmers were asked: 'What gives you a feeling of wealth and well-being?' Their answers included:

   - Fertile land for growing crops
   - Healthy cattle and goats
   - Good roofs on homes to keep the rain out
   - Children or relatives working abroad and sending back money
   - Owning a fridge, TV and bicycle
   - Good neighbours who will give help when needed.

   a) Work in pairs. Think about the answers that someone in the UK might give. Write down *four* likely answers.

   b) How many of these answers are the same as the African ones?

   c) Try to explain why most UK answers would be different.

E Beach living in Mumbai

7 Rich world, poor world

How are differences in wealth between countries measured?

> Understanding the labels given to rich and poor countries
> Looking at where rich and poor countries are in the world

One way to measure differences in wealth is by using GDP (Gross Domestic Product) (see page 12). It is the total value of goods and services produced in a country during the year, divided by its population. This is the best estimate of a country's wealth and is given in US dollars.

In 2003 the top three countries for GDP were:

1. Luxembourg   US $41 950 per head
2. Norway   US $37 020 per head
3. USA   US $35 200 per head

Luxembourg and Norway are small countries, but the USA is large, with 290 million people. The USA is the world's richest large country. The UK was twelfth richest with a GDP of US $23 920.

Three of the bottom four countries for GDP were in sub-Saharan Africa:

- Congo US $100
- Ethiopia US $100
- Burundi US $110

These figures can only be guesses. Most people in these countries grow all their own food. They are called **subsistence** farmers. It is impossible to know how much the food they grow is worth because it is not sold.

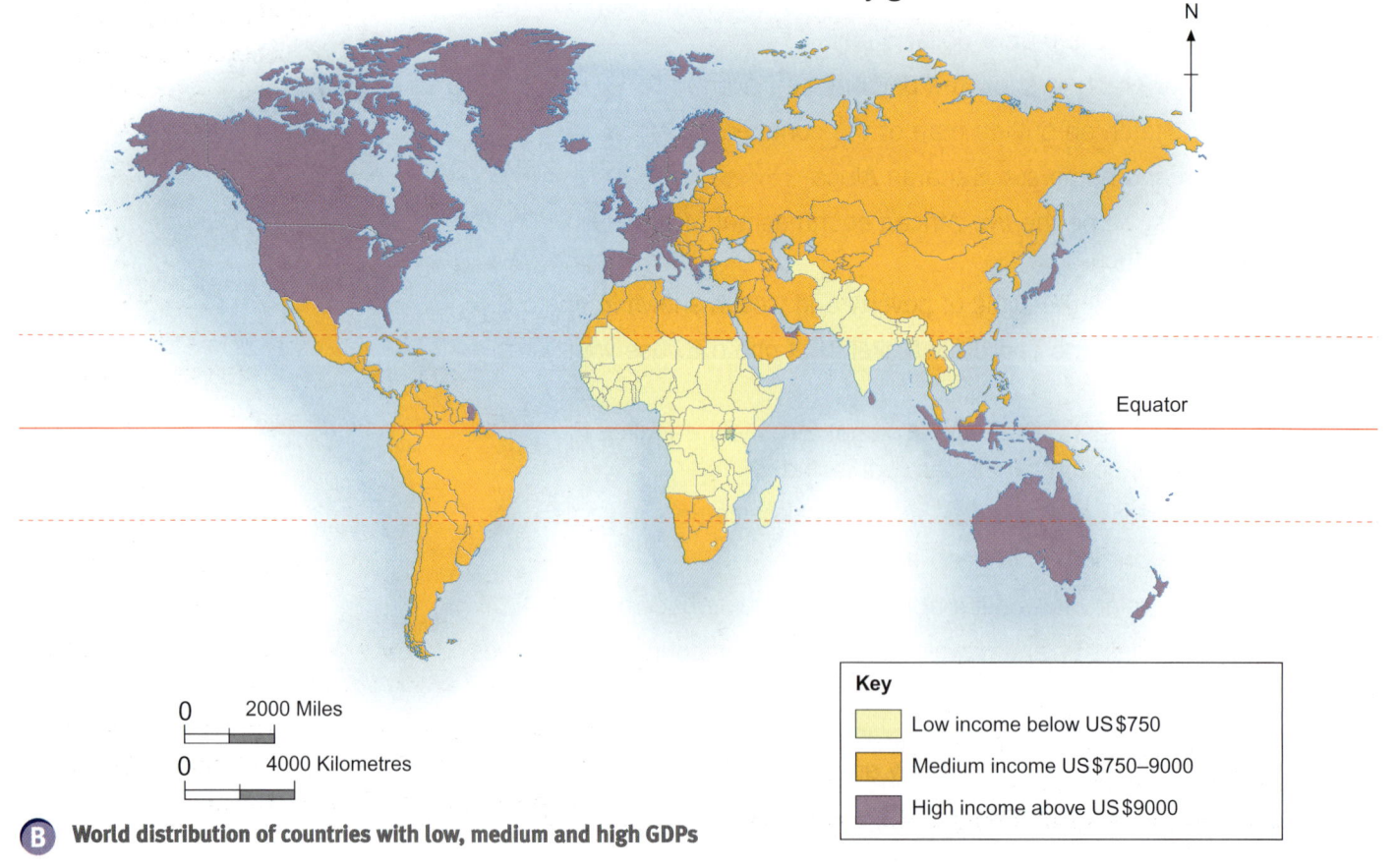

A The value of goods sold at markets like this one in Ecuador in South America is unlikely to be included in the country's GDP

B World distribution of countries with low, medium and high GDPs

Key
- Low income below US $750
- Medium income US $750–9000
- High income above US $9000

DIVIDING THE WORLD INTO RICH AND POOR

In Book 1 the world was divided into

- northern hemisphere and southern hemisphere
- continents and oceans.

These are physical divisions. But in human geography the world is divided into Rich World and Poor World.

The dividing line between rich and poor is shown in map **C**. The rich countries are on the northern side of the line. The line makes a loop around Australia so that Japan and Australia are included with the other rich countries on the 'northern' side of the line. Several different labels are used for the human division of the world into rich and poor.

- **'North' and 'South':** Rich countries are found mainly in North America and Europe. They are well *north* of the Equator. Poor countries lie further *south* in the world, many of them in the tropics in Africa, Asia and South America.

- **'First World' and 'Third World':** 'First World' is another name for rich countries. 'Third World' refers to poor countries. The 'Second World' was made up of **socialist** countries until the collapse of **communist** governments in the Soviet Union and Eastern Europe in the 1990s. We now include these countries in the 'First World'.

- **'MEDCs' and 'LEDCs':** These are the terms used in geography today. MEDCs are rich countries and LEDCs are poor countries.

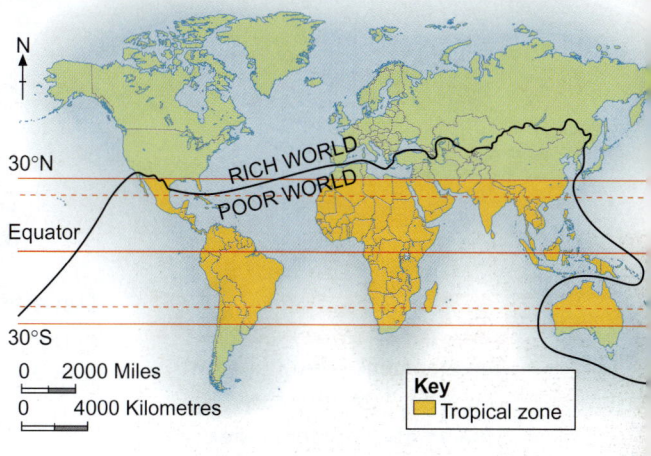

C The dividing line between rich and poor countries

Key words

Communist or **socialist** – countries where the State plans and runs most economic activities
LEDCs – Less Economically Developed Countries; the poorer countries of the world
MEDCs – More Economically Developed Countries; the richer countries of the world
Subsistence – living on what a family grows and produces for itself

Activities

1 Look at map **B**. What are the differences in wealth between:

   a) Europe and Africa?

   b) North America and South America?

2 a) Look at the course followed by the line in map **C** that divides the world into rich and poor. Write out the passage below. Fill in the gaps using each of these words once:

   Africa   Asia   Australia   east   Europe   northern   southern   southwards   South America

   For most of the time the dividing line between rich and poor countries runs from west to _____, with rich countries on its _____ side and poor countries to the south. Countries in North America and _____ are mainly rich countries, whereas countries in the continents of _____ and _____ are mainly poor.

   The dividing line runs through the middle of the continent of _____, before making a sharp turn _____ to keep Japan on the rich side of the line. It makes a large loop around _____ because it is a rich country in the _____ hemisphere.

3 a) Make a frame, then draw and label a sketch of the market scene shown in **A**.

   b) Would you say that the people at the market are rich or poor? Can you find *three* things in the photo to explain your answer?

7 Rich world, poor world   105

What is development?

> Looking at how development can be measured
> Discovering the difference between 'standard of living' and 'quality of life'

Key words

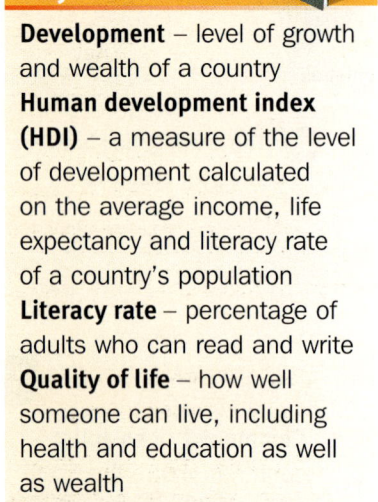

Development – level of growth and wealth of a country

Human development index (HDI) – a measure of the level of development calculated on the average income, life expectancy and literacy rate of a country's population

Literacy rate – percentage of adults who can read and write

Quality of life – how well someone can live, including health and education as well as wealth

Standard of living – how well off and wealthy a person is

Development means that a country is growing and getting richer. More economically developed countries (MEDCs), such as the USA, UK, Japan and Australia, are rich countries. They lie on the northern side of the line in map **C** on page 105. Most people living in these countries have a high **standard of living**. After paying for food, clothing and shelter, there is money left over to buy luxury goods or take holidays. Development is also about improving people's **quality of life**.

Some countries have gone further along the road of development than others. Look at graph **A**. You can see the GDPs for a sample of countries ranging from very poor to very rich. Sierra Leone (US $160) had the fifth lowest GDP in the world in 2003 while Switzerland (US $34 460) had the fifth highest. Countries with a GDP below US $9000 are known as less economically developed countries (LEDCs).

A few countries, mainly in Asia, are developing fast. South Korea is an example of an NIC (Newly Industrialising Country), because of the rapid growth of industry since 1960 (see page 132). Singapore used to be an NIC, but it is now an MEDC. Poor people everywhere dream of becoming as wealthy as people in the USA; they see them all the time on TV and in movies.

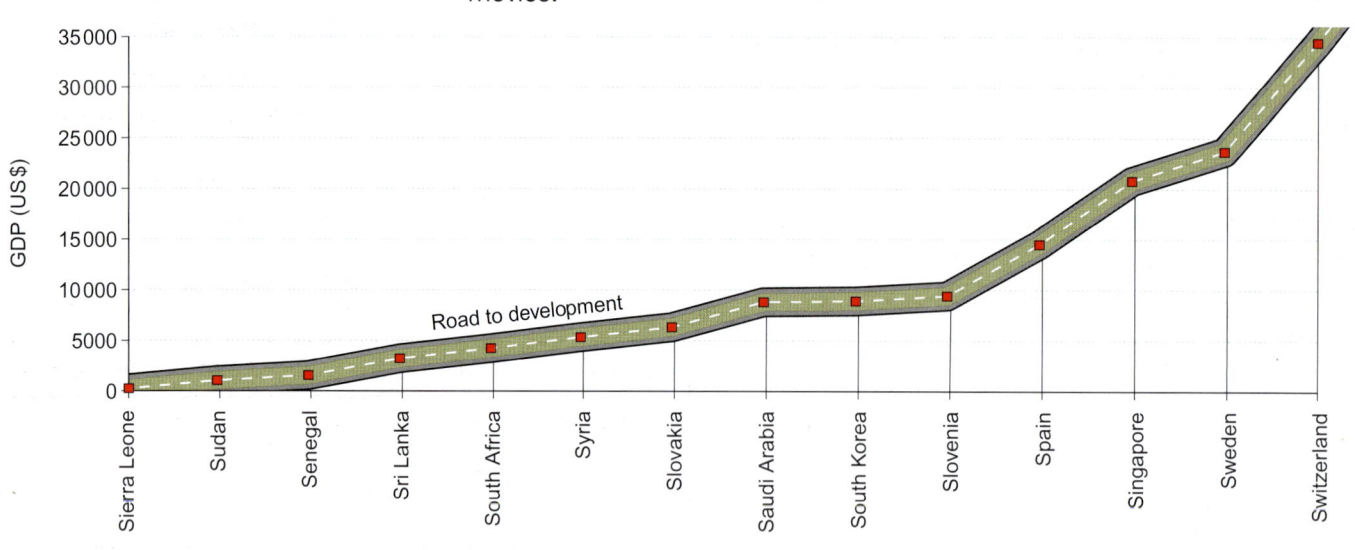

A The road to development – GDPs for a sample of countries from poor to rich

HUMAN DEVELOPMENT INDEX

Another way to measure a country's development is to look at its **human development index** (HDI). This also uses average income per head (like GDP), but also takes two other factors into account – life expectancy and **literacy rate**. These also affect a person's quality of life. Map **B** shows where countries with low, medium and high human development are located.

Look back at map **B** on page 104 and compare it with map **B** on this page. Hopefully you will notice that a similar picture of world wealth and development is given by both of them. There are some exceptions. A few countries with high human development are shown in Asia and South America. Can you name any of them? One is the UAE (United Arab Emirates), an oil-rich state in the Gulf. Another is Argentina in South America, which has the same high levels of literacy and life expectancy as in MEDCs.

What it means to be poor is not the same in LEDCs and MEDCs.

In LEDCs it means:

- hunger
- illiteracy (not being able to read and write)
- many diseases
- lack of health services
- no access to safe water.

In MEDCs it is different because:

- hunger is rare
- literacy rates are close to 100 per cent
- outbreaks of disease are few
- health services exist for all
- safe water flows from taps.

Who are the poor people in the UK? Pensioners, single parents, the unemployed and the homeless are among the poorest. What poverty issues matter most to people in these groups?

B World distribution of countries with low, medium and high human development

Key
- Low human development
- Medium human development
- High human development

Top of human development league

Norway (northern Europe)
Annual income per person
US $30 000
Life expectancy 79 years
Literacy rate 100 per cent

Bottom of human development league

Sierra Leone (West Africa)
Annual income per person
US $470
Life expectancy 34 years
Literacy rate 33 per cent

C Two extremes of HDI

Activities

1. Make a large copy of the table below. Use map **B** on page 104 to fill it in for GDP. Use map **B** on this page for human development.

2. Look at **C**.
    a) Where would you prefer to live – Norway or Sierra Leone?
    b) Give *three* reasons for your answer.

3. Work in groups.
    a) Write down your ideas about what makes for (i) high and (ii) low standard of living in the UK.
    b) Choose what you consider to be the best five ideas for each of high and low standard of living. Show them on two spider diagrams – look at pages 145–155 of *SKILLS in geography* if you need help.

Continent	GDP	Human Development
North America	All high income (above US 9000)	All high
Europe		
Asia		
South America		
Africa		
Oceania		

7 Rich world, poor world

Other measures of development

> Looking at other ways to measure development in a country
> Investigating the effects of poverty

FACT FILE — HOW IS DEVELOPMENT MEASURED?

Figure **A** shows some different ways to compare development.

Economic
GDP per head
LEDC US $2904   MEDC US $15 986
Percentage working in farming
LEDC 61 per cent   MEDC 10 per cent

Education
Adult literacy rate
LEDC 70 per cent   MEDC 99 per cent
Percentage of children not attending primary school
LEDC 22 per cent   MEDC 0 per cent

Health
Life expectancy at birth
LEDC 61.8 years   MEDC 74.1 years
Percentage of people with access to safe water
LEDC 71 per cent   MEDC 99 per cent

A Measures of development

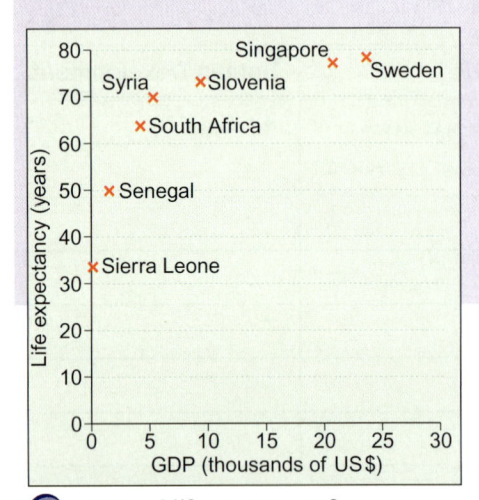

B GDP and life expectancy for countries with different levels of development

You can use a graph to compare GDP with other measures of development. The most useful graph for doing this is a scatter graph (**B**). This graph shows that as a country's GDP increases, the life expectancy of people living there increases as well. There is a positive relationship because both are increasing together.

WHAT DOES THE GREAT DEVELOPMENT DIVIDE MEAN?

Many of the measures of development have other effects. Here is an example:

→ If people do not have clean water to drink, they will suffer more often from water-related diseases such as typhoid and diarrhoea.

→ They will be too weak to work; if they cannot spend as much time growing crops, food production will decrease.

→ Already poor, they will become even poorer, trapped in the poverty cycle shown in **C**.

Charity workers did a survey among villagers in LEDCs. One question they asked was:

'What does poverty mean for you?'

The most common answers were:

'Not enough farm land'

'Having bad housing'

'Having to send our children out to work'

'Short of livestock and farm equipment'

'Not being able to send children to school'

'Not owning the land we farm'

'Being single parents'

'Having more mouths to feed'

'Not having enough healthy people in the family to care for the rest of us'

'Having food security for only a few months each year after the harvest'

If farmers and other people living in villages in the UK were asked the same question, what answers would you expect? Are any of them likely to be the same?

C Poverty cycle

Activities

1 a) Make a table like the one below. Work out the differences between the values for MEDCs and LEDCs given in **A**.

Measure of development	Difference between MEDCs and LEDCs
GDP per head (US $)	US $13 082
Percentage working in farming	
Adult literacy rate	

b) Using the information in **A**, give *one* reason why (i) adult literacy rate and (ii) life expectancy at birth are higher in MEDCs.

2 Draw another flow diagram like the one in **C**. Start with 'Poverty' in a box at the top and four more boxes, as in **C**. Choose the best order for the four statements below and write them in the boxes.

Little contribution to family income   **Unable to read and write**

Cannot afford to send children to school   **Do not have the skills needed to get a well paid job**

3 a) Draw the same type of a sketch as **A** for a farming or village scene in the UK.

b) Label *five* ways in which the UK scene is different from **A**.

7 Rich world, poor world

Why are poor countries poor?

> Finding out about the physical problems of living in the tropics
> Learning about natural hazards and their long-term effects

Geographical location is one reason why poor countries are poor, because most LEDCs are in the tropics (see map **C** on page 105).

PHYSICAL PROBLEMS FOR PEOPLE LIVING IN THE TROPICS

One problem is the amount of rainfall. Where it is hot and wet all year, near the Equator, the land is covered by dense rainforests. After forest clearance, tropical soils are quickly washed away by heavy rain and eroded (photo **A**). Soils soon become infertile once their supplies of new nutrients from dead leaves and branches in the forest are stopped.

There is also the opposite problem – too little rain. Some of the driest places on Earth are in the tropics. What chance do people have of living here? The answer is none, unless they can find an underground source of fresh water.

Natural hazards such as **drought**, flood and violent storms are more common in the tropics than in cooler temperate lands further north. They are also more destructive.

A Soil erosion after rainforest clearance in Malaysia

FACT FILE — TROPICAL STORMS AS AN EXAMPLE OF A NATURAL HAZARD

Map **B** shows places most at risk from **tropical storms**. Hurricanes, cyclones and typhoons are names used for tropical storms in different parts of the world. The only MEDCs regularly at risk from the worst effects of these are Japan and small areas in the USA and Australia. No weather event spreads more fear and panic among people than a tropical storm.

- Wind speeds often above 150 mph (240 km per hour).
- Crops, trees, buildings and power lines brought down and destroyed.
- Think of the strongest gale force wind you have ever known in the UK. Now double its strength. That is the wind speed in a hurricane!
- Rainfall 250 mm or more in less than 24 hours.
- Large areas flooded, no matter how good the flood control systems are.

In September 2004 Hurricane Ivan spread terror and destruction through the Caribbean. Look at the devastation it caused (figures **C** and **D**); it is not surprising that it was given the name 'Ivan the Terrible'.

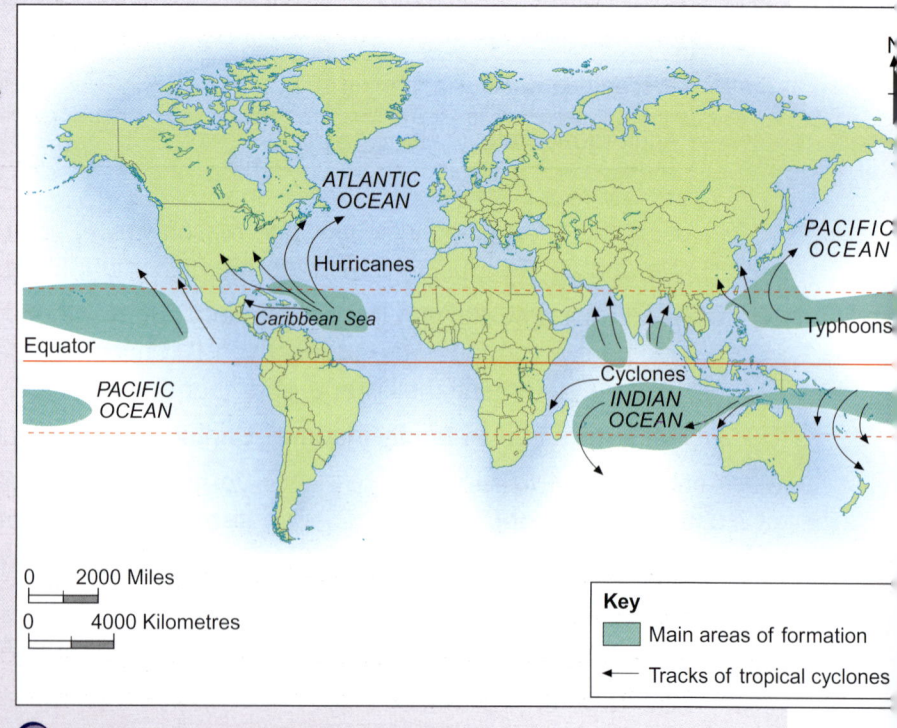

B Tropical storms – main zones of activity

Key:
- Main areas of formation
- Tracks of tropical cyclones

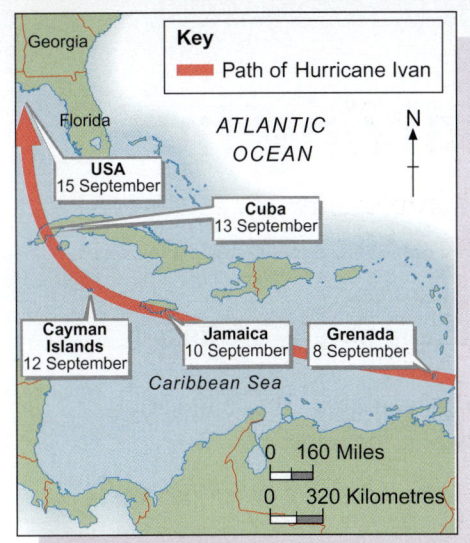

C Hurricane Ivan in September 2004

D Grenada, 10 September 2004 – what 90 per cent hurricane devastation looks like

10 SEPT

HURRICANE IVAN WRECKS GRENADA

90 per cent of houses destroyed, 60 000 homeless. The Spice Island looks like a wasteland of ruined properties and damaged vegetation.

British holidaymaker: 'I was expecting a quiet Caribbean holiday, with the sun, sand and sea promised in the brochure. What I got was a night of noise and sheer terror.'

Grenadian who had lost everything: 'I used to live in paradise. Now I have nothing – no home, no possessions, no food, no money. Who can help me?'

11 SEPT   JAMAICA IN FEAR OF IVAN'S ARRIVAL – WINDS UP TO 150 MPH (240 KM PER HOUR) EXPECTED

12 SEPT   IVAN THE TERRIBLE TAKES ANGER OUT ON JAMAICA

13 SEPT   155 MPH (250 KM PER HOUR) WINDS AND WAVES 2 METRES HIGH BATTER THE CAYMAN ISLANDS

CUBA gets ready for Ivan's arrival: government orders evacuation of half a million people from the western tip of the island. Cubans instructed to store essential supplies of food and water, board up windows and move to hurricane shelters.

E Newspaper headlines and reports about Hurricane Ivan

Activities

1. Percentage loss of life from different natural hazards, 1975–2000:

   Drought 50 per cent   Tropical storms 20 per cent
   Earthquakes 15 per cent   Floods 10 per cent   Others 5 per cent

   a) Draw a pie graph to show these percentages. Look at *SKILLS in geography* pages 145–155 for help with this. Finish it off with a title and key.

   b) Explain how these percentages show that people living in the tropics are at greatest risk from natural hazards.

2. a) Describe the physical problems that make it difficult for people to live in a desert.

   b) Draw a sketch from photo **A**. Label the problems for people that it shows.

3. a) Draw or use a large sketch map to show the route taken by Hurricane Ivan through the Caribbean.

   b) Add to your map some details of the death and destruction that resulted.

4. Is any part of the world being affected by tropical storms at present? Follow the links on Hotlinks (see page 2) and write down the details that you find.

Key words

Drought – period of dry weather beyond that normally expected

Natural hazard – short-term event that is a danger to life and property

Tropical storm – area of very low pressure with high winds and heavy rainfall

7 Rich world, poor world

Other problems for people living in the tropics

> Learning about diseases in the tropics
> Understanding how poor health and poverty are linked

Insects and bacteria love hot, wet, tropical climates. The long list of tropical diseases that damage human health includes:

- malaria, yellow fever, dengue fever – from bites of mosquitoes that breed in water
- cholera, typhoid, hepatitis – from drinking dirty water
- bilharzias, guinea worm infection – from carriers that live in water.

All these diseases are linked with water. Therefore, the risk of local people catching them is greatest in the wet season. This is worst time for farmers to fall ill, because it is their busiest time of the year. If the farmer is not fully fit when it is time to plant crops, the family's food supply for the year will be reduced.

FACT FILE — MALARIA

This is a dangerous disease that affects more than 45 per cent of the world's population in almost 100 countries; it is a major health problem in countries in sub-Saharan Africa (pages 114–115).

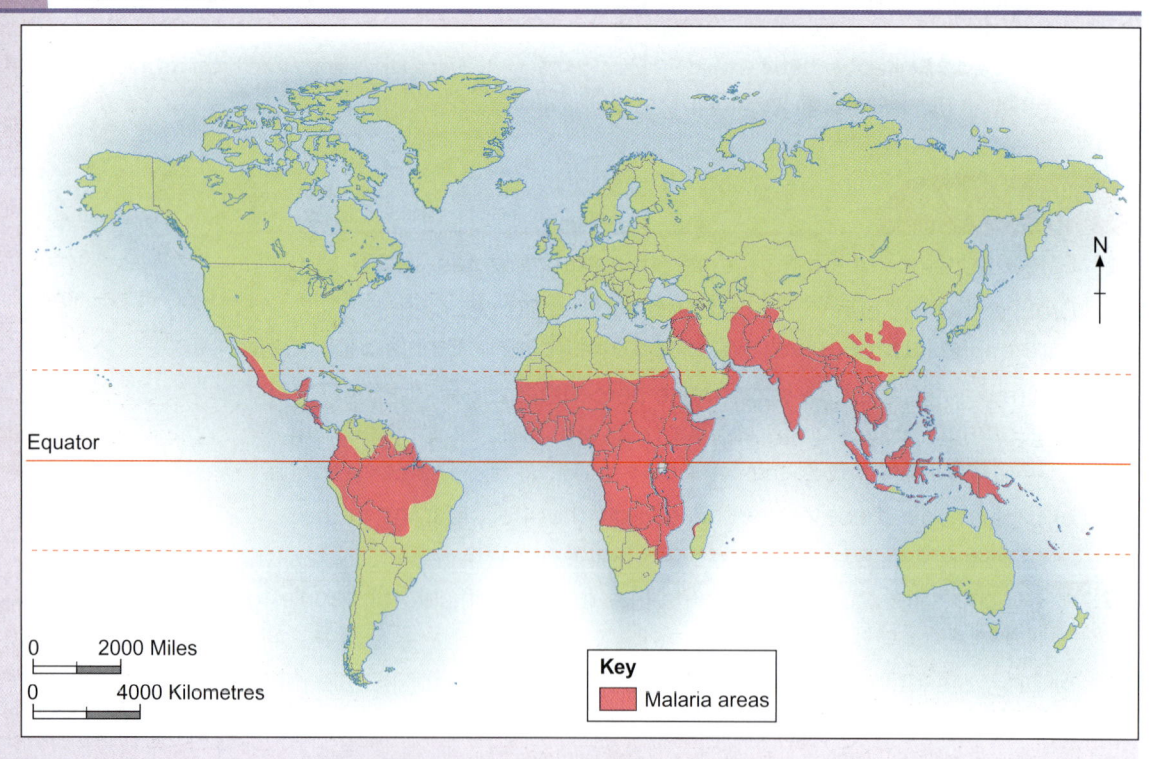

A Malaria – main areas affected

Mosquitoes breed in stagnant water (water that is not flowing). The female mosquito usually bites and sucks blood at night. If the person bitten already has malaria, the disease is spread to the next person bitten by the mosquito.

- Malaria kills 2.7 million people a year.
- 75 per cent of these are African children under the age of five.
- 300–500 million cases of malaria occur every year.
- Symptoms include fever, headache, repeated vomiting, convulsions, coma and, in severe cases, death.

B Malaria – the grim details

geography 360° Foundation Book 2

- Where malarial mosquitoes breed
- Female anopheles mosquito
- Mosquito rests for a couple of days
- Bites a person at night while asleep without the protection of a mosquito net
- Mosquito takes another blood meal; passes on the malaria parasite to the person bitten while sleeping

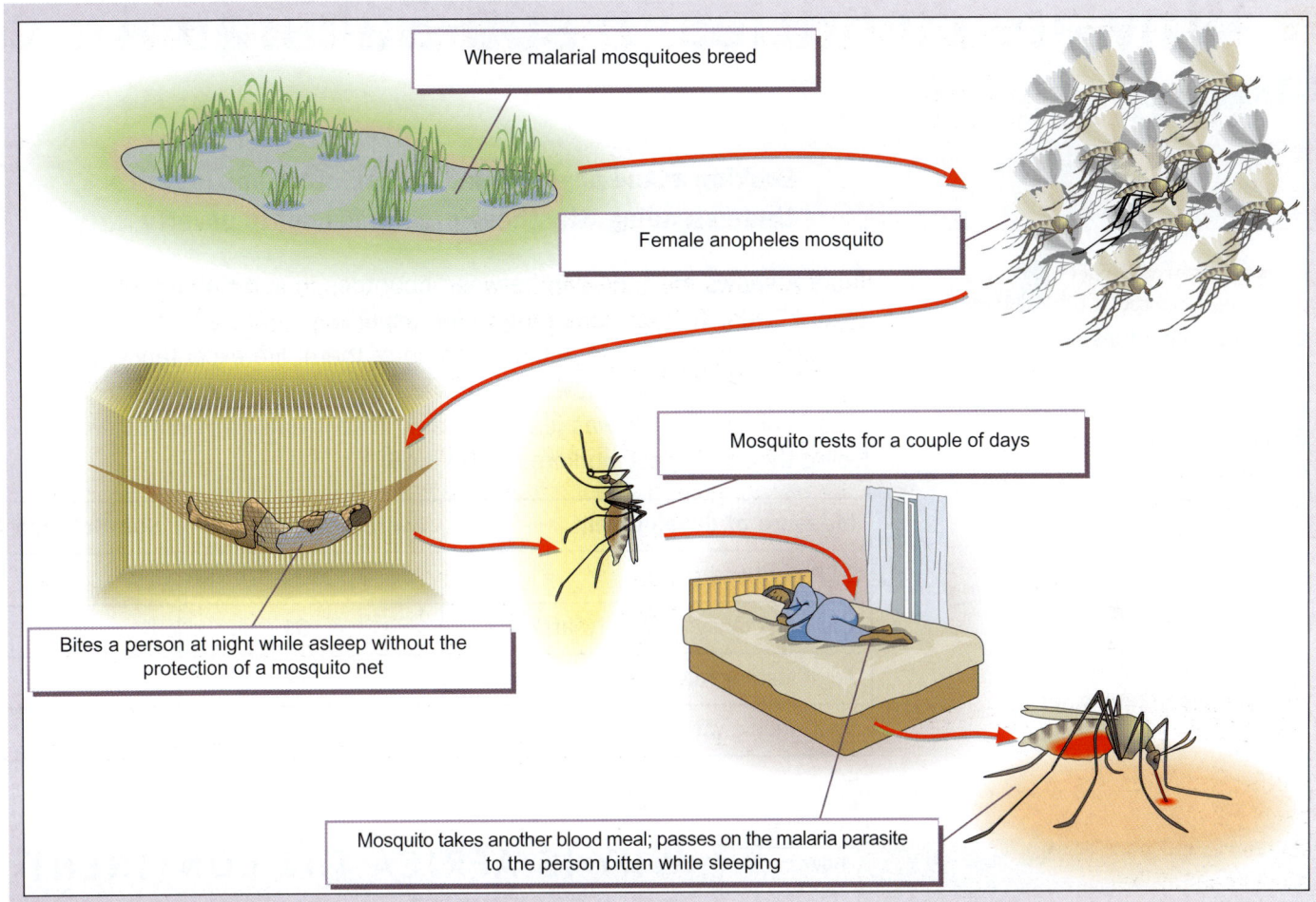

C How malaria spreads

Why has no one found a cure for malaria? After all, hundreds of millions of people in the world are affected by it. There are drugs to fight malaria such as chloroquine; this is a cheap drug, without side-effects, and is perfect for use in poor countries. Unfortunately, new strains of malaria have developed that are resistant to the drug; when people take the tablets, they no longer work.

Big drug companies are based in the USA and Europe. They are often accused of not spending enough money on looking for a vaccine against malaria. Two reasons are given for this.
- Not many people living in MEDCs are affected by malaria.
- If they discovered a new vaccine, poor people would not be able to afford it.

Activities

1. a) Name *three* diseases that are common in tropical countries and not the UK.
   b) How are water and disease linked in the tropics?

2. a) Draw a labelled diagram to show how malaria spreads.
   b) When do visitors to tropical areas need to protect themselves against being bitten by mosquitoes?

3. A charity is asking governments and drug companies to spend more on research into a vaccine against malaria. You have to write a letter to show that malaria is a very serious disease needing urgent attention. You can break up your letter into short paragraphs using the headings:
   - The numbers of people affected
   - Where is malaria found?
   - What malaria does to people
   - Why the old drugs need replacing
   - The benefits of a successful vaccine

   You could also include a map of where malaria is found.

7 Rich world, poor world

Why are countries in sub-Saharan Africa poorest of all?

> Looking at the physical and human problems in Africa
> Understanding why these problems lead to poverty

Key words

Colonies – countries owned and governed by other countries

Primary products – raw materials from land and sea such as minerals and crops

Secondary products – products made from raw materials, such as chocolate bars made from cocoa beans

Soil erosion – loss of fertile topsoil by wind and water

Table **A** shows the wide gap between countries in sub-Saharan Africa and other LEDCs. The gap is getting wider, especially in African countries that are badly affected by HIV/AIDS. In some of them, life expectancy has fallen below 40 years. How many fewer people would you know if life expectancy in the UK was just 40 years? Many families in Africa are losing their strongest workers on the land.

Measure of development	Average for LEDCs	Sub-Saharan Africa
GDP per head (US $)	2904	1377
Life expectancy at birth (years)	61	49
Adult literacy rate (%)	70	56
% of people with access to safe water	71	51

A How sub-Saharan Africa compares with other LEDCs

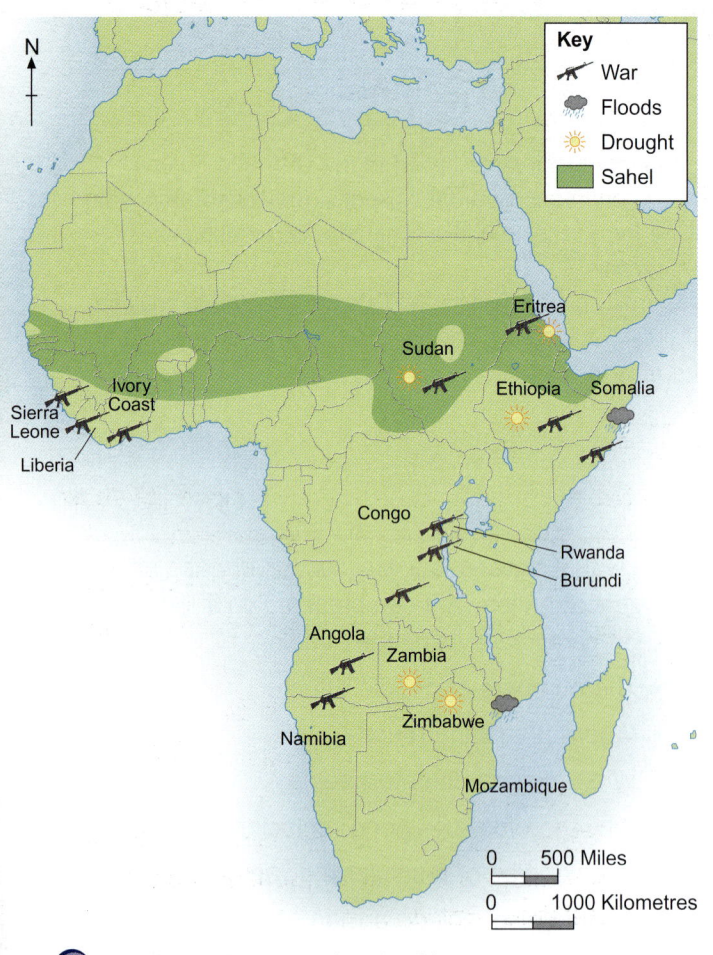

WHY IS AFRICA THE CONTINENT OF POVERTY?

As is usually the case in geography, the reasons are a mixture of physical and human ones (see map **B**).

Physical reasons

Africa is a dry continent. The Sahara is the world's largest desert. Rains that are expected in the Sahel and southern Africa often do not come, resulting in drought. The east coast of Africa can be hit by tropical storms and heavy rains, resulting in the opposite problem – flooding. What chances do poor African farmers have of coping with drought one year and floods the next year?

Human reasons

Wars and armed conflicts between different tribes and countries are common. European countries, mainly Britain, France, Portugal and Belgium, carved up the land between them as **colonies**. Colonies were set up to benefit European countries.

Some African countries are badly governed by dictators who use their country's wealth and resources selfishly. Also, a lot of African countries owe huge sums of money to the World Bank, which means they have less money to develop themselves.

B Physical and human crises in Africa

The wealth of Africa lies in its **primary products** – minerals, tropical hardwoods and crops. These were exported to be used in Europe, where they were made into **secondary products**. African countries still export their valuable natural resources for low prices (see pages 116–117); the pattern of trade remains the same as it was when they were colonies.

FACT FILE — PROBLEMS IN THE COUNTRYSIDE

Figure **C** shows a type of farming found in many parts of West Africa. The tribe keeps a mixed herd of animals. These are taken to grazing land by day and brought back to the village compound at night. Around the village are small fields of subsistence crops such as maize and millet. Wood for fuel is collected from the surrounding woodland. The only source of drinking water for both people and animals are waterholes in the bed of a nearby stream.

Population growth has led to **soil erosion**. The land has been over-used for crop growing and grazing. As the tribe clears more trees for fuel and for farming, more of the land surface is opened up to wind and rain. Strong winds blow away fertile topsoil. Heavy tropical downpours wash away the soil and cut the ground surface into deep valleys.

C Traditional pattern of farming by tribal groups in West Africa

Activities

Look at *SKILLS in geography* pages 145–155 for help with these activities.

1. Look at **A**. Work out and write down the differences between values for LEDCs and sub-Saharan Africa. For example, the difference in GDP is US $1527.

2. a) Look at the list of eight reasons for poverty in Africa below. Sort them into human and physical reasons.

   **colonies   conflicts between tribes
   drought   flooding   desert   wars
   low prices of exports   tropical storms**

   b) Choose *one* reason from each list. Describe how each reason causes poverty.

3. Look at figure **C**.

   a) Make a large frame and draw a sketch to show the landscape and farming in the area.

   b) Add some labels about farming to your sketch.

   c) Complete the paragraph about farming in West Africa below.

   (i) Farmers keep animals such as …

   The daily pattern of farming with their animals is …

   Farmers also grow crops such as … There are many problems for farmers and their families such as …

7 Rich world, poor world

Is world trade fair?

> Understanding why world trade is unfair to LEDCs
> Looking at how MEDCs can help make trade fairer for LEDCs

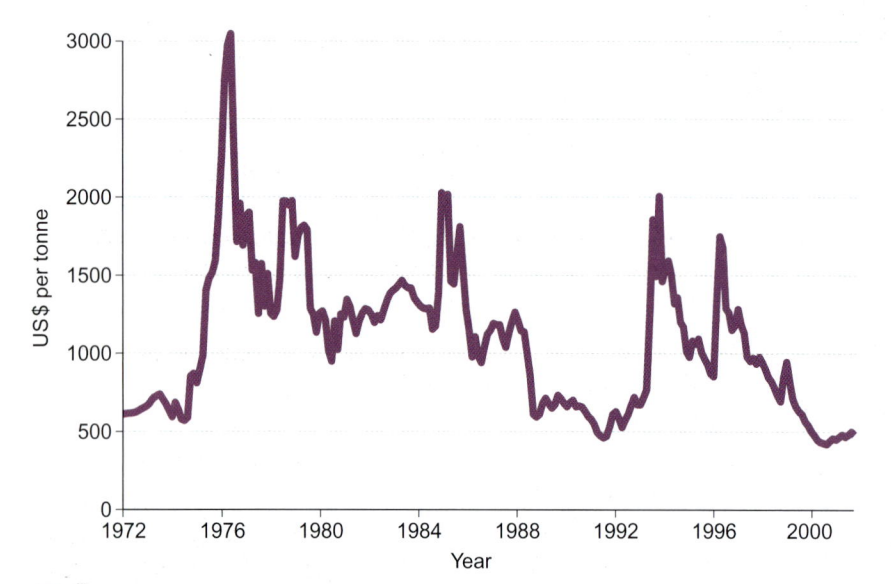

A World coffee prices, 1972–2002

LEDCs don't always benefit from world trade.

- Many LEDCs export minerals (e.g. oil and iron ore) or foods (e.g. bananas, cocoa and coffee). These are low in value per tonne.
- MEDCs export manufactured goods, such as tractors and trucks, which are high in value. Value is added when minerals and crops are made into other products in factories.

For example, farmers in LEDCs need to export a lot of coffee beans to pay for the import of just one tractor or truck.

Another problem for LEDCs is that world prices for minerals and crops go up and down like a yo-yo. Look at the world coffee prices shown in **A**. It was great to be a coffee farmer in 1975, but not so good in 2000 when prices touched a 30-year low.

FACT FILE — COFFEE AND THE FAIR TRADE MOVEMENT

Coffee beans grow on bushes on hillsides in tropical countries such as Brazil and Costa Rica (see **B**). The ripe beans are picked, put in bags and shipped mainly to North America and Europe. Food and drink companies such as Nestlé roast the beans and put the processed coffee in jars for sale in shops.

When you buy a jar of instant coffee for £2, how much goes to the coffee farmer who grew the beans? Take a guess. You can find the answer by looking at **D**. It is about 20 pence (10 per cent of £2.00).

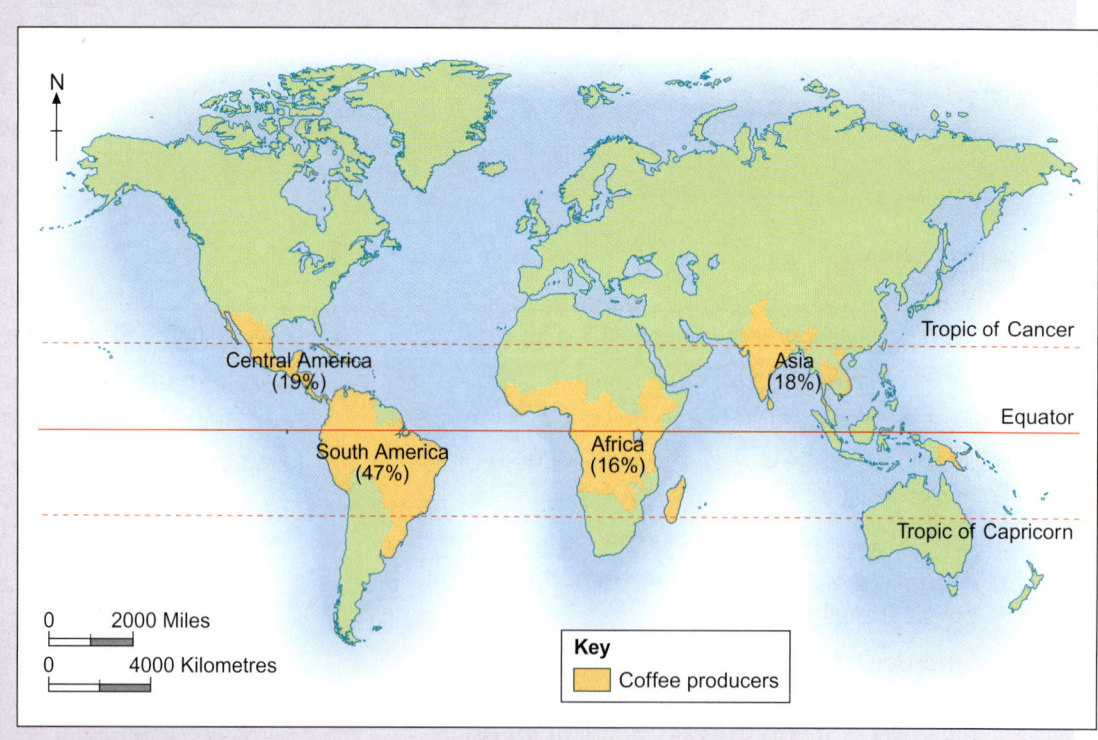

B Coffee-producing areas – are they all in LEDCs?

Central America (19%)
Asia (18%)
South America (47%)
Africa (16%)

116 geography 360° Foundation Book 2

C Coffee farm in the tropical regions of Central America, on the fertile lower slopes of a volcano

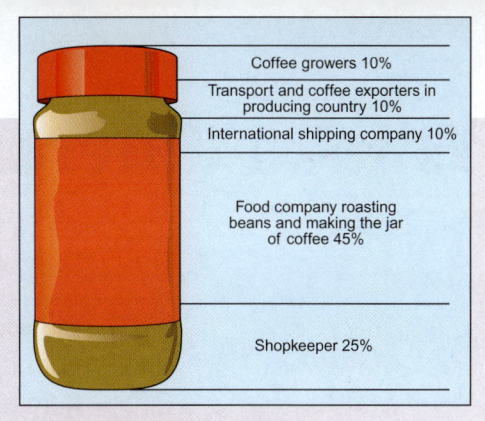

D Who makes the instant profit from a jar of coffee?

- Coffee growers 10%
- Transport and coffee exporters in producing country 10%
- International shipping company 10%
- Food company roasting beans and making the jar of coffee 45%
- Shopkeeper 25%

Another thing that **D** shows – only 20 per cent of the selling price goes to the LEDC where the coffee was grown. Big companies that ship, roast and sell the coffee take 80 per cent; most of these are located in MEDCs. Is this an example of fair trade?

The Fair Trade movement

You can follow the links on Hotlinks (see page 2) to find out about the Fair Trade movement. This movement began in 1993 to try to give small farmers growing cocoa in LEDCs a fair price for their crops. Fair Trade guarantees farmers a minimum price; they will be paid this price even if world market prices drop very low.

For example:

- Fair Trade guaranteed price is US$1600 per tonne.
- World cocoa price drops to US$1000 per tonne.
- Farmer gets US$1600 per tonne.

On top of this, Fair Trade gives US$150 per tonne for community development projects. This money is used for improving everyone's quality of life, not just cocoa farmers. Fair Trade now do this for other crops such as coffee as well (see **E**).

Have you or your family ever bought a Fair Trade product? In UK supermarkets the best-selling Fair Trade products are coffee and chocolate. The higher price reflects what the farmers get for their hard work. The total market for Fair Trade products in the UK for 2004 was £100 million. Nearly five million farmers and their families in LEDCs benefit from these sales.

E Fair Trade coffee – note the Fair Trade logo at the top left. Will the packaging attract shoppers?

Activities

1. Look at graph **A**.
   a) In which year was the coffee price highest? What was the price?
   b) In which two years were coffee prices very low? How low was the price?
   c) Describe how the graph shows that coffee prices go up and down like a yo-yo.

2. Who gets what from the sale of a £1 bar of chocolate in the UK?

   Shop 33p Chocolate company 39.5p
   Government VAT 17.5p Transport and marketing in LEDC 6p Cocoa farmer 4p

   a) Draw a diagram or sketch of a bar of chocolate.
   b) Divide the bar up according to who gets what.

3. Work in groups.
   a) Design a questionnaire to ask people about buying Fair Trade products.
   - Find out if they have bought Fair Trade goods and what they bought.
   - Ask them why they have, or have not, bought Fair Trade goods.
   - Find out if they will buy them in the future.
   - Ask them about what will stop them buying them.

   b) Use your questionnaire with members of the class.
   c) Write about what you have found out. Use your questions as headings for your writing.

What a difference clean water makes

> Looking at the links between clean water and quality of life in LEDCs

Did you know that every ten seconds a child somewhere in the world dies from diseases carried by dirty water? Can you imagine getting your water from a muddy pond or dirty river – for drinking, bathing and washing clothes? This is what many villagers in LEDCs have to do every day.

FACT FILE: TAKING CLEAN WATER AND SANITATION TO RURAL AREAS IN PAKISTAN

A new project in the Punjab in Pakistan (see **A**) aims to provide a clean water supply and safe sanitation systems to 800 000 people in more than 300 villages. These are all poor people with family incomes below US $60 (£40) per month. Tube wells are sunk to reach underground stores of clean water; the safe water brought to the surface is piped to homes.

Village people were asked what they wanted most. The clear message from villagers was that they wanted the chance to:

- send their children to school
- improve health and sanitation
- increase family income.

A safe water supply was seen as the best start.

Facts about Punjab, Pakistan
- Population 84 million
- Largest and most densely populated province of Pakistan
- 60% of people live in rural areas
- 36% live below poverty line
- Only 53% of rural people have access to safe water supplies

A Information about the Punjab in Pakistan

THE KNOCK-ON EFFECTS...

The story of Sughran Bibi, a mother of five, is typical. The project to pipe clean water to homes in her village was completed in 2001.

Before

"We used to get our water from a pond also used by the animals. It was so dirty. Then they dug a well, but we had to queue all day under the sun to get a little water. The water wasn't good. Many children got sick with diarrhoea, and there was cholera in the rainy season. We had no money to go to the doctor. Life was so bad that some families left the village. My girls wanted to go to school but there was no time because we spent five to six hours a day fetching water. Mothers would say to their daughters: 'First you must fetch the water, then you can study!'"

After

"Life is much better now. I have time for sewing and embroidery. I make clothes that I sell. We don't have to skip meals any more. I have time to look after our home vegetable plot. My girls now go to school. They are hardly ever ill. I feel good because I am helping to bring money into the home. My dream has come true."

The new piped supply of clean water has brought other great benefits to village people in the Punjab.

- Water-related diseases have decreased by 90 per cent.
- School attendance has increased by 80 per cent.
- Household incomes have gone up 20 per cent, because women have time to earn extra money from making clothes, keeping chickens and selling goods in town markets.

SMALL-SCALE SCHEMES HELP LOCAL PEOPLE MOST

The Play-Pump uses a children's roundabout to power a water pump (**B**, **C**). It is easy to maintain because it uses low technology, having only two moving parts. Advertising signs around the water tower earn money to pay for repairs. One pump can draw up 1400 litres of water an hour from as deep as 40 metres – more than enough water for one village. This is better than piping and pumping water from a large dam hundreds of miles away.

B Play-Pump in a water playground in South Africa. Reproduced with permission of Roundabout (www.roundabout.co.za)

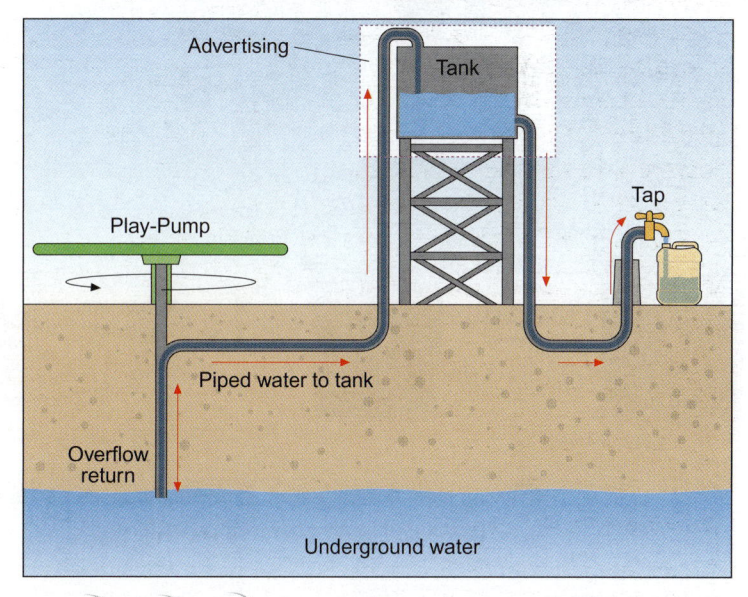

C Diagram showing how a Play-Pump works

Activities

Look at pages 145–155 of *SKILLS in geography* if you need help.

1. Draw a bar graph to show the percentage increases in school attendance and incomes *after* clean water reached the village.
2. Draw two large spider diagrams. Complete them to show 'Quality of Life Before' and 'Quality of Life After' the clean water supply project for Sughran Bibi and other villagers.
3. a) Draw a large labelled sketch to show how the Play-Pump works.
   b) Write down *two* reasons why the Play-Pump is a great success.
4. A charity is trying to raise money for a water project in an LEDC. You have been asked to write about why clean water and good sanitation are so important to this area. Look back through this chapter and make brief notes on: percentage access to safe water in LEDCs, the effects of dirty water on health and poverty, and some examples of the benefits clean water bring. Then write the report.

7 Rich world, poor world

Are poor countries caught in a trade and poverty trap?

> Looking at examples of the poverty trap in LEDCs
> Making connections between different factors

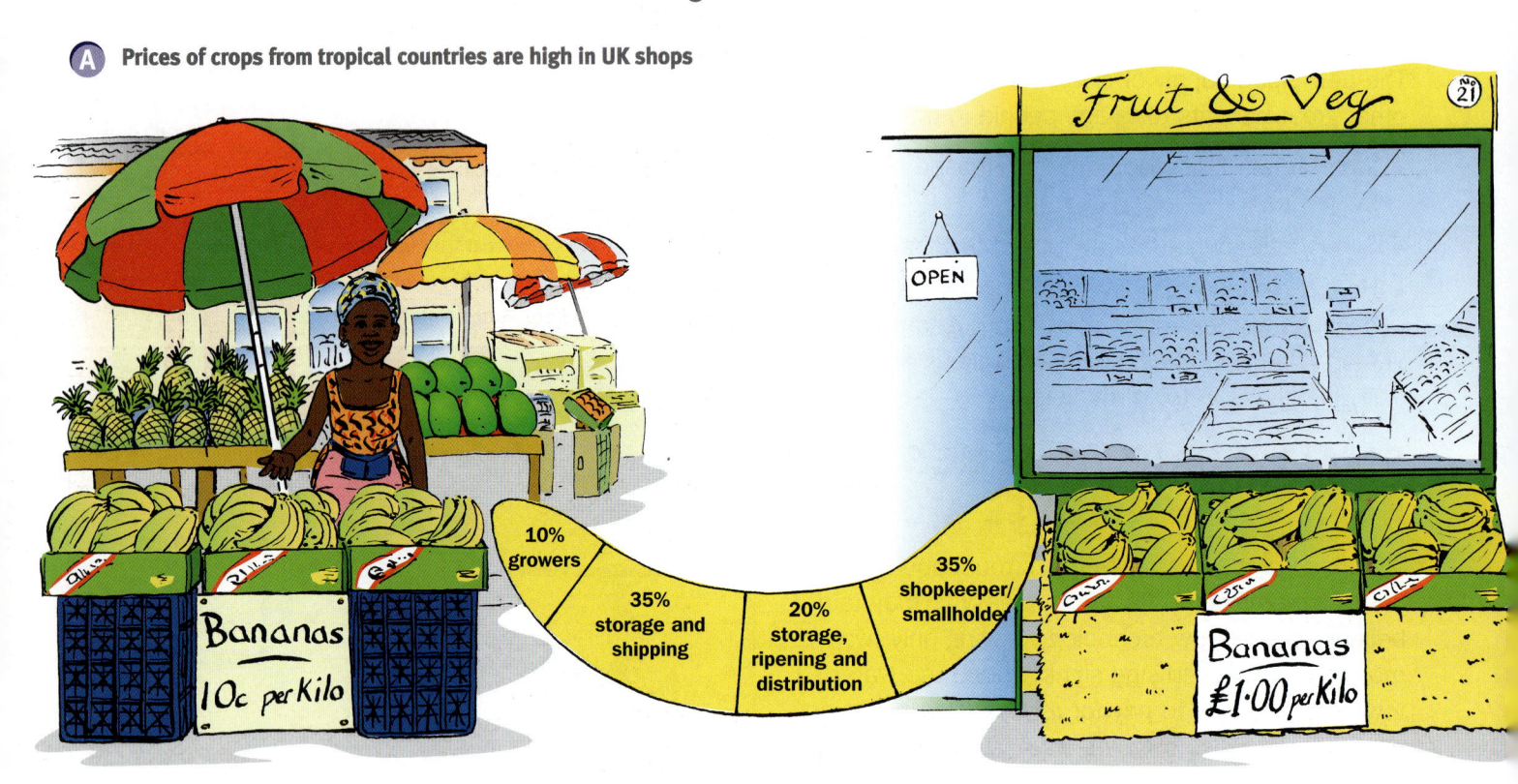

A Prices of crops from tropical countries are high in UK shops

- 10% growers
- 35% storage and shipping
- 20% storage, ripening and distribution
- 35% shopkeeper/smallholder

Bananas 10c per Kilo

Bananas £1·00 per Kilo

B Foreign exchange from exporting crops is a vital source of income for many poor tropical countries

Caribbean farmer:
'My country is too small and too poor to make tractors. All our tractors, trucks and other machines must be imported.'

Government Minister in LEDC:
'We need the money to pay off our debts. Having to sell cheap and buy dear has put the country in debt. The size of our debt keeps on increasing.'

C Finding other ways of earning foreign exchange is difficult

Caribbean farmer:
'I have spent a lot of money on my banana plantation. I cannot pull all the plants out now. Will any other crop give me more money?'

Businessman in LEDC:
'I am told that there is a big demand for sports gear in the USA. Wages are low here but clothes made here are blocked from the USA by high import taxes and quotas.'

D Persuading governments of MEDCs to give development aid is not easy

Government Minister in MEDC:
'We fund major schemes like dam building. They make a big difference to poor countries.'

Charity worker:
'Water and electricity from big dams go to the cities and rich people, not to the village people in greatest need.'

E Solutions using local resources and communities and low technology are often much more effective

Villager in southern Africa:
'The new biogas converter is amazing; it turns dung into methane gas for cooking and lighting. It used to take hours to collect enough wood.'

Activities

1. Study the mind map below. It shows why poor countries are caught in a trade and poverty trap. Describe and explain the links shown, then add notes to explain the links on a copy of the diagram.

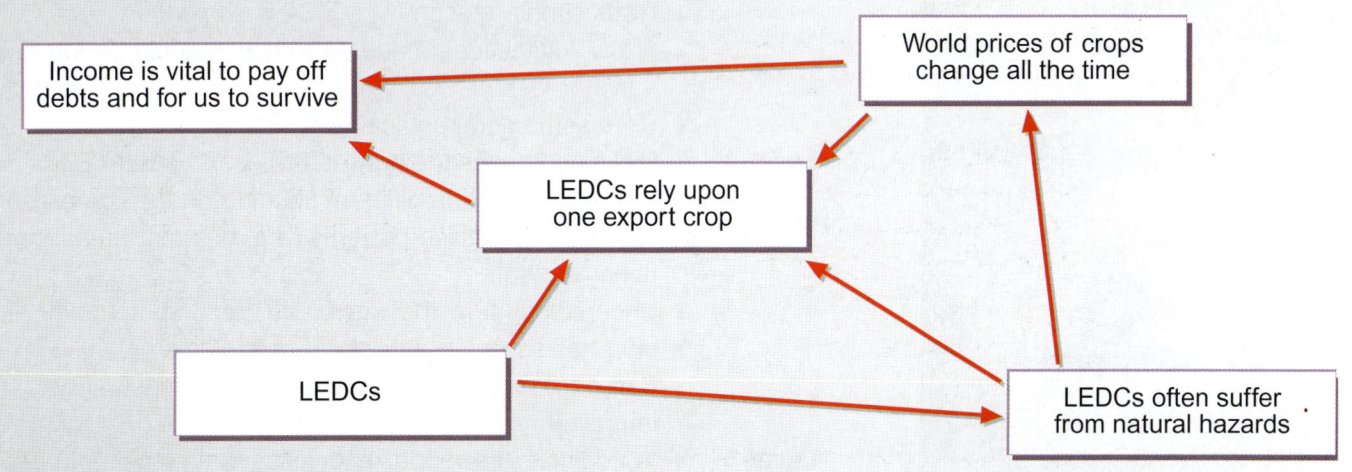

   - Income is vital to pay off debts and for us to survive
   - World prices of crops change all the time
   - LEDCs rely upon one export crop
   - LEDCs
   - LEDCs often suffer from natural hazards

   F Mind map

2. Study the information in **A**.
   a) Draw a pie chart to show how the money from selling a banana is divided up. Look at *SKILLS in geography* pages 145–155 if you need help.
   b) What percentages of the selling price go to LEDCs and MEDCs?
   c) Explain why this is an example of unfair trade.
   d) How would you make the trade fairer?

3. Using sources **B** and **C**, find *two* problems caused by poor countries being paid so little for their exports.

4. Using **A–E**, explain why it is very difficult for countries to get out of this trade trap.

7 Rich world, poor world 121

Assessing 360°

Rich country, poor country

1. Photographs **A** and **B** were taken in Peru, an LEDC in South America.
   a) Make *two* frames. Draw sketches of the two photographs. Add labels to show wealth and poverty.
   b) Write about likely differences in quality of life for the people living in these two places.

2. Work in small groups. Draw up a development plan for improving the life and farming for people in sub-Saharan Africa (SSA from now on). Look back at the sources on pages 114–115 for information and ideas. Use the following as a guide:
   a) How poor are the countries in SSA?
   b) Why are these countries so poor?
   c) Suggest a four-point plan to improve their way of life and farming. Include suggestions on improving their water supply through a water project. Also include a solution to the fuel problem, for example education and money towards growing trees.
   d) Explain how your plan would improve the people's way of life and farming. Would anyone lose out?

Present your reports to the rest of the class. They can use the following mark scheme to give you an assessment of your work.

Level 3
- Makes some simple comparisons between SSA and other LEDCs
- Gives simple reasons why SSA is so poor
- A few suggestions made as to how it could be improved – five or less
- Uses some geographical words

Level 4
- Makes comparisons between SSA and other LEDCs
- Makes reference to different countries in the comparison
- Begins to recognise patterns, e.g. different areas that are richer or poorer
- Understands how the way of life could be improved – plan has several points that are explained
- Can offer their own views about how things will be improved

Level 5
- In addition, the report recognises that places and people are dependent upon others
- Shows some understanding of sustainability, i.e. that the suggested plan will bring lasting positive improvement
- Shows some ability to classify problems or solutions, e.g. into human and physical
- Shows some understanding of ideas such as the trade trap, poverty cycle and fair trade

A City wealth – part of Lima, the capital city, where rich people live

B Poverty in the countryside – a farming village in the Andes

8 South and East Asia

Have you seen washing like this? This is Dhobi Ghats, Mumbai's main laundry where 5000 men work and beat the dirt out of sheets and clothes. A large, hard-working and cheap workforce is one of Asia's main assets. What would happen if these men were replaced by machines?

Learning objectives

What are you going to learn about in this chapter?
- The major features of the physical and human geography of Asia
- The geography of Japan and the reasons for the country's great industrial importance
- South Korea's industrial growth and the problems it has caused
- How China, the world's population giant, is also trying to become an industrial giant
- The geography of the Indian sub-continent and the rise of hi-tech industries in India
- How Bangladesh struggles with its geography because of repeated flooding

A Dhobi Ghats, Mumbai's main laundry

Asia – the big continent

> Learning about the geography of Asia
> Comparing the climates of Asia and the UK

FACT FILE — THE GEOGRAPHY OF ASIA

Everything about the physical geography of Asia is big.

- It is the biggest continent by area.
- Highest mountain range in the world – the Himalaya, with thirteen peaks above 8000 metres.
- Highest mountain in the world – Mount Everest.
- Five of world's ten longest rivers – the Yangtze River in China is the longest in Asia.
- World's largest lake – the Caspian Sea.
- Lowest land on the Earth's surface – the Dead Sea, 403 metres below sea level.
- Second and third largest deserts in the world – Arabian and Gobi.

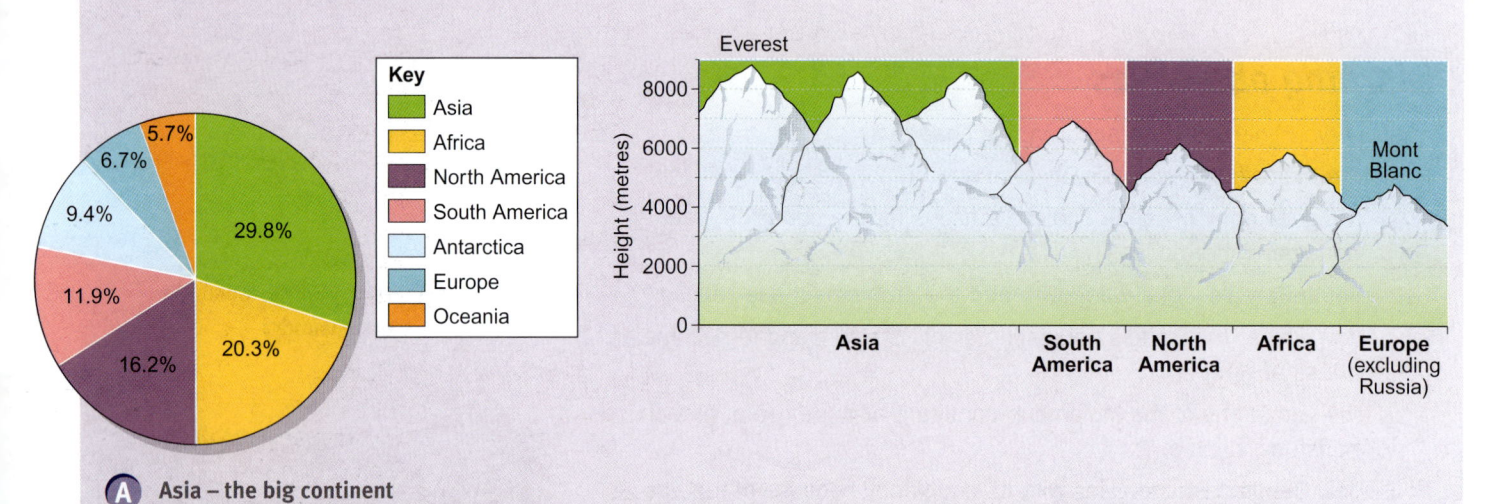

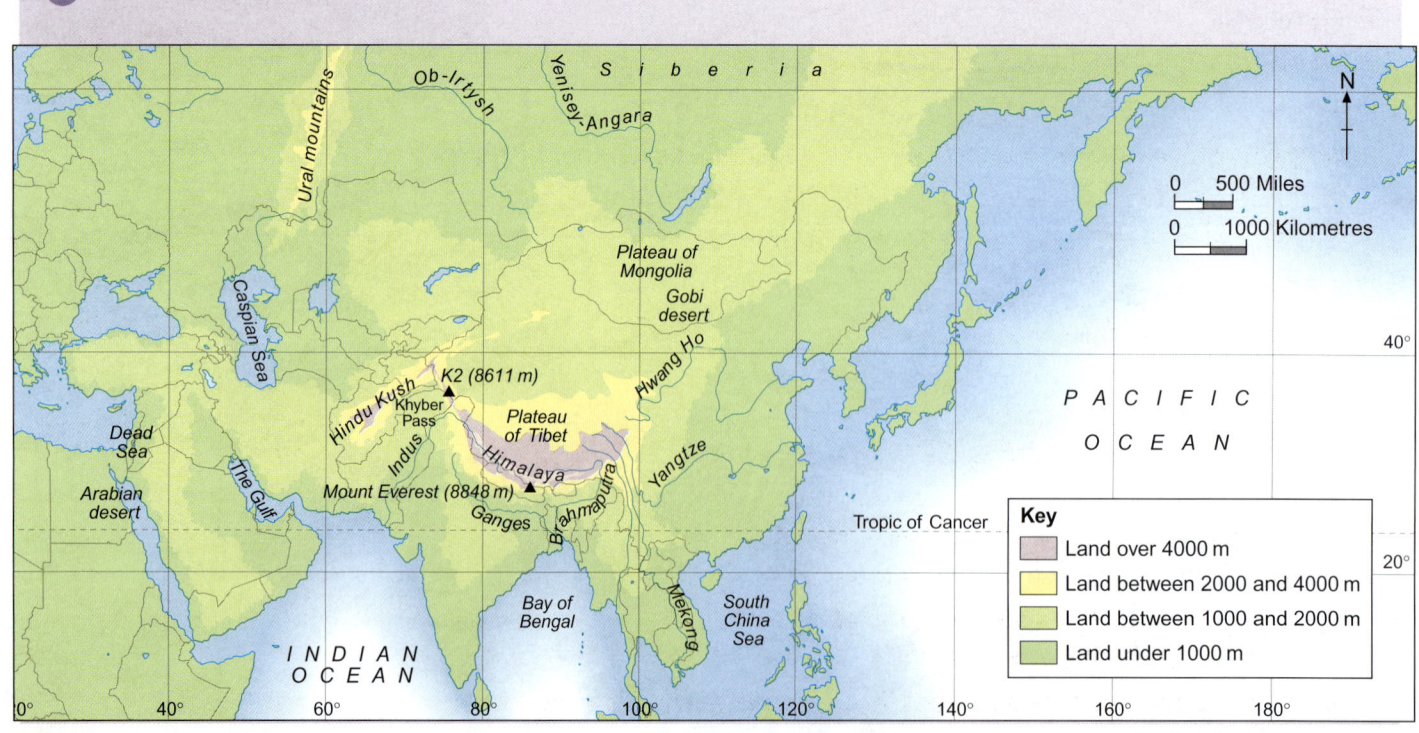

Key
- Asia
- Africa
- North America
- South America
- Antarctica
- Europe
- Oceania

Pie chart percentages: Asia 29.8%, Africa 20.3%, North America 16.2%, South America 11.9%, Antarctica 9.4%, Europe 6.7%, Oceania 5.7%

Mountain heights chart: Everest (Asia), South America, North America, Africa, Mont Blanc (Europe excluding Russia)

A Asia – the big continent

Key (Physical map)
- Land over 4000 m
- Land between 2000 and 4000 m
- Land between 1000 and 2000 m
- Land under 1000 m

B Physical map of Asia

124   geography 360° Foundation Book 2

ASIA – CONTINENT OF BIG DIFFERENCES IN CLIMATE

Asia stretches from south of the Equator (0°) to north of the Arctic Circle ($66\frac{1}{2}°$). There are big differences in weather and climate between places. Look at **C**. Singapore is on the Equator; its climate is hot and wet. Verkhoyansk is in Siberia, north of the Arctic Circle; its climate is very cold and dry. How large is the difference in temperature in January between them?

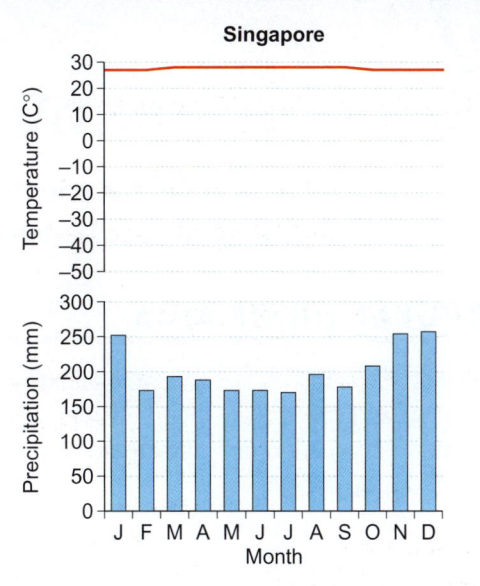

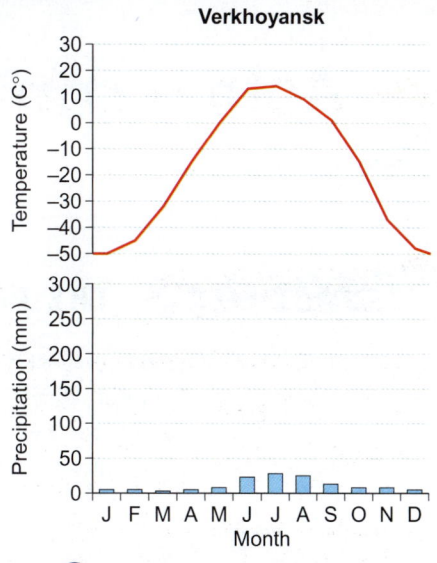

Asia's best known climate is the **monsoon**. One season is dry and the other is wet. In summer, winds blow from sea to land and bring heavy rain to India and the countries around it. Without these monsoon rains rice would not grow. Rice is the **staple crop** that feeds Asia's many billions.

When monsoon winds hit the hills of north eastern India, they are forced to rise. Water falls from the clouds by the bucketful! Cherrapunji (1300 metres above sea level) is the wettest place on Earth, with an average rainfall of 10 799 mm per year. It holds the world record for the amount of rain *in one day* – an estimated 900 mm. London gets only about 600 mm *in one year*.

C Climates of Singapore and Verkhoyansk

SKILLS

How to describe a climate graph

Find the:
1. highest temperature and month
2. lowest temperature and month
3. range of temperature (highest minus lowest)
4. highest precipitation and month
5. lowest precipitation and month
6. precipitation distribution (all year, season with most).

For more help see page 148 of *SKILLS in geography*.

Key words

Monsoon – climate with one season of heavy rainfall, as in India

Staple crop – the most important food in people's diets

Activities

1 Look at **B**.

Write out the paragraph below. Fill each space with one of these names.

| Everest | Ganges | Gobi | Himalaya | Mongolia |
| Ob | Siberia | Tibet | Yangtze | Yenisey |

In the middle of Asia is the world's highest mountain range, the _____. The River _____ begins here and flows into the Bay of Bengal. The name of the world's highest mountain is Mount _____. North of this mountain range is the high plateau of _____. This is where Asia's longest river starts, the _____ River, which flows east through China. To the north is the _____ desert, some of which extends to the plateau of _____. Between here and the Arctic Ocean is _____, the cold eastern part of Russia; it is crossed by north-flowing rivers like the _____ and _____.

2 You are going to describe differences in climate between Singapore and Verkhoyansk, using the method given in the *SKILLS* box.

a) Make a large table for your answers using three columns and six rows. Complete the table.

b) State the *two* biggest differences in climate between Singapore and Verkhoyansk.

Asia – continent of many people

> Learning about the population of Asia
> Comparing the populations of Asia and other parts of the world

FACT FILE — THE POPULATION OF ASIA

Asia has four of the world's largest countries by area: Russia, China, India and Kazakhstan. Russia and China cover great areas of land, mainly in the north and centre of Asia (see **A**). Here the climate is cold and dry. Smaller countries are found in the south and east of Asia, closer to the Indian and Pacific Oceans. Indonesia, Philippines and Japan are countries with many islands.

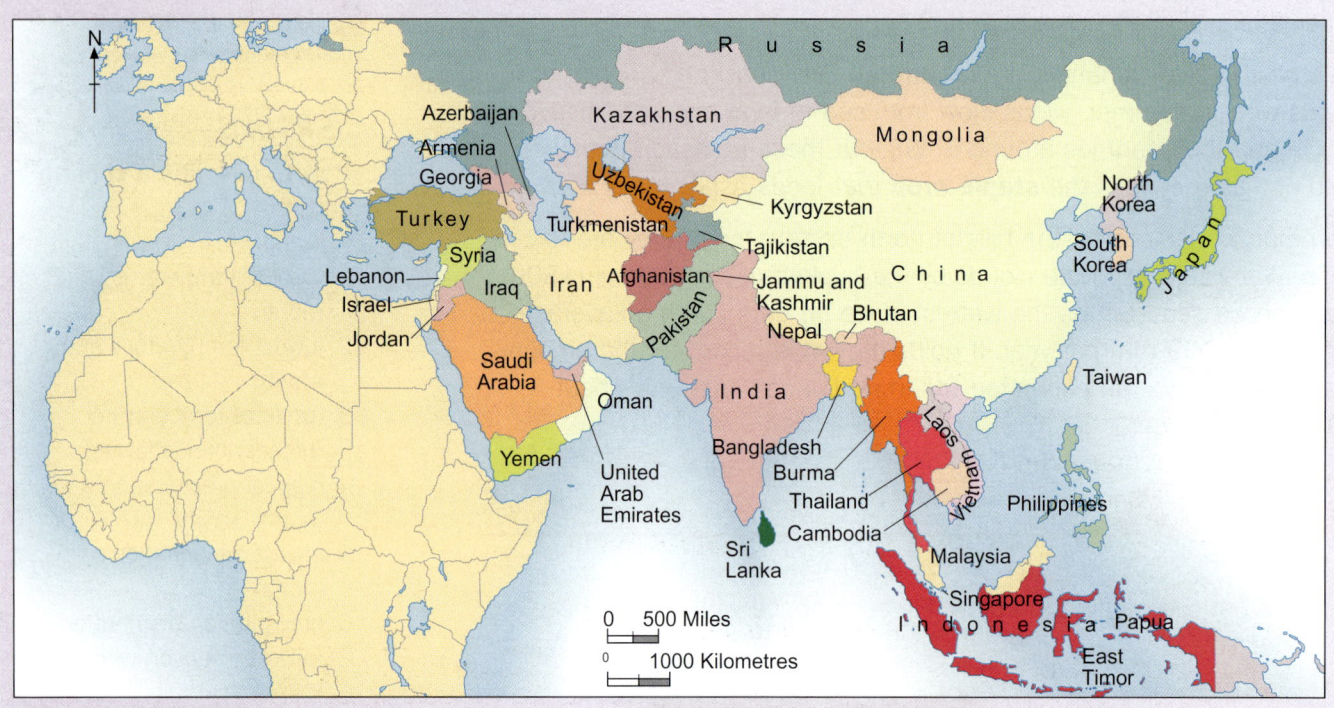

A Political map of Asia

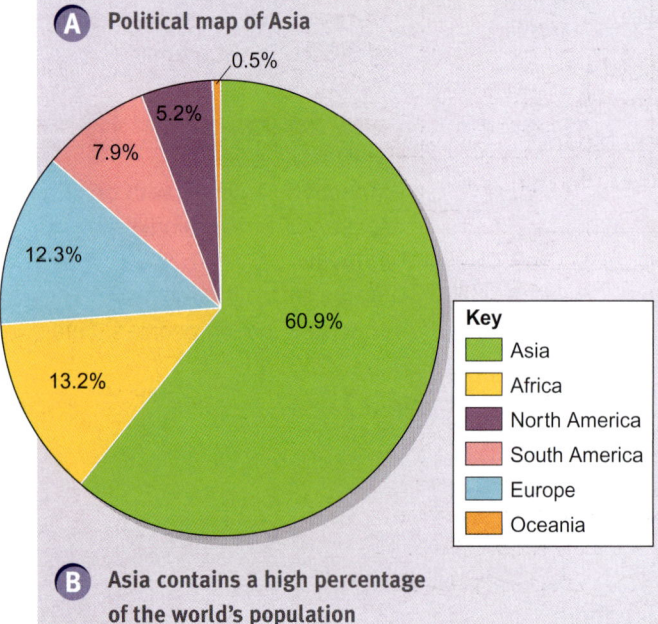

B Asia contains a high percentage of the world's population

Pie chart key:
- Asia: 60.9%
- Africa: 13.2%
- North America: 5.2%
- South America: 7.9%
- Europe: 12.3%
- Oceania: 0.5%

C The ten countries with the largest populations in 2001 (millions)

1	China	1285.0
2	India	1025.1
3	USA	285.9
4	Indonesia	214.8
5	Brazil	172.6
6	Pakistan	145.0
7	Russia	144.7
8	Bangladesh	140.4
9	Japan	127.3
10	Nigeria	116.9

Large numbers of people live in Asia. In fact, six out of every ten people on Earth live in Asia (see **B**). More than one-third of the world's people live in just two Asian countries, China and India.

126 geography 360° Foundation Book 2

SOUTH AND EAST ASIA – DRAMATIC INDUSTRIAL GROWTH

Japan is the world's second largest industrial country after the USA. It is called 'the locomotive' because it is pulling other Asian countries behind it along the road of development (see Chapter 7 page 106).

Hong Kong (**D**), Singapore, Taiwan and South Korea were the first to follow Japan. These NICs (Newly Industrialising Countries) are known as 'East Asian Tigers' because of the speed at which they grew. Now they have been joined by 'new tigers' such as Thailand, Indonesia, Malaysia and the Philippines.

At present Japan is the economic giant of Asia, but will China and India overtake it by 2025?

D Hong Kong was one of the original East Asian Tigers before it was handed back to China in 1997; it has one of the world's great natural harbours

Activities

1 Look at the Asian countries in **A**.
   a) (i)   Name *five* countries that are all islands.
      (ii) Name *three* countries that are landlocked (do not have a coastline).
      (iii) Name *one* country partly on an island and partly on the mainland of Asia.
      (iv) Name *one* country with land both north and south of the Equator.
   b) **Odd one out**. Which one is the odd one out in each group below? Say how it is different from the others.
      (i)   Sri Lanka   Philippines   South Korea
      (ii) Mongolia   Nepal   Pakistan
      (iii) China   India   Japan

2 a) Draw a bar graph to show the population estimates for 2050 in **E**. Use a different colour or shading for the bars for countries in Asia.
   b) What is expected to be different about China and India in 2050 compared with 2001 (look back at **C**)?

3 a) Use **D** and draw a labelled sketch to show what Hong Kong looks like.
   b) Does it look rich or poor? Write out and finish this sentence: 'I think Hong Kong looks … because … .'

1	India	1 530
2	China	1 400
3	USA	400
4	Pakistan	350
5	Indonesia	300
6	Nigeria	260
7	Bangladesh	250
8	Brazil	240
9	Ethiopia	170
10	Congo	150

E Estimated sizes of the largest countries in 2050 (millions of people)

Japan – geography and people

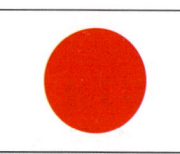

> Understanding the geography of Japan
> Learning about traditional and western culture in Japan

A Two quizzes about Japan

Do you know anything about the geography of Japan? Try to answer the quiz questions below before looking at the rest of the page.

QUIZ 1
JAPANESE GEOGRAPHY

Fuji	Hiroshima	Hokkaido	Honshu
Kyoto	Kobe	Kyushu	Narita	Osaka
Sapporo	Shikoku	Tokyo	Yokohama

1. Name the largest island in Japan.
2. Which is the capital city?
3. Name the highest mountain.
4. Which was hit by a big earthquake in 1995?
5. Name the chief port.

QUIZ 2
JAPANESE COMPANIES AND BRAND NAMES

Canon	Fuji	Hitachi	JVC	Mazda	Minolta
Mitsubishi	NEC	Nikon	Nintendo	Nissan	Panasonic
Sharp	Sony	Subaru	Suzuki	Toyota	Yamaha

1. Name a maker of play-stations and games.
2. Which company makes mobile phones?
3. Name one maker of TV sets.
4. Which company has a car factory in the UK?
5. Name one company that makes cameras.

Did geography win? Probably not. Most of you will have done better in Quiz 2 because you have bought goods made by Japanese companies.

FACT FILE — WHAT IS JAPAN REALLY LIKE?

Look at **B**.

- Japan is an island country like the UK. Of the four big islands, Honshu is the largest and most important.
- Japan is in the temperate zone like the UK, but a little further south. Its summer climate is hot and humid, especially in Tokyo and the south.
- The south coast of Japan can be hit by tropical cyclones in autumn (page 110). These are called *typhoons* in Japan.

B Japan

Mountains make up 75 per cent of Japan. The scenery is beautiful in the Japanese Alps – jagged peaks, rocky gorges, waterfalls and thick forests. Mount Fuji (3276 m) is the highest peak (**C**). Most Japanese people live on the flat plains near the coast. Over 100 million people are squeezed into the lowlands, which are very densely populated. There is little room to spare in Japan's busy cities.

C Mount Fuji, a perfect cone-shaped volcano

A TRADITIONAL CULTURE IN A MODERN WORLD

Space is in such short supply in the cities that most families live in apartments that are tiny by UK standards. Most people sit on cushions on the floor and sleep on padded quilts called futons, which take up less space than chairs and beds in **western** homes. Not many people live in houses with gardens and garages. When land was needed for new projects, such as new airports for Osaka and Nagoya, it was 'made' by **reclamation** of land from the sea.

In Japanese society the group is considered to be more important than the individual. The working day in many Japanese offices and factories begins with group exercise sessions. The Japanese are more formal than we are; they always bow when meeting and greeting others.

First-time British visitors to Japan often notice these things.

- Japanese formality – everyone bows in shops, hotels and everywhere.
- Cities packed with people – crowds on the trains, in the streets, everywhere
- Many school groups, all immaculately dressed in uniforms.

The spread of Western culture

Western culture is spreading fast to Japan, and to young people in particular.

- Clothes – young Japanese follow western fashions and designs.
- Food – young people no longer eat rice with every meal. They eat more meat, bread and dairy produce than their parents. McDonald's and other American diners are popular eating places.
- Sport – although Japanese sports like judo, karate and sumo wrestling are still popular, baseball and football have many supporters. Big European clubs like Manchester United and Real Madrid make pre-season tours, because their Japanese fan clubs are so large. In 2002 Japan jointly hosted the World Cup with South Korea.

D Traditions survive longest in the countryside, where most people are rice farmers, growing some crops in terraced fields on the mountainsides

Activities

1. Make a poster to show the great scenery in the mountains of Japan. Choose a type that could be used by the Japan Tourist Office to attract visitors to Japan.
2. Write down *two* differences between:
   a) mountains and plains in Japan
   b) old (traditional) and new (modern) Japan.
3. **Postcard from Japan**
   Imagine that you are on a visit to Japan. Write to a friend and tell him/her about all the things that are different in Japan.
4. Find out what these are. They are all related to Japan.
   a) bullet train   b) kimono   c) origami   d) sake   e) sushi

Key words

Reclamation – making land useful for settlement or farming
Terraced – where level strips of land are cut out of hillsides
Western – lifestyles in Europe and North America as opposed to those in the East, mainly Asia

Japan – industrial powerhouse of Asia

> Understanding Japan's industrial success
> Finding out which industries have grown in Japan

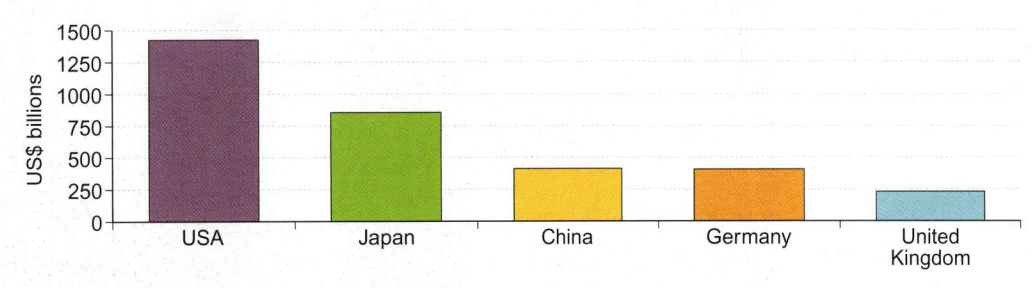

Japan is the world's second largest industrial country (see **A**). Growth of manufacturing industry since 1950 has been fast. Why?

A Top five countries for manufacturing output in 2003

FACT FILE — INDUSTRIAL TAKE-OFF

The Japanese success story began with **heavy industries** such as steel, shipbuilding and chemicals. New shipyards, filled with modern machinery, were built. Ships could be built faster and cheaper than in the UK. Japanese shipbuilders captured markets throughout the world. British shipyards were unable to compete and closed down.

Then the Japanese moved into **consumer goods** such as TVs, music systems, cars and cameras. Again they were successful, because they improved quality and reliability. At the same time they brought down the prices.

One reason for their success was the great use made of robots on factory assembly lines (see **B**). Japanese factories have some of the most advanced equipment in the world. Japanese companies keep on investing in new technology and stay in front of other companies in the world.

Technology take-off

Times were hard for Japanese makers of electronics goods in the 1990s.

- Wage rates were high in Japan and costs were going up.
- Wage rates were low in other Asian countries like South Korea and China.

Japanese companies were saved by the new **digital technology**. They were rewarded for spending so much on Research and Development (R&D) during the 1990s.

B Car assembly in Japan, where the emphasis is on quality, reliability and value for money

Across the world consumers are switching to digital.

From	To
Cameras with film	Digital cameras
Analogue TVs with big tubes	LCD or plasma flat-panel TVs
VCR video recorders	DVDs
Fixed-line phones	Mobiles with colour screens and cameras

Japan dominates the digital world. Seventy per cent of all digital consumer products made in the world are made in Japan.

THE CROWDED SOUTHERN COAST OF HONSHU

Half of Japan's people live in the coastal strip from Kobe to Tokyo. The built-up area stretches for over 300 km (200 miles) along the south coast. Most Japanese industries are located here. There is great competition for land and space.

The Tokyo **metropolitan** area includes the port city of Yokohama and the industrial city of Kawasaki. Together they form the world's biggest city with about 27 million people (London's population is 8 million).

You can see signs of wealth everywhere in Japanese cities:

- modern skyscraper offices
- streets lined with department stores, posh shops and expensive high-rise apartments
- roads filled with the latest expensive cars.

C Tokyo – a bustling modern city, full of traffic and people

Activities

1. a) From graph **A**, state the values for manufacturing output for Japan and the UK.

   b) Give *one* reason why Japan is a more successful industrial country today than the UK.

2. a) (i) Which digital goods do you and your family own?

   (ii) Look at the brand names – how many are made by Japanese companies?

   (iii) Why are more and more people buying digital goods?

   b) Finish this sentence:

   Japan is benefiting most as the world changes to digital products because …

3. a) Make a frame and draw a sketch or trace of Tokyo from photo **C**.

   b) Label *three* features that show that it is a rich and modern city.

4. **Brainstorm**

   a) Work in pairs or in groups. Think about what it would be like living and working in Japan.

   b) Choose the best ideas. Make a large table with one column for advantages and another for disadvantages of living and working in Japan. Would you like to live and work in Japan?

Key words

Consumer goods – products made for people to buy

Digital technology – converting audio and video signals into a form that can be processed by computers and accurately reproduced (through the use of numbers, i.e. digits)

Heavy industries – making large or bulky products such as ships and steel girders

Metropolitan – built-up area around the main city

South Korea – country of chaebols

> Finding out what a chaebol is
> Investigating the link between chaebols and pollution in South Korea

Have you heard of any of these South Korean companies: Samsung, LG (Lucky Goldstar), Hyundai, Daewoo? Each of them is a chaebol. Chaebols are the big Korean companies that dominate economic life in South Korea. Each chaebol produces many different types of goods, such as ships, cars, electrical and electronic goods (TVs, microwave ovens, etc.).

A Samsung's head office in Seoul; Samsung is now four times larger than LG, its nearest rival chaebol

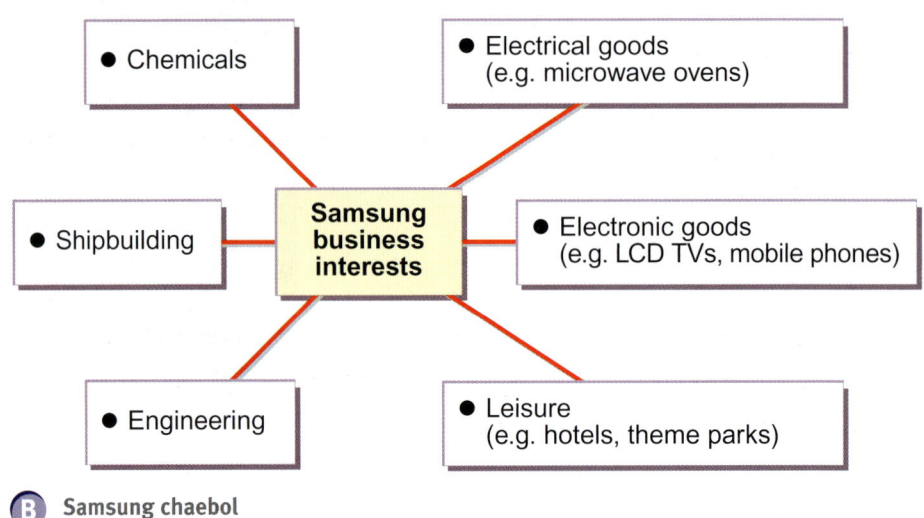

B Samsung chaebol

THE KOREAN MIRACLE

Dramatic industrial growth began in the mid 1960s. Before this time South Korea was a backward and poor farming country. Until 1948 Korea was one country. Now it is split along line of latitude 38°N. In communist North Korea the government does not encourage the growth of consumer industries as in the South.

Today the South has changed into a modern industrial country, exporting everything from ships to hi-tech goods. South Korea is very ambitious. It keeps trying to catch up with Japan.

What made the Korean miracle possible?

- Very low wages.
- No trade unions.
- Workers prepared to work long hours.
- Workers willing to put up with poor working conditions.
- High customs duties on imports.
- Easy export of goods across the Pacific Ocean to rich markets in Japan and USA.

geography 360° Foundation Book 2

Can the miracle last?

By 1990 many South Korean workers were fed up. They had worked long hours for low wages in terrible conditions for many years. Many of them went on strike. Wages have improved, but this makes South Korean goods more expensive than they used to be. Competition from China gets greater every year.

Samsung is switching to hi-tech digital goods, such as:

- LCD (Liquid Crystal Display) flat-panel TVs
- mobile phones – connected to the Internet with colour-screen cameras.

Higher profits are made on these more expensive goods. Samsung is the world's third largest maker of mobile phones after Nokia (of Finland) and Motorola (of Japan).

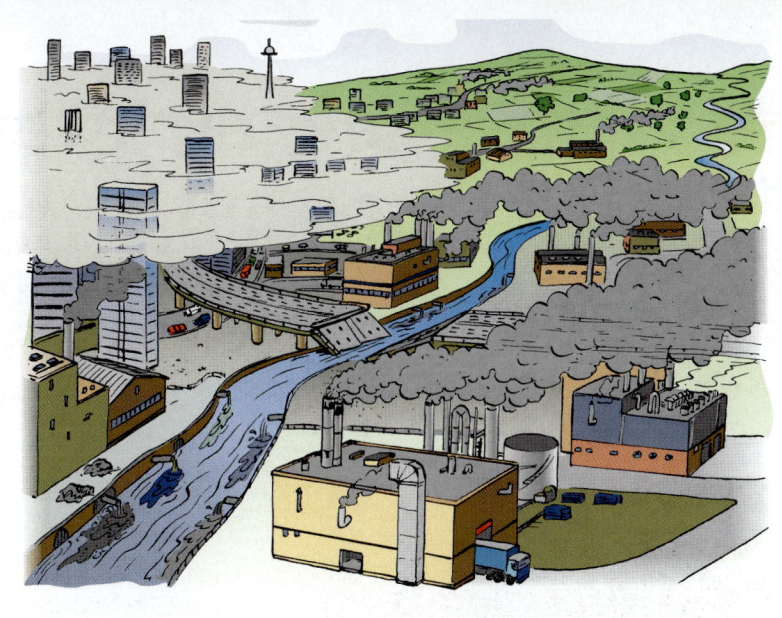

C South Korea after its Industrial Revolution

Problems for the environment

Pollution is a big problem:

- air pollution from traffic and industrial fumes in big cities like Seoul
- dead rivers full of industrial and domestic waste
- Yellow Sea contaminated by toxic wastes.

Factory-owners are more interested in making money than in protecting the environment.

Poor quality of work is another problem.

- A motorway bridge collapsed in 1994 killing 32 people.
- A shopping mall in Seoul collapsed in 1995 killing 500.

Building faults were discovered in both of them.

	1960	2000
Agriculture	62	10
Industry	10	28
Services	28	62

D Employment structure in South Korea (percentages)

Activities

Look at pages 145–155 of *SKILLS in geography* if you need help.

1. a) Use table **D**. Draw pie graphs for 1960 and 2000.

   b) Write out the paragraph below filling the gaps.

   The percentage working in agriculture fell by _____ between 1960 and 2000. In industry the percentage increased by _____ . The percentage increase in services was _____ . This shows that many people had left farms in the countryside and moved to live in _____ . Some are workers in factories, owned by large _____ like Samsung which exports goods such as _____ and _____ all over the world. Many service sector jobs are in offices, shops and transport. Examples of types of jobs done by workers in services include _____ (*list four or five different jobs*).

2. a) What was the miracle in South Korea?

   b) Name *three* things that made the miracle possible.

3. Work in groups.

   a) **Brainstorm**: look at **C** and think of ways to reduce pollution and clean up the environment in newly industrialising countries.

   b) Draw posters (i) to educate people and (ii) to show what places could look like after pollution control and clean-up.

China – geography and history of development

> Understanding the geography of China
> Finding out why China is not like Japan and Korea

FACT FILE   CHINA

A China

China is a huge country. In the north and west are the Gobi Desert, Himalayan mountains and Plateau of Tibet, all of them places where few people live. Instead most Chinese people live on the sides of the big rivers in the lowlands of the east.

The fertile floodplains of China's big rivers are good places for growing wheat and rice, the two main food crops in China. Wheat is grown in the Hwang-Ho (Yellow River) valley in the north; it is made into noodles and bread. Rice is grown in the Yangtze valley and in the south, where the climate is warmer. Farming is very important in China.

- 74 per cent of Chinese people live in villages in the countryside
- 60 per cent of Chinese workers are farmers.

The capital Beijing is in northern China. All the other big cities are in the east. The largest city and main port is Shanghai in central China. It lies at the mouth of the Yangtze River, the longest and largest river in China.

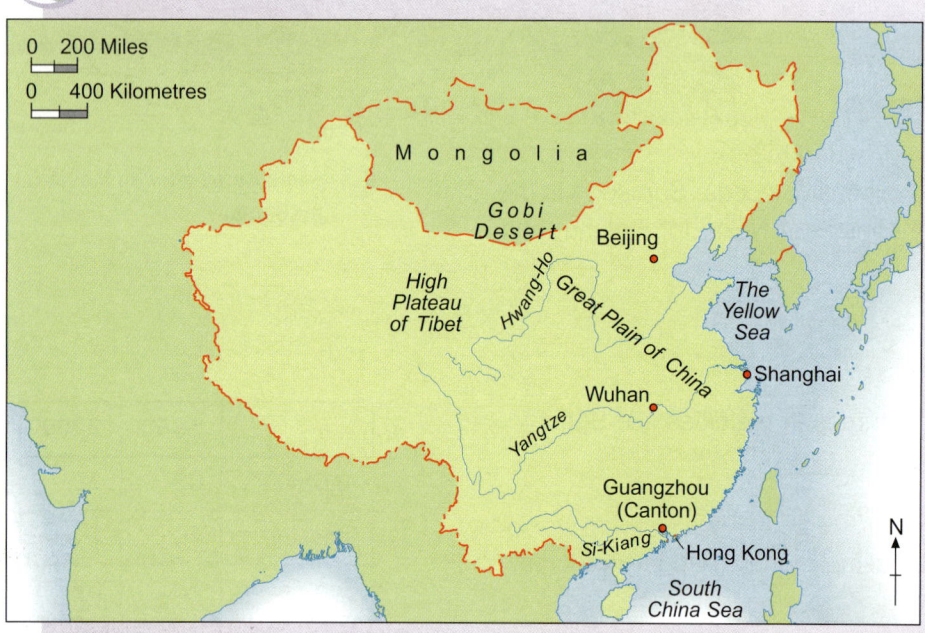

Typical house
- Built of mud bricks, clay bricks or stone; roof made of tiles or straw; three or four rooms.

Services
- Most have electricity except in remote areas, but few have piped water in the house.

Possessions
- Many own a bicycle, radio and sewing machine.
- Fewer people than in cities have a TV set, washing machine or motor scooter.

Daily life
- Work many hours per day, especially at busy times like planting and harvesting.
- Attend political meetings and night classes, where they learn how to read and write and how to use improved methods of farming.
- Have little time for recreation.

B Village life in rural China

A HISTORY OF SLOW ECONOMIC GROWTH

The Chinese civilisation is very old; it began 5000 years ago. Chinese people are proud of their culture and have always tried to keep invaders out. The 5000 km long Great Wall of China (photo **C**) was built to keep out the Mongols. Traders from Europe in the eighteenth and nineteenth centuries were just as unwelcome.

In 1949 the new communist government came to power in China and made big changes. It took control of all farming and industry. Heavy industries like steel and chemicals grew, but there was little trading with other countries.

Then in 1979 the communist government changed their minds. Big companies from Europe, America and Japan, such as VW cars and Pepsi-Cola, were allowed to set up factories in China for the first time. Industry started to grow and from 1995 growth has been very fast. The GDP of China grew twice as fast as the world average (see **D**), showing that China is getting richer.

C Part of the Great Wall of China, one of the human wonders of the world; building began as early as the third century BC

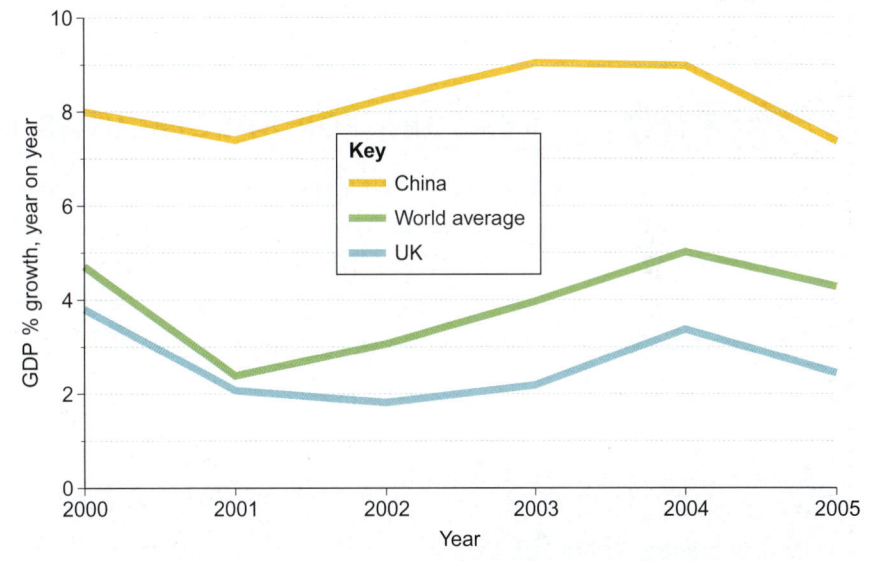

D GDP percentage growth, 2000–5

Activities

1. Write out and complete these sentences.
   a) Few people in China live in _____ .
   b) Most Chinese live in _____ because _____ .
   c) The two main food crops in China are _____, which are grown in _____ .
   d) Most workers in China are _____ who live in _____ .

2. a) Make a scale of dates from 1945 to 2005 for a time column (see the *SKILLS* box).
   b) Add information about China to the time column for these dates.

   1949   1950–1978   1979   1980–1984   1997   1995–2005

3. Work in pairs or in a group. You are going to make a pictorial map of China, i.e. a map with sketches and pictures to show what different parts of China look like. Look at *SKILLS in geography* pages 145–155 for help with this.
   a) Search the Internet to find a holiday company that does tours to China.
   b) Each person should look at a different tour and make lists of (i) main places visited and (ii) what visitors can see in each place.
   c) On a large outline map of China, add sketches, pictures and information about places.

SKILLS

How to make a time column

1. Make a scale of dates down the side of the page.
2. Write in what happened at key dates.
3. Use } for a block of dates and write in what happened.

For more help see page 155 of *SKILLS in geography*.

8 South and East Asia

China – the giant stirs

> - Understanding manufacturing in China
> - Finding out how this affects the rest of the world

China is different from other industrial countries because the government owns all the large factories. Industrial output increases by 5–10 per cent a year. China is now the third largest industrial country in the world after the USA and Japan (see **A** on page 130).

Some people estimate that China's share of world industry will go up from 7 per cent in 2005 to 25 per cent by 2025. Others think that the growth bubble will burst before that date.

FACT FILE — REASONS FOR SPECTACULAR INDUSTRIAL GROWTH

Think of all the things on sale in the UK with 'Made in China' written on them. Pencils, calculators, electrical goods, sports wear, Christmas crackers … can you add to the list?

Why are companies from Europe, America and Japan rushing to set up factories, offices and stores in China?

- Reason number 1: Low **costs of production**

  Wages are low and there are plenty of workers. The Chinese make good workers because they are skilful and hard-working.

- Reason number 2: **Market**

  People living in the cities are richer now and the Chinese market for goods is growing. With 20 per cent of the world's population, can any big company afford not to be in China?

Many city people already own a bicycle, TV set and one or two household appliances (see **A**). How will this change as Chinese people become richer? VW sold more cars in China in 2003 than it did in Germany. B&Q's largest store is in Shanghai.

Overseas companies help China's industry to grow because:

- they build modern factories using all new machines
- they train their workers, giving them new skills.

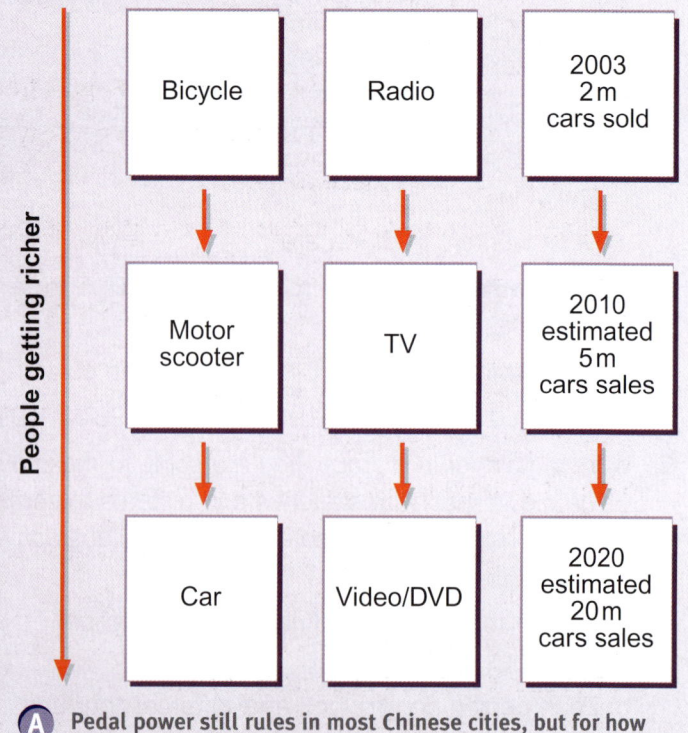

People getting richer →

Bicycle	Radio	2003 2m cars sold
Motor scooter	TV	2010 estimated 5m cars sales
Car	Video/DVD	2020 estimated 20m cars sales

A Pedal power still rules in most Chinese cities, but for how much longer?

THE CONSEQUENCES OF CHINA'S GROWTH

1 Scrap prices at record levels in UK
- Prices doubled for many types of scrap in 2003–4.
- China was taking all that was collected for steel-making in China for use in its other industries. Even disused cars in the UK were worth £70 by the middle of 2004.

2 Growth in demand for oil and other minerals/metals
- World market prices at record levels in 2004 for oil and copper.
- China is power-hungry because of its fast-growing economy.

3 Dynamic cities
- Coastal manufacturing centres are richer than they have ever been. The results of spectacular progress can be seen best in Shanghai, the great trading and industrial city at the mouth of the Yangtze River.

4 Poverty in the countryside
- There is a widening gap between rich cities and poor villages.
- City incomes are on average three times higher than rural ones.
- One in eleven rural residents subsists on less than 637 yuan (about £40) per year.
- The expected trickle-down of wealth from city to countryside is not happening.

5 Pollution in the cities
- A World Bank survey shows that sixteen of the world's twenty most polluted cities are in China.
- Haze and smog caused by low-grade petrol used in cars are worst in Beijing.
- Doctors blame smog for sharp rises in cases of bronchitis and lung cancer.

Activities

1. Draw *two* pie graphs to show China's percentage share of world industry in 2005 and 2025.
2. Think of *two* reasons why overseas companies are rushing to set up businesses in China.
3. a) Make a frame and draw a sketch of Shanghai from photo **B**.
   b) Add *three* labels to show that it is a modern city.
4. Write out and finish these sentences.
   a) Prices for scrap metal in the UK have gone up because _____ .
   b) City people in China are richer than country people because _____ .
   c) Air pollution in Beijing is very bad because _____ .
5. Work in pairs or small groups.
   a) **Brainstorming session**. Note down costs and benefits resulting from the recent spectacular growth of industry in China. Use two headings: (i) for China itself and (ii) for other world countries. Think of as many as you can.
   b) Draw *four* spider diagrams (for i and ii above) for costs and benefits of China's industrial growth.
   c) Do you think the benefits to China are greater than the costs? Explain.

B Shanghai – does it look any different from an American or European city?

Key words

Costs of production – amount of money needed to make something
Dynamic cities – urban areas changing fast due to rapid economic growth
Market – place where goods are sold

8 South and East Asia

The sub-continent – India, Pakistan and Bangladesh

> Understanding the geography of India, Pakistan and Bangladesh

In the years before 1947 India was ruled by the British as one country, despite being 30 times larger than the UK and having people with many different religions and languages.

PHYSICAL GEOGRAPHY

The Indian sub-continent splits neatly into three natural regions (see **A**). The Great Plain is the most important region for people. It stretches across all three countries.

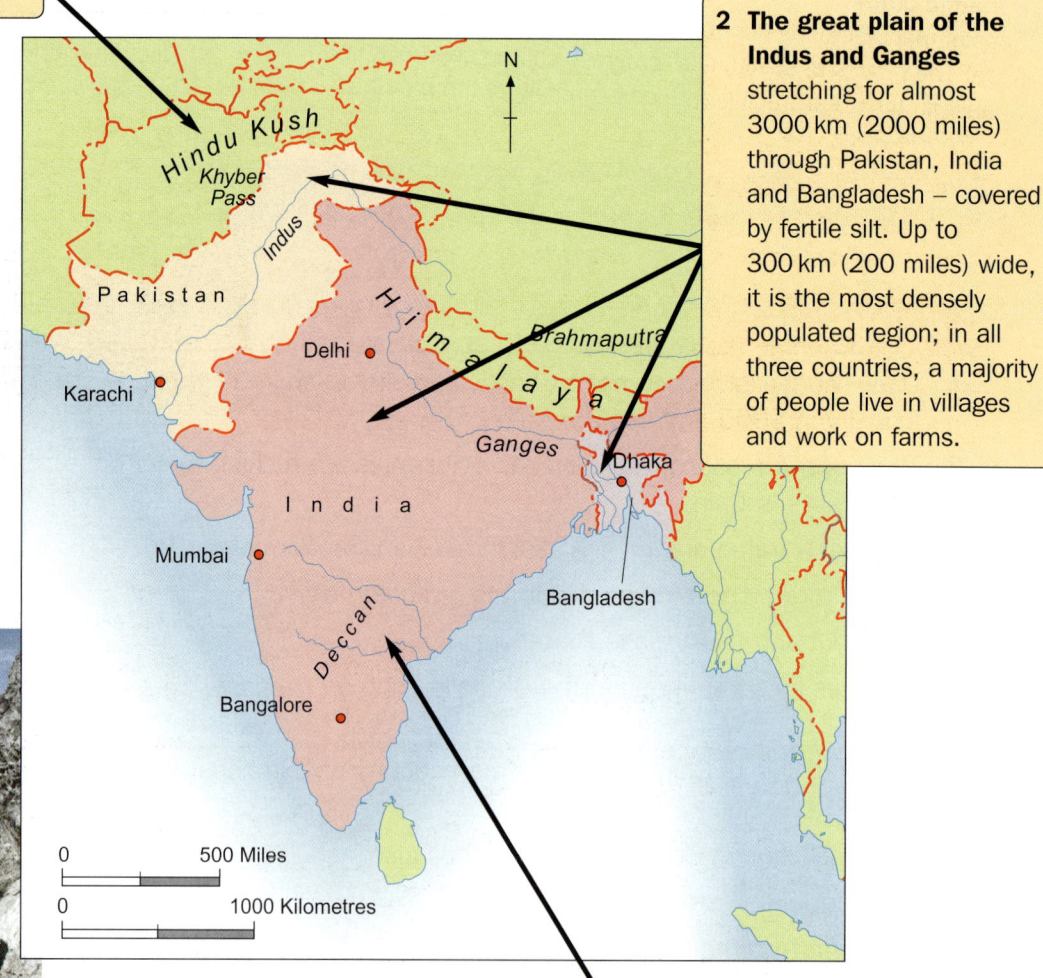

1. **Himalayan mountains** leading into the Hindu Kush range in the north west – a great natural barrier with peaks more than 8 km high. At the top, the mountains are an uninhabitable world of snow, ice and bare rock. Routes through this formidable mountain barrier are few and far between; one of the best known is the Khyber Pass (see **B**).

2. **The great plain of the Indus and Ganges** stretching for almost 3000 km (2000 miles) through Pakistan, India and Bangladesh – covered by fertile silt. Up to 300 km (200 miles) wide, it is the most densely populated region; in all three countries, a majority of people live in villages and work on farms.

3. **The Deccan plateau** in peninsular India – a large triangular area of land. Mountain ranges border its eastern and western sides before the land drops down to coastal plains next to the Indian Ocean. Shortage of water is a problem in some parts. Population densities vary greatly from high to low.

B The Khyber Pass links Afghanistan and Pakistan; it has been important for trade between the West (Europe) and the East (India and Far East) for centuries

A Natural regions

HUMAN GEOGRAPHY

India is much larger than the other two countries. All three are poor countries with many people (see **C**). In the cities, streets and trains are always full of people (photo **D**).

In all three countries religion plays a very important part in the daily life of people. When British rule in India ended in 1947, Pakistan was created as a country for Muslims. Most Indians are Hindus. Muslims and Hindus have different customs, which is why they wanted to live in different countries.

At first Pakistan was split into two parts, West Pakistan and East Pakistan, but they were cut off from each by more than 1600 km (1000 miles). Except for the Muslim religion, they had little in common. In 1971 West Pakistan became Pakistan (where Urdu is the main language) and East Pakistan became Bangladesh (meaning 'land of Bengali-speaking people').

India and Pakistan are great rivals. When they play each other at cricket, every match is like a cup final. Cricket is the number one sport in both countries.

	India	Pakistan	Bangladesh
Total population (millions)	1025	145	140
Population density	312	180	975
Population growth (% per year)	1.5	2.4	2.0
GDP per head (US $)	470	400	330
Life expectancy (years)	64	61	61
Adult literacy (%)	58	44	35
Trade (US $ billions):			
Value of exports	44.0	8.5	6.0
Value of imports	50.1	9.3	9.4
Main export	Textiles and clothing	Textiles and clothing	Textiles and clothing
Main import	Crude oil and oil products	Machinery	Machinery

C Country profiles (2003)

D Suburban shopping area and train in Mumbai, India's largest city

Activities

1 Study **C**.

  a) Draw bar graphs to show the values of imports and exports in the three countries.

  b) Work out the size of the **trade gap** in each country (value of imports minus value of exports).

  c) India is better developed than the other two.

    (i) Write down *two* pieces of information from **C** to show this.

    (ii) How do they show that India is better developed? Start your answer with: 'This shows that India is better developed because …'.

2 a) Make a frame and draw a sketch from the photograph of the shopping area in **D**. Add labels to show how it is different from a shopping street in the UK.

  b) Draw a sketch or find a photo showing a suburban shopping area in a UK city. Add labels to highlight the differences between the UK and India.

3 Look at the result from the 2001 Census below. It was for one of India, Pakistan or Bangladesh.

Hindus 80.2 per cent   Muslims 13.4 per cent
Others 6.4 per cent

  a) Draw a pie graph to show this data.

  b) Can you work out which country this result is for? Explain why you chose this country.

Key word

Trade gap – the difference between the value of imports and exports in any country

8 South and East Asia

Old India awakes

> Finding out how India is becoming competitive in the world market
> Discovering what problems this has caused for India

Until 1990 industry in India was not growing as quickly as in other Asian countries.

- Goods were of poor quality.
- Design of goods was out-of-date.
- Overseas companies were not welcomed.

From 1991 industrial growth has been faster. Computer software companies have done well. As in China, the main attraction for overseas companies is the huge market.

INDIA CALLING

Banks, airlines, credit card and telephone companies are moving work to Indian cities such as Mumbai, Delhi and Bangalore. On average India is 40–50 per cent cheaper than the UK.

'Differences in labour costs are crucial. In 2004 average wage costs including benefits for a call centre worker in the UK are £16 800, compared with £2300 in India and £4200 in Malaysia.'

'India is a highly educated country. It turns out two million graduates a year and most of them speak English. Workers in UK call centres are educated to A level at best.'

There are many advantages for India. Each new phone job creates at least one other new job in the service sector, such as driving, catering or cleaning. Indian workers learn new skills. Plenty of people want one of these jobs because they are well paid.

It's a dream job for Aditi Ekbote answering calls from HSBC customers. She has been at the bank's Hyderabad call centre for seven months... Aditi, 20, lives about 30 minutes from the call centre. She says, 'I dreamed about coming to work here since I was at university. My sister Poonam was already here and I saw what a good job it was.'...

Aditi works an eight-and-a-half hour shift including breaks... [She] earns about £2000 a year, but also has health insurance and is in the HSBC provident fund, the equivalent of a pension scheme. The bank also provides transport for staff to and from their homes.

A View from a call centre in Hyderabad, central India. Reproduced from *The Mail on Sunday*, 22 February 2004.

BANGALORE – THE SILICON VALLEY OF INDIA

Bangalore is a city in the south of India with a population of six million. It is the main IT centre in India, home to more than 250 hi-tech companies. The city is booming and growing fast.

IT companies are located on large new technology parks such as Electronics City (see **B**). It was built for companies in the fields of information technology, software development, telecommunications, financial services and what are described as 'other non-polluting hi-tech industries'. Both overseas companies (e.g. Siemens and Digital) and Indian companies (e.g. Infosys and Velankani) are found here.

Many of Bangalore's longer established textile and engineering companies are located at Peenya Industrial Park (see **C**). Why do new hi-tech industries not use it?

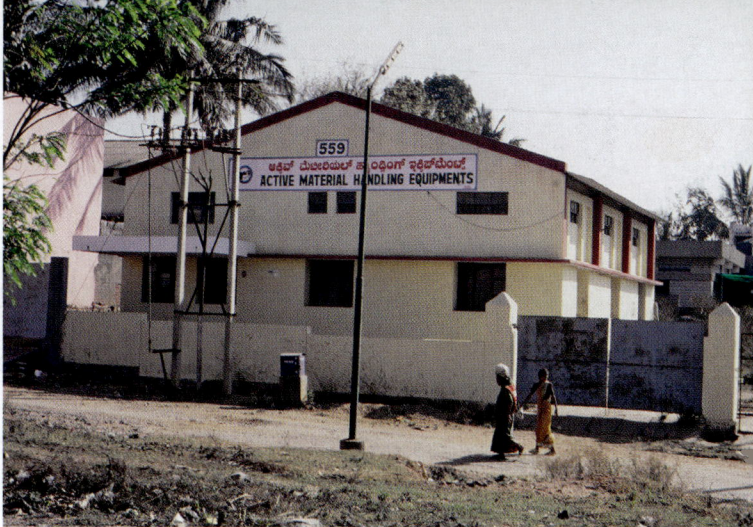

B Electronics City on the southern side of Bangalore

C Peenya Industrial Park

Public services in the city have not been able to keep pace as the city's population has doubled in the past fifteen years. Urban problems resulting from fast growth include:

- roads clogged with traffic
- frequent power cuts
- water shortages
- housing shortages: newcomers must build their own shelters (see **D**).

Activities

1. What is the main reason for UK companies moving jobs to India?
2. Draw a spider diagram to show the advantages of new call centre jobs for India and Indian people.
3. List some of the disadvantages affecting India's quick growth.
4. a) Make a table to show the differences between Electronics City (photo **B**) and older industrial parks (photo **C**) in Bangalore. Use these two headings:

   (i) What the buildings look like
   (ii) What the area around the buildings looks like
5. Draw a poster to advertise Electronics City in Bangalore. Use Hotlinks (see page 2) to find out more about IT in Bangalore.
6. Look at the comments in **E** about companies moving to India.
   a) Which one is not worried about more jobs going to India?
   b) Explain why the other two are worried about UK jobs going to India.

D 'Homes' of new arrivals on the edge of Electronics City

Businesswoman:
'There are 800 000 call centre jobs in the UK. The estimate for India is 60–80 000.'

Trade Union leader:
'200 000 UK jobs in banking and insurance could go by 2008.'

Labour MP:
'This is a drip, drip process. People in my constituency are extremely worried about the future of business in the town.'

E Comments made in the UK in 2003

8 South and East Asia

Bangladesh – struggling with its geography

> Finding out about Bangladesh's unique geography
> Understanding the advantages and disadvantages of its geography

Bangladesh is a very poor country. The main feature of its geography is that it lies on the world's largest delta, formed by two of Asia's big rivers, the Ganges and Brahmaputra.

What is *good* about living on a delta?
1. Very fertile silt soils – another layer of silt is deposited in every flood.
2. All the land is flat.
3. There is plenty of water for growing crops.

Rice (the staple food) and jute (exported to use for sacking and for backing on carpets) are the two main crops. More than 60 per cent of workers in Bangladesh are farmers.

What is *bad* about delta living?
1. Rivers, lakes and swamps cover 10 per cent of the land area.
2. More than half the country is less than one metre above sea level.
3. Flooding occurs almost every year.

Both monsoons and cyclones dump great amounts of rainwater from time to time. In September 2004 Dhaka, the capital city, had its worst rains for 50 years: 350 mm of rain fell in 24 hours on 13 September.

FACT FILE — FLOODING IN BANGLADESH, 2004

The flood that sank a nation

The people of Bangladesh used to expect the mighty Brahmaputra River to overflow about every 20 years, bringing death and destruction in its wake.

Then came a 1960s master plan for flood prevention... millions of pounds [of] aid were pumped into massive engineering projects. The depressing result was that the floods came even faster.

The gap between big floods shortened to 14 years, then 10 years and... 6 years after the devastating floods in 1998, much of Bangladesh is under water again.

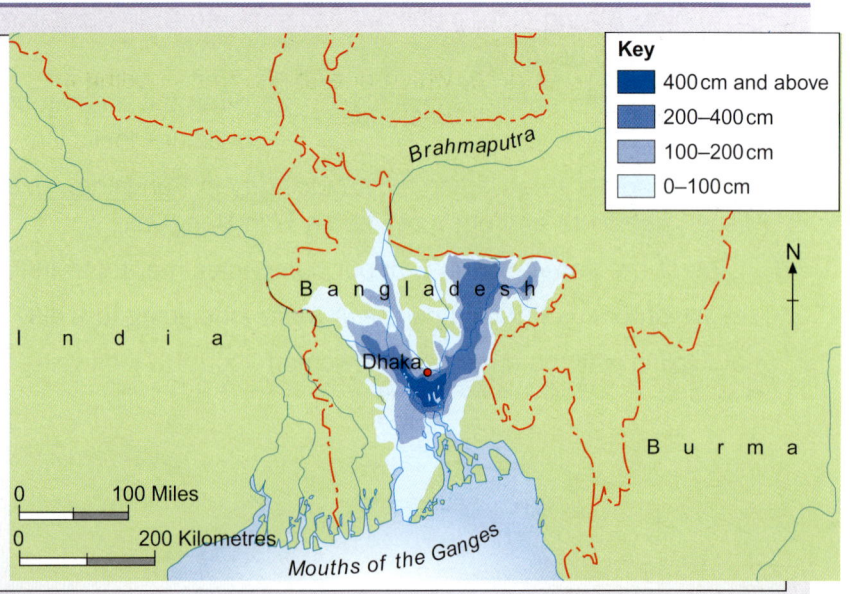

A Adapted from a newspaper report by Leonard Doyle, *The Independent*, 28 July 2004. © *The Independent* (2004).

B Devastating floods in 2004 – depth of flood water

Key:
- 400 cm and above
- 200–400 cm
- 100–200 cm
- 0–100 cm

- Floods covered half of Bangladesh, killing more than 760 people, directly affecting more than 35 million
- An estimated 8.5m homes were destroyed
- More than a million children are at risk of illness or death due to acute malnutrition within the next two months without more intervention, according to UN
- Worst rain in Dhaka for 50 years, with 35 cm falling in 24 hours on September 13
- Dhaka government puts cost of repairs to roads, agriculture and industry at $6bn (£3.3bn); World Bank estimate is $2bn
- Rice crops, fish farming and salt production badly affected
- World food programme distributing high-energy biscuits daily for next 10 months to 80,000 children in worst-hit districts.

C Flood facts, September 2004. Newspaper report by Lucy Ward, *Guardian*, 29 September 2004.
© Guardian Newspapers Limited (2004)

Activities

J	F	M	A	M	J	J	A	S	O	N	D
18	31	58	103	194	321	437	305	254	169	28	2

D Average monthly rainfall in Dhaka (mm)

1 a) Use **D** to draw a bar graph to show rainfall in Dhaka.
  b) In which months is the risk of flooding (i) very high and (ii) very low?
  c) Name the *two* causes of heavy rainfall in Bangladesh.

2 You are going to produce a project about flooding in Bangladesh in 2004. Include the following:
- Causes of the flooding
- Number of people dead and how they died
- Other damage caused by the floods
- Labelled sketches to show how bad the flooding was
- Why it will take Bangladesh and its people a long time to get over the flooding.

3 Read the comments in **E**.
  a) (i) Out of the three, which one thinks that flooding in Bangladesh can be stopped?
     (ii) Why has it not been stopped?
  b) (i) Out of the three, which one thinks that the flooding cannot be stopped?
     (ii) Why not?
  c) (i) Do you think that flooding in Bangladesh can be stopped?
     (ii) Write down as many good reasons as you can in support of your answer.

Government Minister:
'Bangladesh is water and water is Bangladesh: floods are nothing new to us.'

Bangladeshi newspaper against the government:
'Flood control projects remain unfinished due to corruption. Builders bribe politicians to build blocks of flats and shopping plazas on waterways used for flood water.'

Overseas expert on flood control:
'The flooding can never be stopped. The real problem is a population growing by leaps and bounds so that millions of poor people are forced to live on the flood plain.'

E Comments made on the 2004 floods

Assessing 360°

Taking a different look at the world

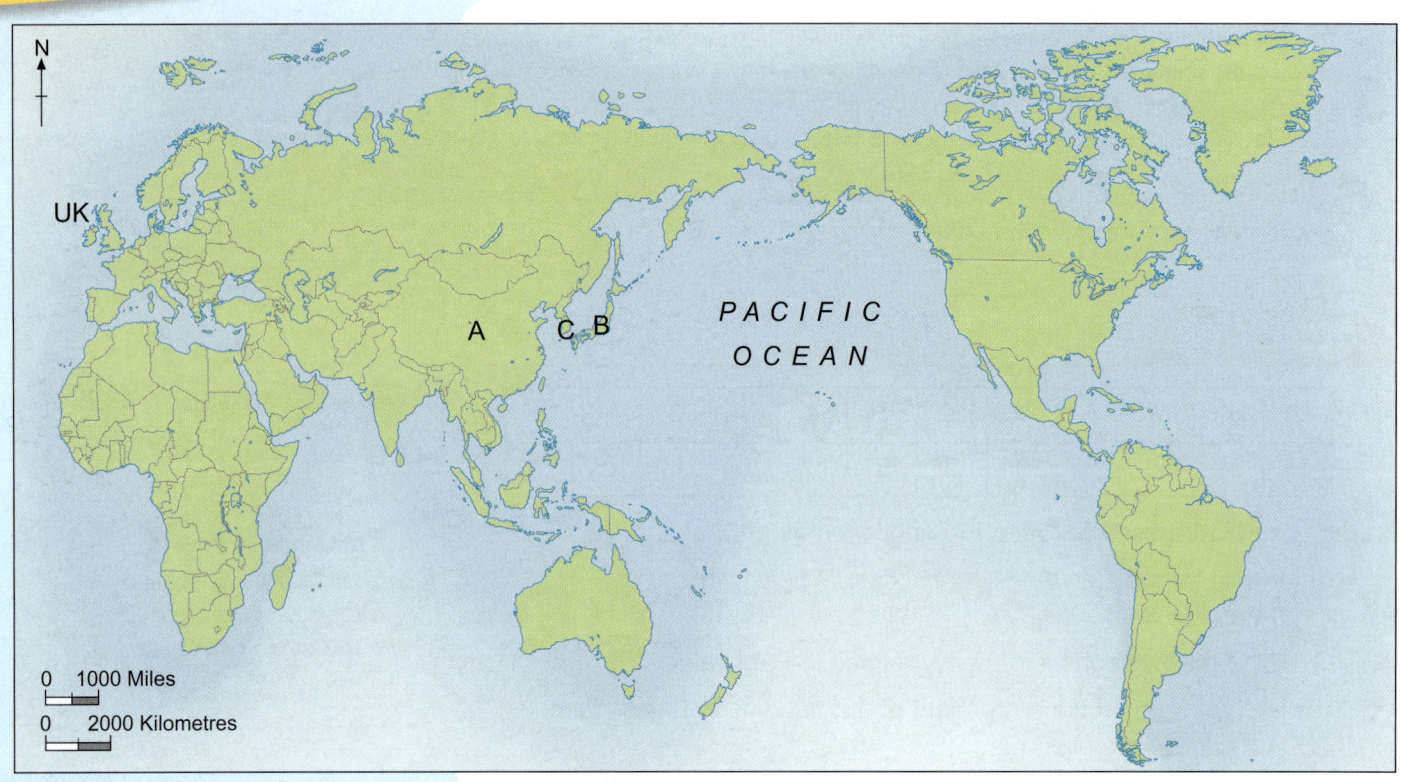

A World map

B Wealth of nations in 2000. This map does not show the real size of countries and world regions, but size according to total GDP (i.e. according to wealth).

1 a) Find the UK on map **A**. How is its position different from on most other maps of the world you have seen?
b) Name the countries lettered A–C on map **A**.
c) Which country matches each of these descriptions?
  (i) Population giant   (ii) Industrial giant of Asia
  (iii) Newly industrialising country and Asian Tiger

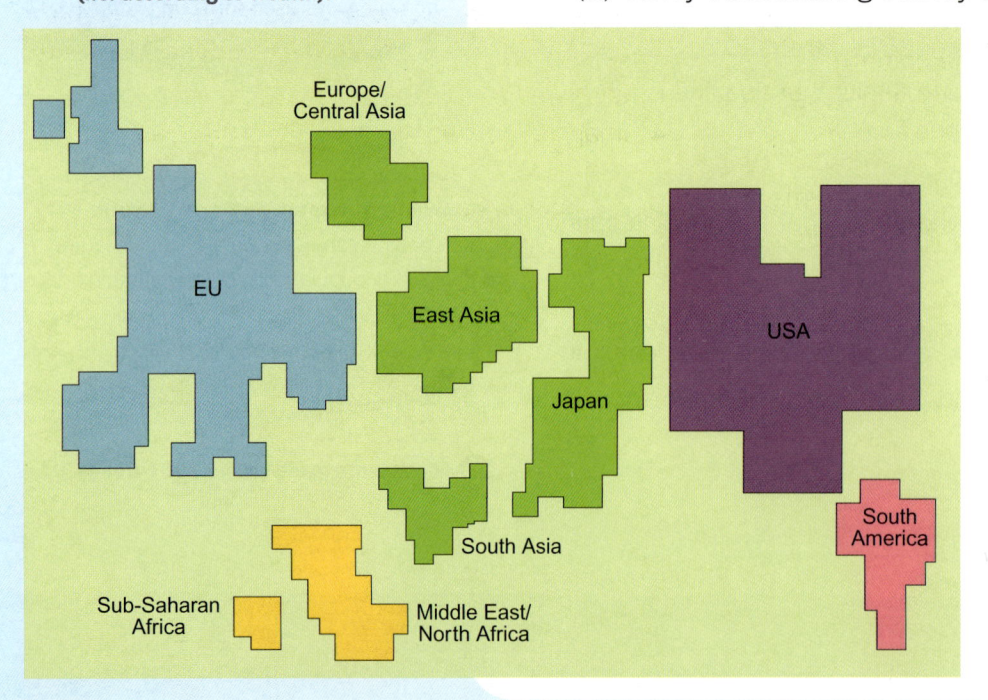

2 a) Find the UK and Japan on map **B**. How are their sizes different from on map **A**? Why is this?
b) Which is richer – the UK or Japan?
c) Write about the differences in wealth shown on map **B** between Asia and Africa.

3 a) Look at map **B**. *Many of the world's most important countries lie around the sides of the Pacific Ocean.* Is this statement true or false?
b) Explain your answer.

144 geography 360° Foundation Book 2

SKILLS in geography

1 ATLAS SKILLS

A How to use an atlas 1 – Countries of the world
1. Find the 'Contents' page in the front of your atlas.
2. Look for the heading 'World maps'.
3. Then search for a world 'political map'.

B How to use an atlas 2 – Finding a place
1. Turn to the 'Index' at the back of your atlas.
2. Places are named in alphabetical order.
3. The page for the map you need is given first.
4. Its square is given second.
5. Next its latitude is stated, and then its longitude.

Example:

Oxford, UK	**5**	**5E**	**51° 46´N**	**1° 15´W**
	Page	Square	Latitude	Longitude
			51 degrees	1 degree
			46 minutes	15 minutes
			North	West

The amount of information given, and the order, varies from one atlas to another.

2 OS MAP SKILLS

A How to give a four-figure grid reference
1. Write down the number of the line that forms the left-hand side of the square – the easting – 31.
2. Write down the number of the line that forms the bottom of the square – the northing – 77 (see **A**).
3. Always write the numbers one after each other – do not add commas, hyphens, brackets or a space.
4. Write the number from along the bottom of the map first, then the number up the side – 3177.

B How to give a six-figure grid reference
1. Write down the numbers of the line that forms the left-hand side of the square – the easting. These are the same as the first two numbers in a four-figure grid reference – 31.
2. Imagine the square is then further divided up into tenths (see B). Write down the number of tenths the symbol lies along the line – 319.
3. Write down the number of the line that forms the bottom of the square – the northing. This is the same as the second two numbers in a four-figure grid reference – 77.
4. Imagine the side of the square is divided into tenths. Write down the number of tenths the symbol lies upwards in the square – 774.

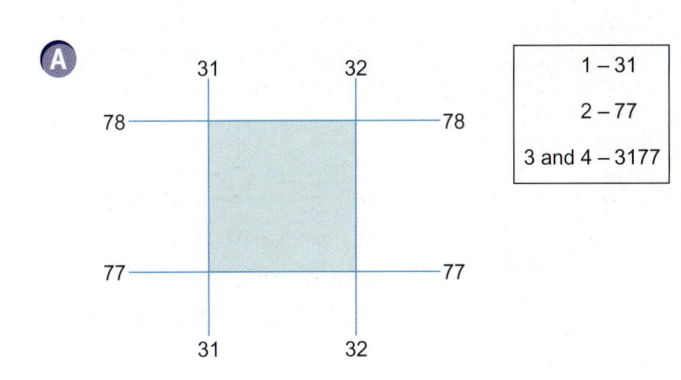

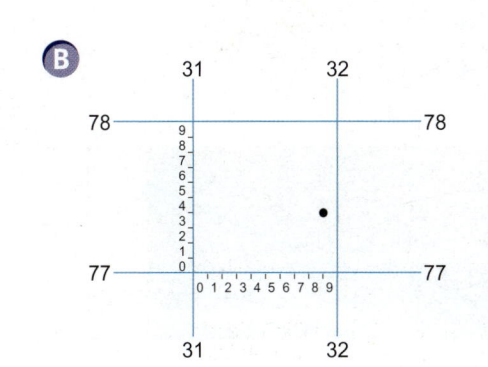

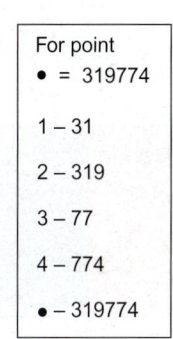

A
1 – 31
2 – 77
3 and 4 – 3177

B For point
● = 319774
1 – 31
2 – 319
3 – 77
4 – 774
● – 319774

Skills in geography

C How to draw a cross-section

When drawing a cross-section from an OS map, you will need to find out the height of the land. See the example below.

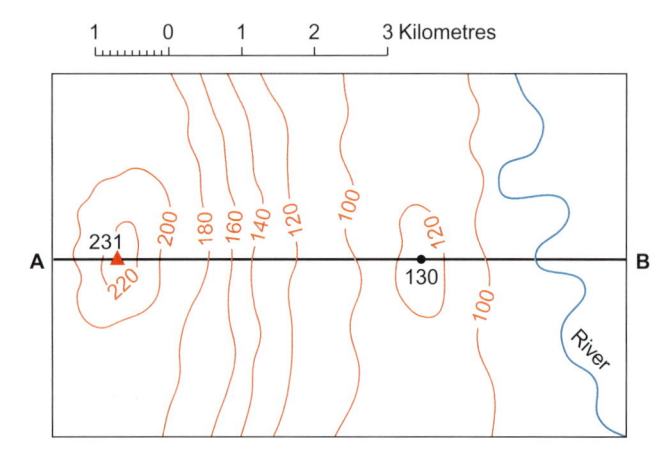

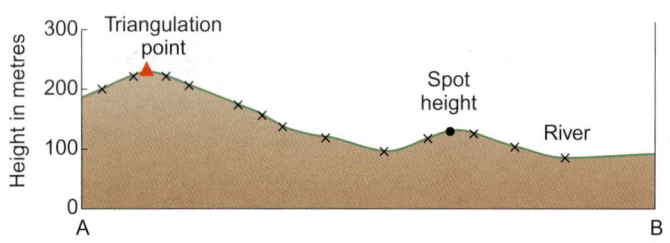

1. Place the straight edge of a piece of paper along the section and mark the start and end point of your section on the paper (AB).
2. Carefully mark on the paper the place where each contour line crosses. Note carefully the heights of the contour lines.
3. Mark on any interesting features, e.g. rivers, roads, spot heights.
4. Now draw a graph of your results. Draw a graph outline (see above). Note the lowest and highest contour height and use this to mark the vertical axis from 0 metres.

NB. Think carefully about the scale up the side – a good guide is 1 cm to 100 m for a 1:25 000 map.

5. Place your paper along the base of the graph and put small crosses on your graph at the correct heights and locations
6. Join the crosses together with a smooth curve – it is best to draw this freehand.
7. Add a title and labels for any key features, e.g. names of hills, rivers and roads.

3 GRAPHS THAT SHOW A TOTAL OF 100 PER CENT

This type of graph allows you to show the parts which make up a total. Think of using one of these four graph types whenever you have to present any data that has a total value of 100 (%). Graphs A–D all show the data in the table on the right.

Vehicle type	Number
Buses	20
Cars	70
Lorries	10
Total	100

A ten-minute traffic count near the centre of a UK city

1. Add up the values and make a total.
2. Draw a bar for the total value.
3. The bar can be either vertical or horizontal.
4. Add the scale to the sides of the bar.
5. Plot the different values.

B Pictograph

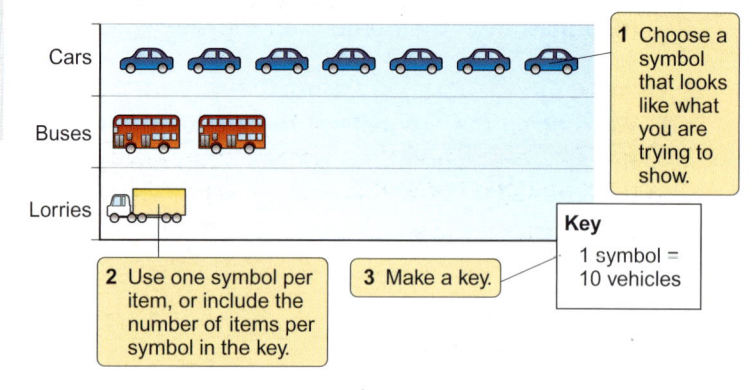

1. Choose a symbol that looks like what you are trying to show.
2. Use one symbol per item, or include the number of items per symbol in the key.
3. Make a key.

Key
1 symbol = 10 vehicles

A Divided bar graph

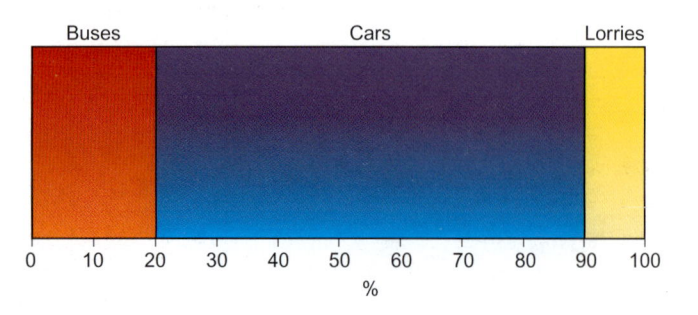

146 geography 360° Foundation Book 2

C Pie graph

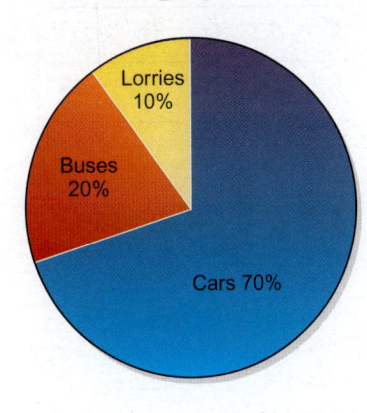

1 If you need to, turn the figures you are using into percentages.
2 Draw a circle.
3 Start at the top (12 o'clock) and draw the segments (from largest to smallest).
4 Make a key or label the segments.

D Block graph

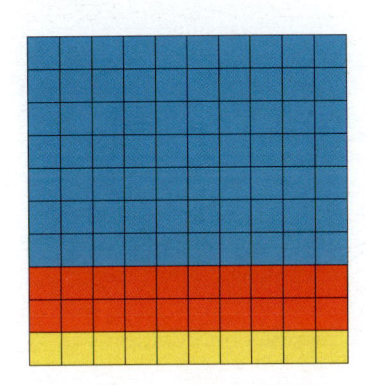

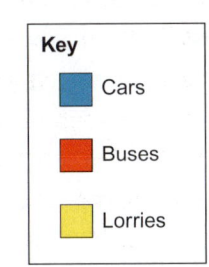

Key
- Cars
- Buses
- Lorries

1 Make a grid of 100 squares. Each square in the block shows 1 per cent.
2 Choose a different shade or colour for each value.
3 Shade or colour in the number of squares for the percentage.
4 Make a key.

4 OTHER GRAPHS

There are many different types of graphs. They are used all the time in geography. Sometimes it does not matter what type of graph you use. At other times, the type of data being shown needs a certain type of graph.

A Line graph

Always use a line graph to show **continuous data**. For example, the only way to show temperature is in a line graph:

J	F	M	A	M	J	J	A	S	O	N	D
4	5	7	10	13	16	18	17	15	11	8	5

Average monthly temperatures in London (°C)

1 Draw the two axes, one vertical and one horizontal.
2 Label what each axis shows.
3 Look at the size of the values to be plotted.
4 Choose the scales and mark them on the axes. 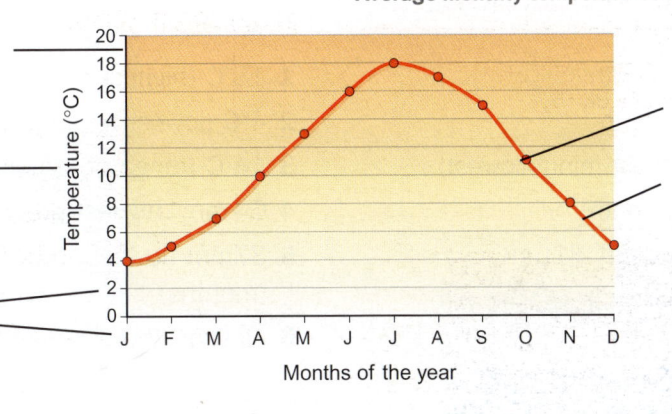
5 Plot the values by a dot or cross.
6 Join up the dots or crosses with a line.

Skills in geography

B Vertical bar graph

This graph is useful for showing data that changes every month, or every year. For example, the best way to show rainfall is as follows.

J	F	M	A	M	J	J	A	S	O	N	D
54	40	37	37	46	45	57	59	49	57	64	48

Average monthly rainfall in London (mm)

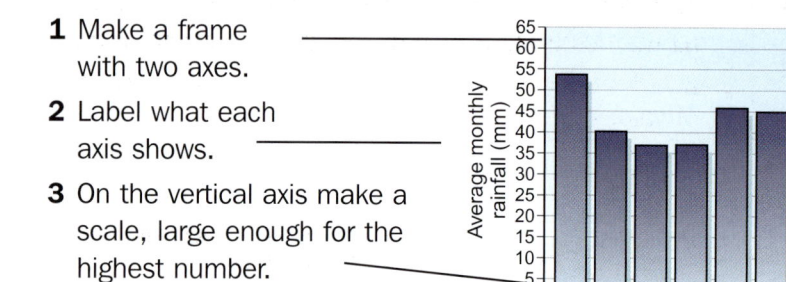

1 Make a frame with two axes.
2 Label what each axis shows.
3 On the vertical axis make a scale, large enough for the highest number. 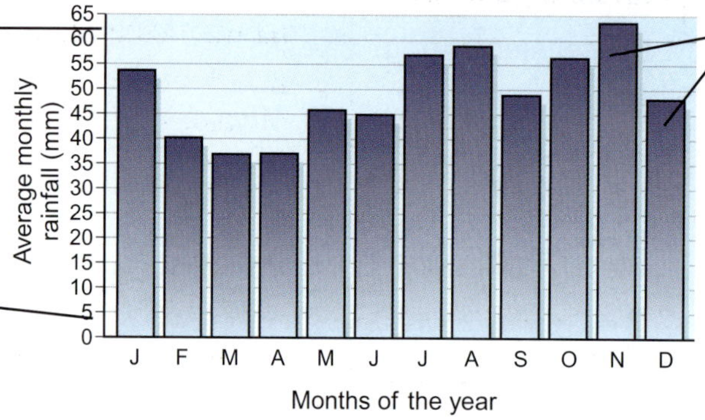
4 From the horizontal axis draw bars of equal width.

C Climate graph

How to draw a climate graph

1 Draw graph axes like those in the example here.
2 Allow 12 cm on the horizontal axis for twelve months. Label these J, F, M, etc.
3 Put a scale for rainfall on the lower part of the vertical axis.
4 Above this put a scale for temperature.
5 Plot the monthly rainfall figures as a bar graph.
6 Plot the monthly temperature figures as a line graph. Place each cross or dot in the middle of the column because it is the average temperature for the month.
7 Add a title and label the axes.

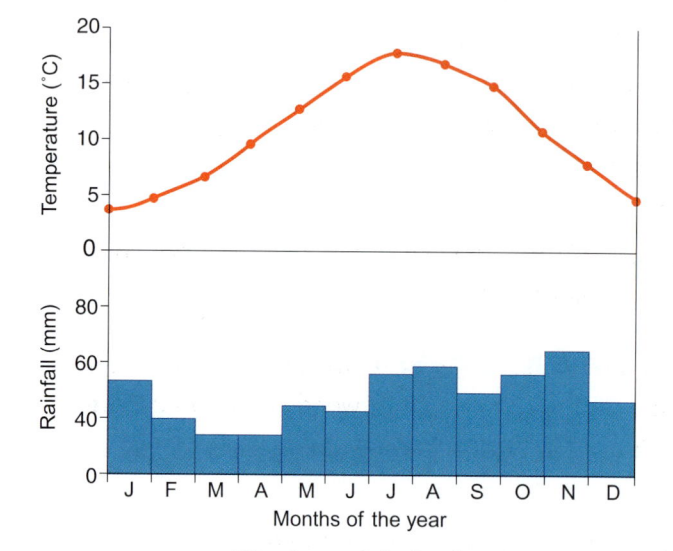

Climate graph for London, UK

How to describe climate graphs

Climate graphs show a lot of data. So, where do you start? The guide below is to help you select the information that is most important. It will make it easier for you to compare the climates of two or more places.

Find the:

1 highest temperature and month
2 lowest temperature and month
3 range of temperature (highest minus lowest)
4 highest precipitation and month
5 lowest precipitation and month
6 precipitation distribution (all year, season with most).

These are the answers for the climate graphs shown.

1 18°C (highest temperature) in July (month)
2 4°C (lowest temperature) in January (month)
3 14°C (range of temperature)
4 64 mm (highest precipitation) in November (month)
5 37 mm (lowest precipitation) in March and April (months)
6 All year (there are no dry months)

geography 360° Foundation Book 2

D Scatter graph

This type of graph is used to show the relationship between two sets of data.

Year	Number of working age (15–64) for every person 65 years and older	Estimates for pension costs as a percentage of GDP
2000	4.3	12.6
2010	3.8	13.2
2020	3.3	15.3
2030	2.8	20.3
2040	2.4	21.4

1 Draw the two axes for the graph.
2 Label the two axes.
3 Choose suitable scales to cover the range of values.
4 Place a cross or dot at the point where the two values meet.
5 Do not join up the dots.
6 If possible, draw a straight line which is the 'best fit' for all the points.

This graph shows a negative relationship (see below). As the number of people of working age **decreases**, pension costs **increase**.

If a relationship exists, it is possible to draw in the line of 'best fit' for all the points. The best fit line is always a straight line. It does not have to go through all the points. It is a summary line which shows the general relationship that exists between the two sets of values.

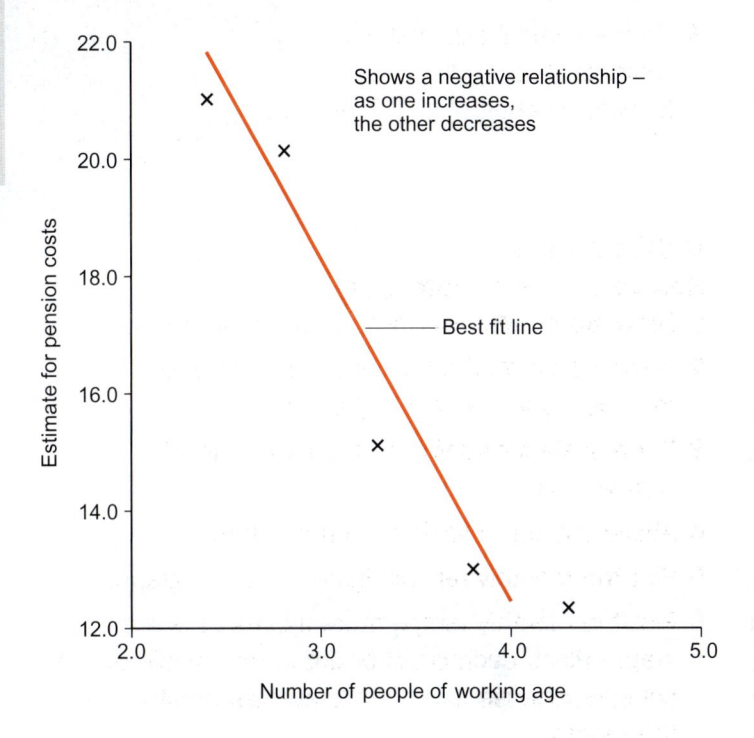

Shows a negative relationship – as one increases, the other decreases

What does the scatter graph show?
The three types of relationship are shows in graphs A–C below.

A Positive relationship
As the value of one increases, the value of the other increases as well. Both values increase at the same time.

B Negative relationship
As the value of one increases, the value of the other decreases. One is increasing and the other is decreasing.

C No relationship
It is impossible to see a relationship. The values are scattered all over the place. Drawing a best fit line on the graph is impossible.

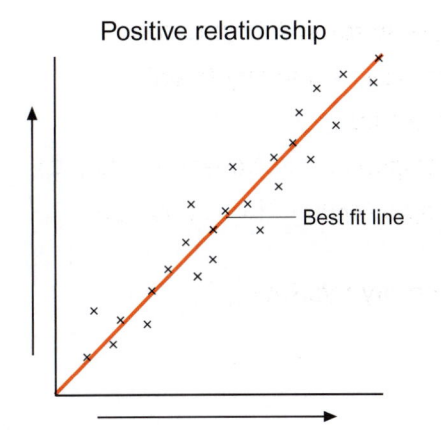

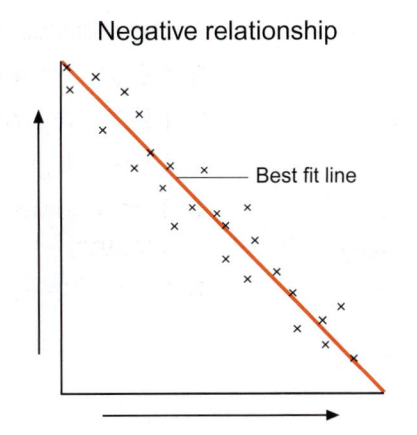

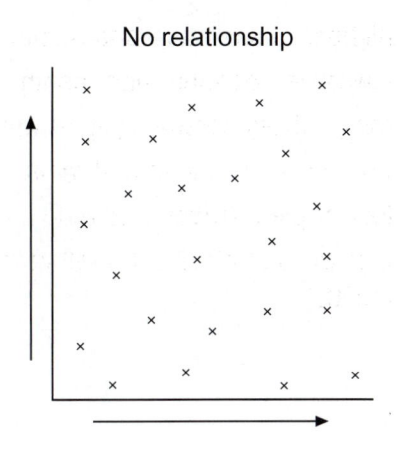

Skills in geography

E Population pyramid

1. Show the male population on the left and the female on the right.
2. Draw a horizontal axis with 0 in the middle. The scale can be in either percentages or numbers.
3. Draw a vertical axis from the 0. Divide into age groups, e.g. 0–4, 5–9, 10–14, etc.
4. Draw bars horizontally for each age group and gender.
5. Label the axes and add a title.

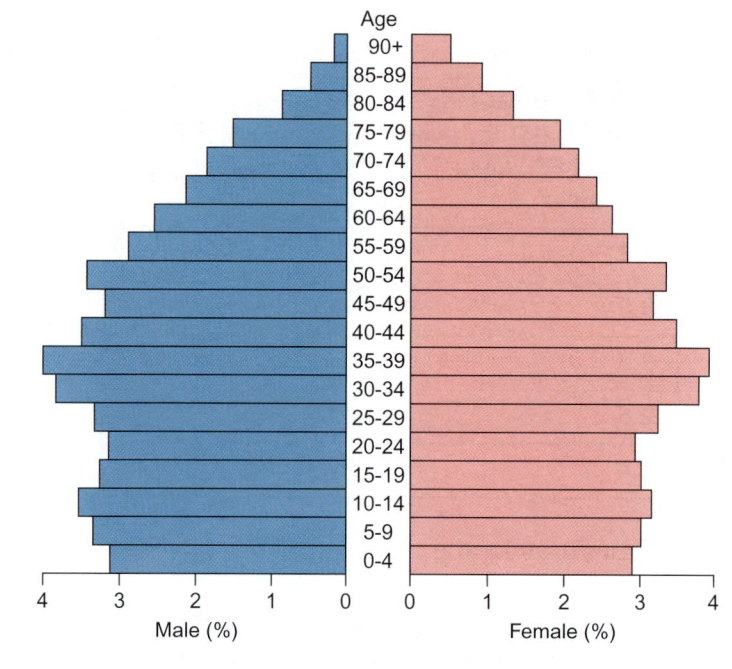

Percentage male and female population

F Block bar graph

Block bar graphs are useful to show two or more values on the same graph. They can be vertical, as here, or horizontal.

1. Draw vertical and horizontal axes.
2. Draw bars for one set of values.
3. Above them draw bars for the second set of values, and so on.
4. Colour in each of the divisions and add a key.
5. Label the axes and add a title.

	Primary	Secondary	Tertiary
India	65	30	5
Japan	8	30	62
UK	4	26	70

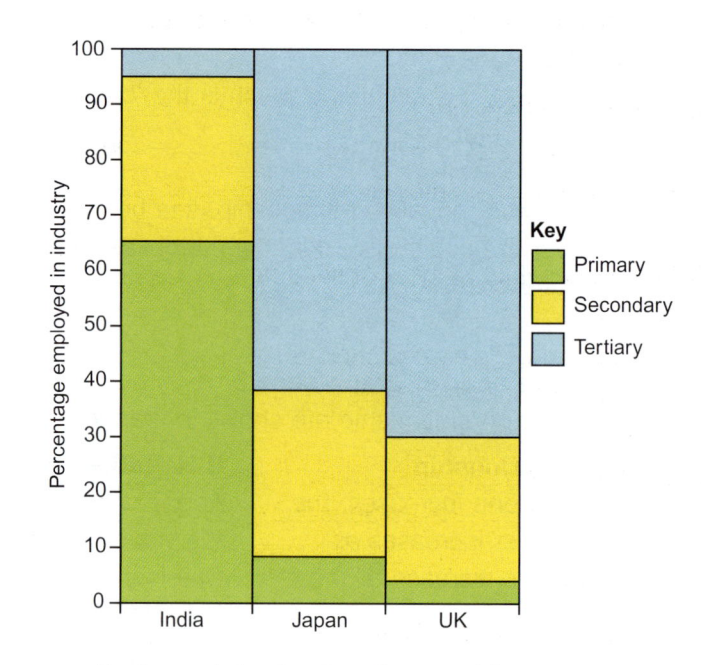

Employment structure in various countries

150 geography 360° Foundation Book 2

G Living graph

1. Draw your graph outline and label the axes. Put the years or time along the bottom and the other value (e.g. *How Laura feels*) up the side.
2. Plot the graph to show how the value changes over time.
3. Add the labels in the correct places on the graph.
4. Add a title to your graph.

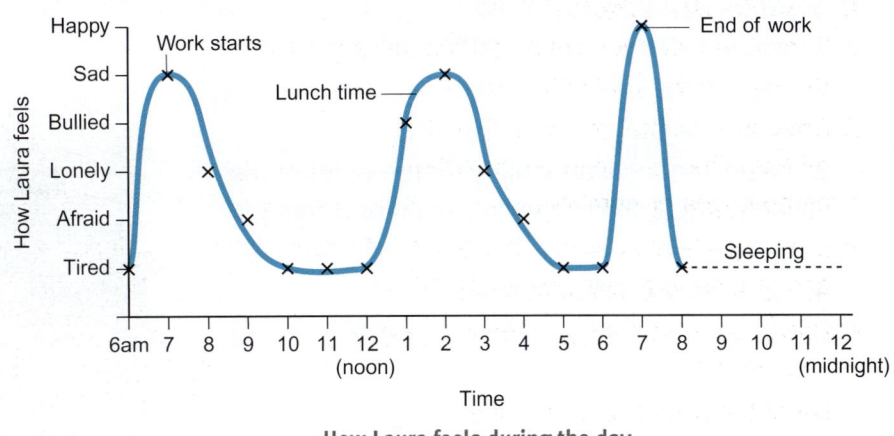

How Laura feels during the day

5 OTHER TYPES OF MAPS

A How to draw a shading (choropleth) map

Shading (choropleth) maps show data for areas. If you have a table of data for named areas of the UK (or for anywhere else), it can be used to make a choropleth map.

1. Look at the highest and lowest values in your table of data, e.g. the highest and lowest wage.
2. Split the values up into four or five groups of equal size.
3. Choose a colour or type of shading for each group.
4. Very important – always choose darker colours for the data groups with the highest amounts (values).
5. Look at your data to see which areas on the map match each value group you set up in step 2. Shade or colour in each area correctly.
6. Remember to add a key!

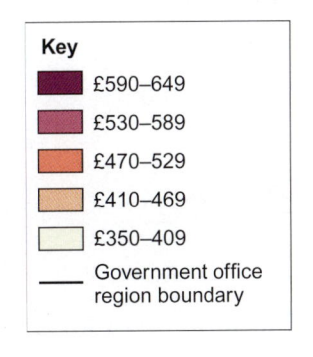

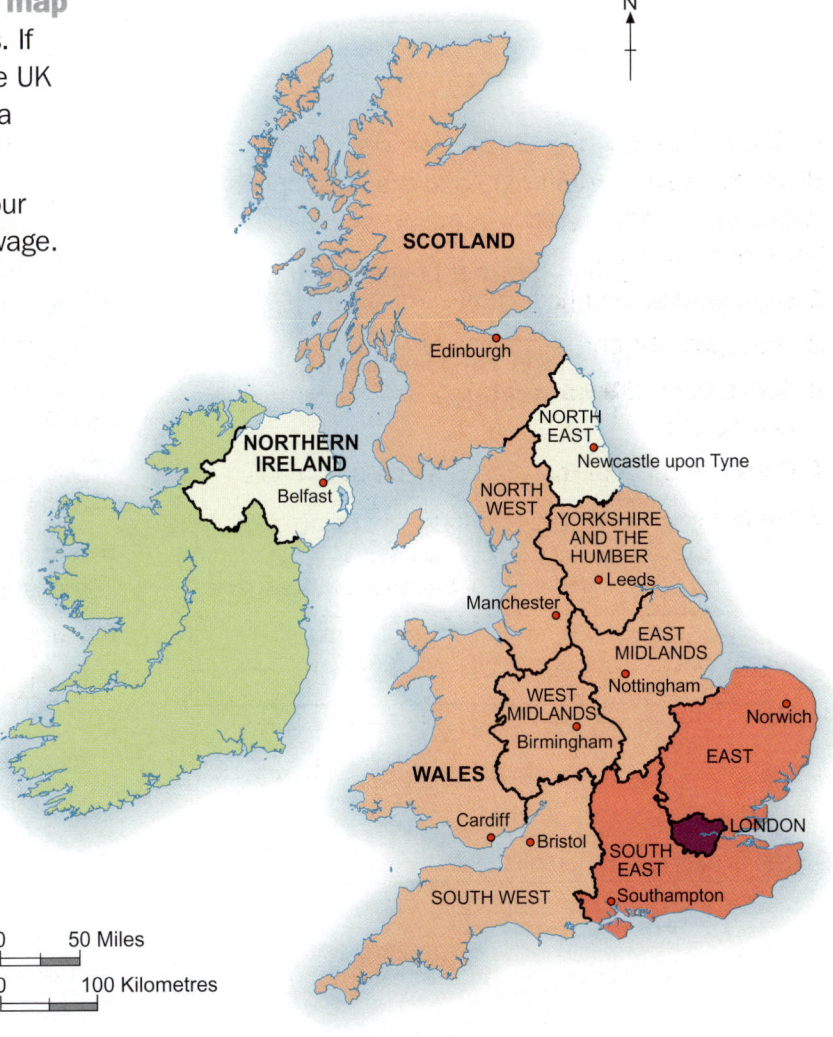

Key
- £590–649
- £530–589
- £470–529
- £410–469
- £350–409
- Government office region boundary

Skills in geography

B How to draw a flow map

1. Use a base map showing the places named.
2. Look at the size of the values and the space on your map.
3. Decide on a suitable scale for the width of the lines, e.g. 1 mm for each person or 2 mm for every 5 people, according to the space available.
4. Work out the different line widths.
5. Plot lines of varying width from areas A, B and C to the town.
6. Add a scale and a title to your map.

Where people travelled from	Number of workers
Place A	40
Place B	20
Place C	5

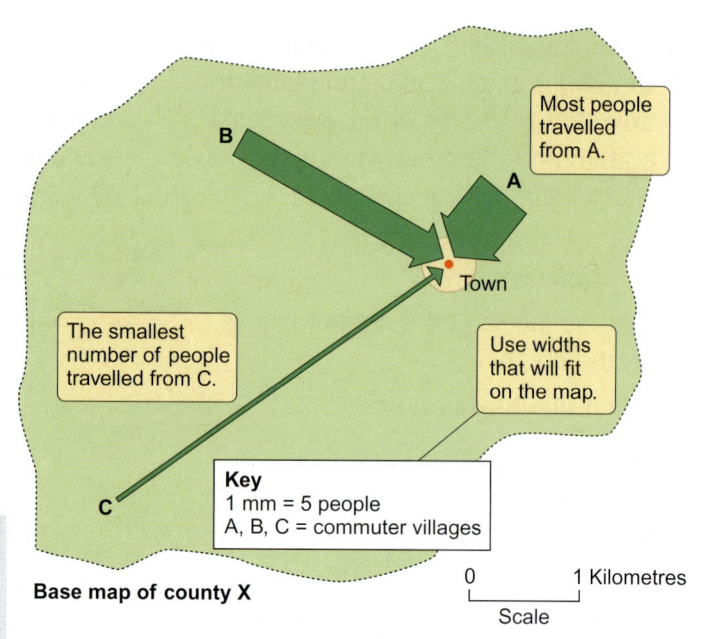

Most people travelled from A.

The smallest number of people travelled from C.

Use widths that will fit on the map.

Key
1 mm = 5 people
A, B, C = commuter villages

Base map of county X

C How to measure distances on a map

Using the cross-section map and the instructions below, you can see that:

The distance between the spot height and the river along line A–B = 1 km

The distance between the trig point and the spot height along line A–B = 2.9 km

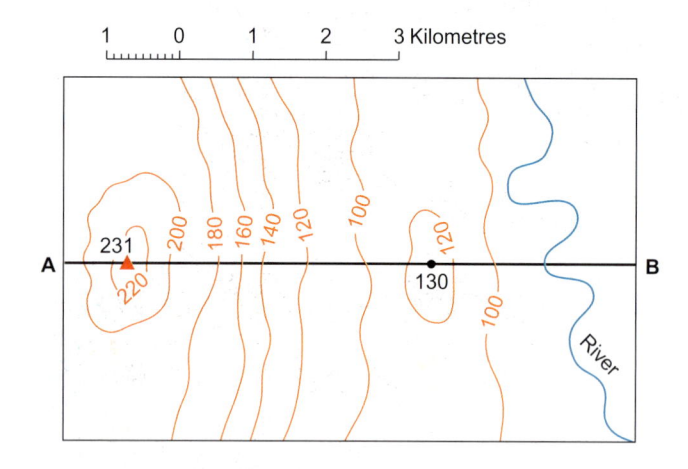

1. Using a piece of paper (or string if it is a winding distance) accurately mark the start and end point of the distance being measured.
2. Transfer the paper or string to the linear scale for the map.
3. Put the left-hand mark on the zero and accurately mark the total number of kilometres on the paper.
4. Measure the bit that is left using the divided section of the scale. This will be in metres.
5. Add the two together to give the final distance measured.
6. Remember to give the units (kilometres or metres) in your answer.

geography 360° Foundation Book 2

D How to draw a pictorial or mental map

Both use symbols, sketches and diagrams to show locations of geographical features on maps. Below is an example of a pictorial map to show farming. In a pictorial map, the map outline is always accurate and true. In a mental map, the map outline can be accurate, but it may also be distorted.

Pictorial map

This shows what is actually located in an area.

1. Draw or trace accurately an outline map of the area.
2. Make up symbols, sketches, diagrams etc. which look like the features to be shown.
3. Put these in a key
4. Place them on the map where the features are located.

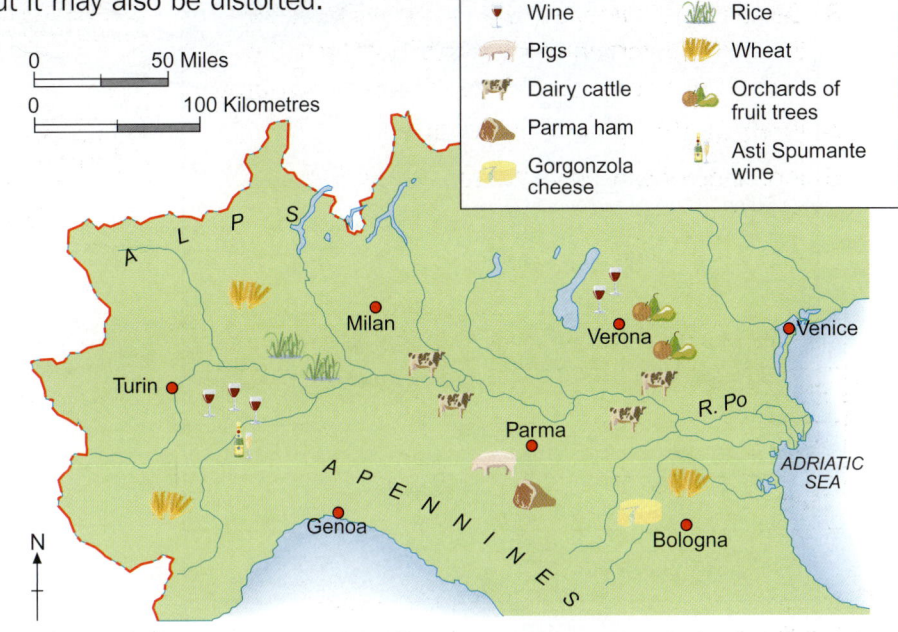

Key
- Wine
- Pigs
- Dairy cattle
- Parma ham
- Gorgonzola cheese
- Rice
- Wheat
- Orchards of fruit trees
- Asti Spumante wine

Mental map

This shows what people think is located in an area; for geographical features actually located there, it shows what people think they look like.

1. Draw an outline map so that the area can be recognised, even if it is not totally accurate. Remote areas can be made to look further away than they really are.
2. Make up symbols, sketches, diagrams etc. which look like people imagine the features to be shown. Features can be made to look better or worse than they really are.
3. Put these in a key.
4. Place them on the map where people think the features are located.

Skills in geography 153

6 SKETCHES

A How to draw a sketch map

The sketch map below was drawn to show differences in relief and drainage.

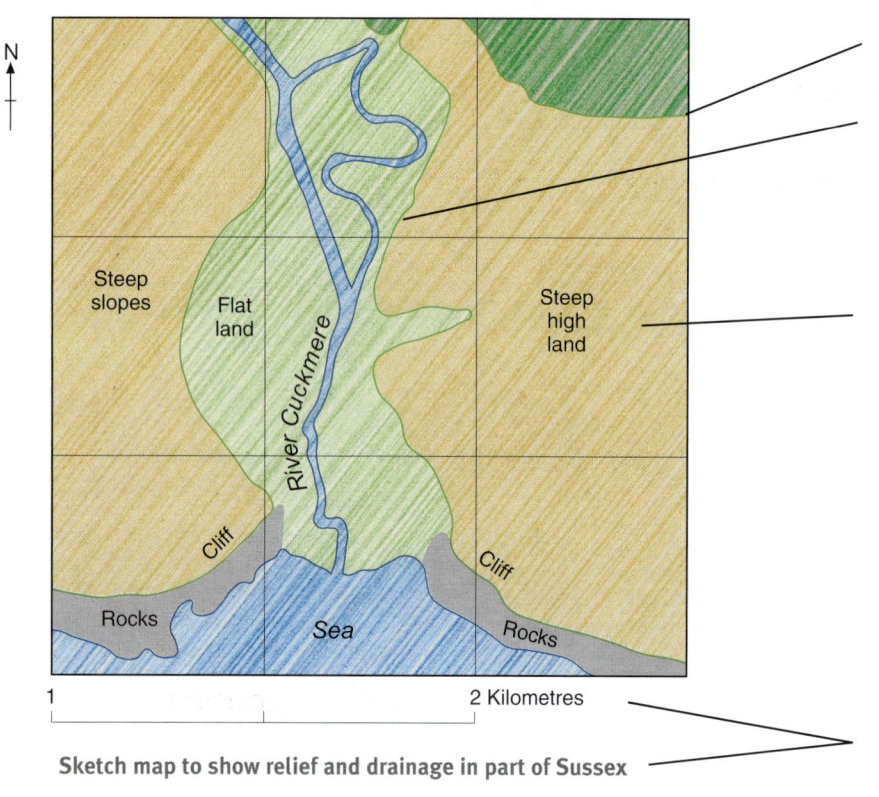

Sketch map to show relief and drainage in part of Sussex

1 Draw a frame for your sketch map – think about its size and shape.
2 In pencil, sketch the features you wish to show. Start with some accurate major features such as a coastline or road, or even lightly mark on the gridlines and numbers.
3 Colour in your sketch map. Add a key for the symbols and colours you have used.

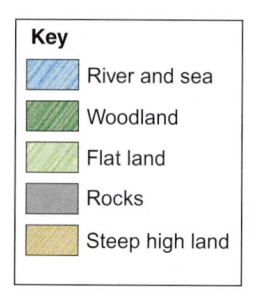

Key
- River and sea
- Woodland
- Flat land
- Rocks
- Steep high land

4 Add a title, north sign and scale.

B How to draw a labelled sketch from a photograph

Cley next the Sea, Norfolk

1 Make a frame the same size as the photograph.
2 In the frame, draw or trace the main features shown.
3 Label the main physical and human features.
4 Give your sketch a title.

154 geography 360° Foundation Book 2

7 TIME COLUMNS

These are used to show what changes happened at key dates in the history of a place. The information contained helps with an understanding of its geography today.

How to make a time column
1 Make a scale of dates down the side of the page.
2 Write in what happened at key dates.
3 Use } for a block of dates and write in what happened.

Date	Information / changes	
1350	Farming village	⎫ Farming village
1900	Most houses around the sides of the village green	⎭
1901	Mine opened; terraced houses built around the mine	⎫
1906	Railway station opened	⎬ Mining settlement
1957	Mine closed	⎭
1963	Railway station closed	
1971	Motorway built nearby	⎫
1974	Housing estates built	⎬ Modern commuter settlement
1994	Becomes a commuter settlement	⎭

8 DIAGRAMS

How to draw a spider diagram
1 Draw a circle (the 'body') in the middle of your page. Write the title in it, e.g. *Factors affecting farming*.
2 Draw lines ('legs') away from the circle.
3 Write an advantage at the end of each line, e.g. *Sunshine, Rainfall, Soil*.
4 You could draw a small sketch beside each advantage.

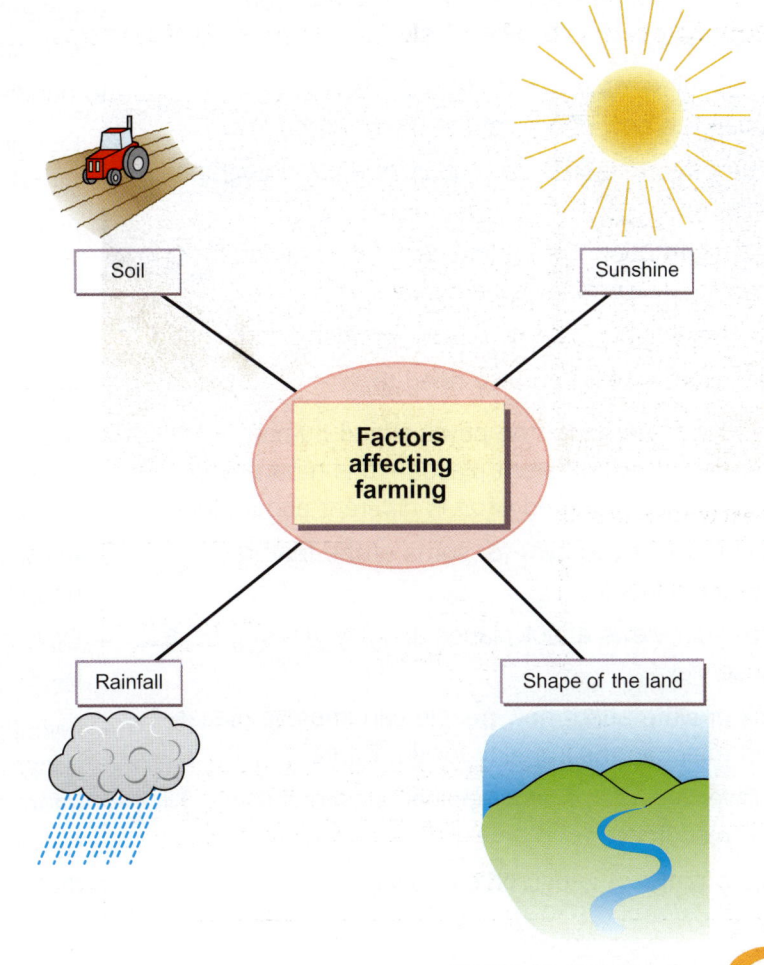

Skills in geography

Knowing your levels

Key Stage 3 attainment targets

The targets set out below should help you measure your current level of attainment or realise what needs to be done to achieve your overall Key Stage 3 attainment target.

Attainment descriptions

When looking at your own work or that of your classmates, try to use these bullet points to help you assess the work. Think about what you would need to do to get a piece of work to the next level.

To achieve **Level 2** you need to:

- Recognise physical features in the local area e.g. rivers, woods
- Recognise human features in the local area e.g. houses, shops, villages, roads
- Write about (describe) physical and human features in the local area
- Show an awareness of places outside of your local area
- Give your views about an environment or place
- Recognise how people affect the environment
- Select information from resources e.g. photographs, maps
- Use information from resources and what you have seen to answer and ask questions
- Use geographical words in your speaking and writing.

To achieve **Level 3** you also need to:

- Be able to compare the physical and human features of two different places – this means saying what is the same and what is different about places
- Give reasons (explain) for some of the features found in places
- Give your views about places and say why you have those views
- Talk or write about how people can improve places and maintain their quality for the future
- Answer a range of geographical questions using skills and resources
- Use a range of geographical vocabulary.

To achieve **Level 4** you also need to:

- Study a wider range of places and environments – at different scales and in different parts of the world
- Write about geographical patterns or distributions – be able to say where things are and where they are not
- Describe or write about physical processes e.g. river erosion and human processes e.g. migration
- Begin to understand how these processes can change a place and affect the people who live in an area
- Understand how people can improve or damage environments
- Give reasons for your own views and those of other people about a change to the environment
- Suggest geographical questions and investigate places/environments
- Collect primary and secondary data and present it in different ways and write about what it shows.

To achieve **Level 5** you also need to:

- Explain geographical patterns – why are some things found in some places but not in others?
- Explain the physical and human processes
- Describe how the processes lead to similarities and differences in environments and people's lives
- Recognise some links and relationships that make places and people dependent on others
- Suggest reasons for the ways human activity may change an environment and the different views people have
- Know what sustainable development is and how people try to achieve it
- Explain your own views about environments and places
- Begin to suggest geographical questions and issues
- Investigate places and environments using geographical skills and different ways of presenting information
- Select information, present it, write about it and draw sensible conclusions.

To achieve **Level 6** you also need to:

- Study places at a whole range of scales from local to global
- Describe and explain physical and human processes
- Recognise that processes interact to produce distinctive characteristics of places e.g. the climate in Europe is good for settlement and farming so many people live in this part of the world
- Describe how processes can interact and produce patterns and lead to changes in places e.g. over the last 50 years people have moved out of the centres of cities causing decline in inner cities – the pattern. This has led to a lot of redevelopment in inner cities and people are now moving back – changes.
- Appreciate the links and relationships that make places dependent on each other
- Recognise that there may be conflicting demands on an environment
- Describe and compare different approaches to managing environments
- Appreciate that people, including yourself, have different values and attitudes and that this results in different effects on people and places
- Carry out investigations to answer geographical questions and issues – collect primary and secondary data in different ways, present them using a range of skills, describe and explain what the data show and draw conclusions.

Glossary

Ageing population Increasing percentage of old people (aged 65 and over) in a country.
Air mass A huge block of air, thousands of kilometres across, with the same temperature and moisture content.
Air pressure The 'weight' of the air pressing down on the Earth's surface.
Altitude The height in metres above sea level.
Anticyclone An area of high pressure where winds blow outwards.
Aquifer Underground store of water in permeable rock.
Asylum-seeker A refugee who applies to stay in another country because they face persecution and possibly death in their home country.
Atmosphere The 'envelope' of air masses that surrounds the Earth.
Barometer Instrument used to measure air pressure.
Bauxite A mineral from which aluminium is made.
Birth rate The number of births per 1000 people per year.
Channel Area between the banks where the river flows.
Climate An area's average weather over a period of time.
Cloud Millions of tiny water droplets or ice crystals.
Colonies Countries owned and governed by other countries.
Communist or socialist Countries where the State plans and runs most economic activities.
Condensation When water vapour, a gas, is changed into water as a liquid in water droplets and clouds by cooling.
Consumer goods Products made for people to buy.
Convection current When warm air rises through the air.
Core region Area most attractive for settlement and most densely populated in a region.
Costs of production Amount of money needed to make something.
Death rate The number of deaths per 1000 people per year.
Depression A swirling system with low pressure at the centre and fronts.
Development Level of growth and wealth of a country.
Digital technology Converting audio and video signals into a form that can be processed by computers and accurately reproduced (through the use of numbers, i.e. digits).
Distribution How the population of an area is spread.
Drainage basin Area of land drained by a river and its tributaries.
Drought Period of dry weather beyond that normally expected.
Dynamic cities Urban areas changing fast due to rapid economic growth.
Economic migrant Someone who moves to another country for a better standard of living.

Eco-tourism Allows tourists to have a good holiday but conserves the environment and involves the local people (also called green tourism).
EU The European Union, many countries in Europe have joined.
Evaporation When water from lakes and seas is changed into water vapour, a gas, by heating.
Evapo-transpiration Loss of water into the atmosphere from all surface sources.
Fertility rate Average number of children born to a woman in her lifetime.
Floodplain Area of flat land on the sides of a river.
Fold mountains Mountains formed by rocks being folded and uplifted.
Front The zone where two blocks of air meet.
GDP (Gross domestic product) The amount of money a country makes from the production of goods and services divided by the total population; the higher the GDP the richer the country.
Gender The sex of a person, male or female.
Gorge Deep, narrow, steep-sided valley.
Groundwater flow Movement of water through spaces and holes in rock.
Heavy industries Making large or bulky products such as ships and steel girders.
Human attractions Facilities for tourists built by people.
Human development index (HDI) A measure of the level of development calculated on the average income, life expectancy and literacy rate of a country's population.
Infiltration Downward movement of water into soil.
Infrared Radiation that is similar to light but invisible to humans; it can be used in photography.
Interception When rain is prevented from reaching the ground by trees.
Isobar A line on a weather map that joins together places with the same air pressure.
Landscape The natural scenery of an area and what it looks like.
Lateral erosion Wearing away the sides of the channel and valley.
Latitude The distances north or south of the Equator; lines of latitude are parallel to the Equator.
Leakage When much of the money paid for a holiday goes to companies based in richer countries instead of the country visited.
LEDCs Less Economically Developed Countries; the poorer countries of the world.
Levees Raised banks on the side of a river forming a natural embankment.

Life expectancy The average age to which people in a country are expected to live.
Literacy rate Percentage of adults who can read and write.
Load All materials transported by a river.
Market Place where goods are sold.
Meander Large bend in the river.
MEDCs More Economically Developed Countries; the richer countries of the world.
Meteorologist A person who studies the weather.
Metropolitan Built-up area around the main city.
Migration The movement of people.
Millibars Units used to measure air pressure.
Monsoon Climate with one season of heavy rainfall, as in India.
Mouth Point where a river goes into the sea.
Natural decrease When death rate is greater than birth rate.
Natural hazard Short-term event that is a danger to life and property.
Natural increase When birth rate is greater than death rate; birth rate minus death rate is the growth rate of the population.
Natural resource Something that occurs naturally that people can use.
North Atlantic Drift A warm ocean current.
Onshore wind When a wind blows from the sea to the land.
Ox-bow lake Semi-circular lake on the side of a river.
Package holiday An all-inclusive deal from a travel agent; the package usually includes travel, accommodation, food and some entertainment.
Peninsula An area of land surrounded on three sides by the sea.
Periphery Areas in a region that do not have very many people and do not favour settlement.
Permeable rock Rock with spaces and holes that allow water to pass through it.
Physical attractions Natural features that attract tourists, e.g. climate, rivers, mountains.
Physical geography The natural features on the Earth's surface.
Population The people who live in a place.
Population density The number of people per square kilometre.
Population pyramid A graph showing the population structure of an area, country or region.
Population structure The numbers of males and females in different age groups in a population.
Precipitation All forms of moisture that reach the ground surface, e.g. snow, rain, sleet, dew.
Primary products Raw materials from land and sea such as minerals and crops.
Quality of life How well someone can live, including health and education as well as wealth.
Reclamation Making land useful for settlement or farming.
Refugee A person who is forced to move to another country, usually as a result of civil war, persecution or a natural disaster.
Region Area of land with one or more similar features.
Relief The height and shape of the land.

Reservoir Artificial lake used to store water for human use.
Runoff Movement of water over the ground surface after precipitation.
Satellite image A photograph taken by a satellite camera high above the Earth's surface.
Seasonal unemployment When jobs are only available for part of the year, leaving people without work at other times.
Secondary products Products made from raw materials, such as chocolate bars made from cocoa beans.
Service industry Industry where people provide a service instead of making a product.
Shanty town Area of slums with hand-built shacks where the poorest people live.
Silt Fine-grained sediment carried and deposited by rivers.
Soil erosion Loss of fertile topsoil by wind and water.
Source Point where a river starts to flow.
Standard of living How well off and wealthy a person is.
Staple crop The most important food in people's diets.
Subsistence Living on what a family grows and produces for itself.
Sustainable tourism Tourism that does not damage the environment or the way of life of the local people.
Terraced Where level strips of land are cut out of hillsides.
Tornado A rapidly moving and vicious spiral of air that is smaller than a hurricane.
Tourism The industry that caters for visitors.
Tourist A person who travels away from home for a short time and intends to return home afterwards.
Trade The selling of goods between countries.
Trade gap The difference between the value of imports and exports in any country.
Transpiration Loss of water from plants to the atmosphere.
Treaty An agreement between different countries.
Tributary Smaller river that flows into a larger one.
Tropical storm Area of very low pressure with high winds and heavy rainfall.
Vertical erosion Wearing away land in a downward direction.
Vicious cycle Where one thing leads to another, which leads to another so that the situation gets worse and worse.
V-shaped valley River valley that is lowest in the centre.
Water cycle The movement of water between the air, the oceans and the ground.
Water vapour Water as a gas in the atmosphere.
Waterfall Where the river suddenly drops in height.
Weather The state of the atmosphere at any one time: whether it is sunny or raining, cloudy, hot, cold, etc.
Weather forecast A prediction of what the weather will be like.
Weather station A place used to record the weather with meteorological instruments.
Western Lifestyles in Europe and North America as opposed to those in the East, mainly Asia.
Wind Moving air from an area of high pressure to an area of low pressure.

Index

Africa 102–3, 104, 114–15, 122
anticyclones 36, 37
Asia 123–7
asylum-seekers 24–7

Bangalore (India) 140–1
Bangladesh 126, 127, 138–9, 142–3
Boscastle (Cornwall), flood 74–5

chaebols 132–3
China 126, 127, 134–7
climate 42–5, 46, 52–3, 54, 58, 94
  Asia 125, 142
  Europe 38, 42, 46, 52–3
  Italy 85, 88, 90, 91
  tropical 110
  UK 38, 39, 44, 67
clouds 34, 36, 39, 40
coffee 116–17

depressions 36, 37, 39, 40–1
development 106–9, 114–15, 122, 140–1
diseases 112–13, 118–19

EU (European Union) 10–14, 52–3, 87, 100
Europe 5–9, 31
  climate 38, 42, 46, 52–3
  migration 22–7
  population 15–19, 30, 100
  tourism 49, 50, 52–7

Fair Trade 116–17
farming 44–5, 120, 129, 134
  coffee 116–17
  Italy 88, 89, 91, 92
  subsistence 104, 105, 115
fieldwork, on rivers 78–81
flooding 72–7, 82, 110, 114, 142–3

GDP (Gross Domestic Product) 12, 13, 104, 106, 108, 114, 144
graphs to come
  climate graph 44, 125
  scatter graph 99

HDI (human development index) 106–7

India 125, 126, 127, 138–41
industry 88–9, 91, 92–3, 130–3, 135–7, 140–1
Italy 83–5, 94–5, 98–9
  regional differences 86–93
  see also Venice

Jamaica, tourism 58–9, 60, 61
Japan 126, 127, 128–31

LEDCs (Less Economically Developed Countries) 104–15, 118–22
  and trade 116–17, 120–1

malaria 112–13
Malta 13, 50
maps to come
  mind map 62
  pictorial map 88
MEDCs (More Economically Developed Countries) 104–8, 116
Menorca, tourism 56–7, 62
migration 18, 22–7, 87, 100
Mumbai (India) 103, 123, 139

NICs (Newly Industrialising Countries) 106, 127
North Italy 86–7, 88–9

OS (Ordnance Survey) maps 74, 75, 145–6

Pakistan 118–19, 126, 127, 138, 139
pensions 98–9, 100
Poland 12, 28–9
population
  Asia 126, 127, 139
  density 15, 16–17, 28, 29
  Europe 15–19, 30, 100
  Italy 98–9
  Poland 28, 29
  UK 21, 28, 29, 30
population pyramids 20–1, 98, to come
poverty 86–7, 90–1, 101–3, 107, 108–15, 118–21, 137

pressure 33, 36–7
Punjab (Pakistan) 118–19

quality of life 28–9, 106, 118–19

rainfall 33, 34, 35, 36, 39, 67, 142
rivers 63–5, 68–71, 78–81
  see also flooding

satellite images 40, 41
sketches to come
South Italy 86–7, 90–3
South Korea 106, 127, 132–3
spider diagrams to come
sub-Saharan Africa 102–3, 104, 114–15, 122
subsistence farming 104, 105, 115

time columns to come
tourism 44, 46–51, 60–2
  Europe 49, 50, 52–7
  Italy 94–5
  Jamaica 58–9, 60, 61
  UK 49, 52, 54–5
trade 10, 115, 116–17, 120–1, 135, 138, 139
tropical countries 110–13, 120
tropical storms 110–11, 114, 128, 142

UK (United Kingdom) 12, 21, 28, 30
  climate 38, 39, 44, 67
  flooding 72, 73, 74–5
  migration 23, 24, 25, 26–7
  tourism 49, 52, 54–5
  water supply 66–7
  weather 38, 39, 40–1, 45
unemployment 12, 86, 87
  seasonal 50, 51, 57, 60

Venice (Italy) 96–7

water, safe (clean) 107, 108–9, 112, 114, 118–19
water cycle 34, 35, 64–7
water supply 66–7, 88, 91, 92, 118–19
wealth 12, 13, 86–9, 101–9, 144
weather 31–41, 42, 46